Introducing Strategic Information Systems Planning

Dan Remenyi PhD

NCC Blackwell

MANCHESTER • OXFORD

British Library Cataloguing in Publication Data

Remenyi, D. (Dan), *1944 –*
  An Introduction to Strategic Information Systems Planning
  1. Management Information Systems. Applications of computer systems
  I. Title
  658.40380285

  ISBN 0-85012-814-5

First published 1991 by

NCC Blackwell Limited, 108 Cowley Road, Oxford OX4 1JF, England.

Reprinted 1993, 1994

Editorial Office: NCC Blackwell Limited, Oxford House, Oxford Road, Manchester M1 7ED.

Typeset in 10pt Palatino by TechTrans Ltd, Kidmore End, Reading, RG4 9AY; and printed by Hobbs the Printers of Southampton.

ISBN 0-85012-814-5

Foreword

This book has been written to introduce the concept of Strategic Information Systems Planning (SISP) to general managers, including managing directors, financial directors and accountants as well as those members of the Information Systems profession who have not yet undertaken a SISP study. The book will also be of interest to computer and management consultants in addition to information systems and corporate planning academics.

It is the intention of the book to introduce the reader to the reasons why SISP has become such an important part of Information Systems (IS) management and then to explain the approach or philosophy to conducting a SISP. The actual work of a SISP is quite technical and this book deliberately avoids going into great detail on the technical issues.

Therefore this is not a step-by-step guide for those who want to undertake a Do-It-Yourself SISP, but rather a document which will stimulate thought and discussions within the firm about whether it should undertake a SISP, and if so, what it can expect to achieve and what resources will be required. It is not intended to be a definitive work on the subject of SISP but rather an overview of the important issues which must be addressed to successfully implement a SISP in the firm.

In Appendix 3 there is a list of consultancy firms and hardware manufacturers which market detailed methodologies which may be used for the purpose of implementing a SISP. This is not an exhaustive list as there are more than 100 firms offering this type of service. Appendices 4 to 11 describe eight of the better known methodologies. Readers wishing to begin developing a SISP could obtain advice from any of these firms.

Finally it is worth mentioning that this is the third book in the NCC series on SIS by the same author. More complete details on the nature of SISs and case studies on how they are formulated and implemented are provided in *Increase Profits with Strategic Information Systems* and *Strategic Information Systems, Development, Implementation, Case Studies.*

Contents

Appendix

Introduction to the Concept of SISP

STRATEGIC INFORMATION SYSTEMS PLANNING

The subject of SISP presents a series of challenges to both the practitioner and theorist. These particular challenges lie in the fact that the conceptual frameworks which SISP addresses stem from two quite distinct disciplines both of which are legendary for their complexity.

SISP requires a synthesis of the concepts and working practices of corporate strategy as well as the principles and procedures of information systems management. Corporate strategy is a subject which deals with business issues in their broadest sense. This frequently means looking at the long-term implications of markets, products, clients, staff and other stakeholders. At this level in business there are no simple techniques to quickly and easily identify problems and find solutions. Furthermore there is often a considerable difference of opinion as to the nature of strategic problems or opportunities. It has been frequently pointed out that business is not so much about solving problems as about finding out what went wrong in the first place, or alternatively discovering what opportunities are available to the firm.

The dual nature of SISP has frequently led to a misunderstanding of the nature of the subject. Some practitioners believe that SISP should only address the issues of Information Systems Planning. Others suggest that SISP is more relevant to planning Strategic Information Systems.

This book takes the view that SISP must address both issues. Further, as planning is an ongoing activity, SISP must also become a regular and continuous process in the firm. This means that new prominence must be given to strategy and strategic processes.

To add to this already complex situation concerning the growing body of Information Systems (IS) theory, there is the fact that IS is a very young subject. It has not been in existence for long enough to have developed an extensive tradition of research and management practice. The rate of change in the technology further complicates the issue as does the fact that there are still many executives are seriously computerphobic.

In bringing these two disciplines – strategy and planning – together, a whole new set of jargon comes into existence. Many users of SISP terms are not consistent in their use of the vocabulary which means that the same words may be used to mean different things at different times. In fact it has been observed that the language of SISP is reminiscent of Alice's conversation with Humpty Dumpty which went as follows:

"And only one for birthday presents, you know. There's glory for you."
"I don't know what you mean by 'glory'", Alice said.
Humpty Dumpty smiled contemptuously.
"Of course you don't – till I tell you. I meant – there's a nice knock-down argument for you!"
"But 'glory' doesn't mean 'a nice knock-down argument'," objected Alice.
"When I use a word", Humpty Dumpty said, in rather a scornful tone, "it means what I choose it to mean – neither more or less."
"The question is", said Alice, "whether you can make words mean so many different things."
"The question is", said Humpty Dumpty, "which is to be master – that's all."
Alice was too puzzled to say anything.

Through the Looking Glass – Lewis Carroll

Furthermore when debate takes place, especially between experts in the SISP field, the content of the discussion sometimes sounds more like this:

You have two sides one out in the field and one in.

Each man that's in the side that's in goes out and when he's out he comes in and the next man goes in until he's out.

When they are all out the side that's out comes in and the side that's been in goes out and tries to get those coming in out.

Sometimes you get men still in and not out.

When both sides have been in and out including the not outs that's the end of the game.

Explanation of a Cricket Match – Anonymous

There are a number of different approaches to SISP. Many management consultancy firms as well as computer vendors have developed their own SISP methodology. In this book the author has drawn from a number of these methodologies as well as discussing how to develop an independent approach.

In summary SISP requires considerable application to come to terms with the two disciplines involved. Firms who are starting out on the SISP route need to reorient the attitudes of both senior business management and IS management. This is no simple task and results should not be expected immediately. Nonetheless, if the firm perseveres with this relatively new approach to planning, a very substantial improvement in performance may be achieved.

1 What Is SISP and Why Is It Important ?

1.1 THE IMPORTANCE OF SISP

What is SISP and why is it considered to be one of the most important management issues for both IS people and general management in the 1990s?

A SISP is the process of establishing a program for the implementation and use of IS in such a way that it will optimise the effectiveness of the firm's information resources and use them to support the objectives of the whole enterprise as much as possible. The products of a SISP will typically include a short term plan for the next 12 to 18 months as well as a longer term plan for the next three to five years. SISP is believed by many to be one of the most important issues facing management today. It can make a significant impact, not only on IS practices, resources and management, but also on the overall performance of the firm.

SISP is a concept which has been evolving over the last ten years. It is a development which has grown out of a realisation that the hardware/software requirements approach to IS planning was not producing adequate results for the IS department, or the firm as a whole. SISP involves matching the computer applications with the objectives of organisations so as to maximise the return on the efforts of the Information Systems Department (ISD), as well as the return earned by the organisation as a whole.

Although SISP has its roots in traditional strategic planning, today it places strong emphasis on how firms can identify strategic information systems, or information systems which will give the firm a competitive edge. However, SISP does not end there, as it also encompasses issues of data and applications architecture. It also considers how proposed applications should be filtered for viability and financial success, as well as risk.

SISP therefore has a dual nature which includes detailed planning and budgeting for the ISD at one level, and strategic issues and formulation at another. One of the characteristics of SISP is that in some cases it leads management to reassess the appropriateness of the enterprise's objectives and strategies and it has occasionally been known to lead to major strategic reformulations.

SISP is an intricate and complex planning activity which requires the input of a relatively large number of members of staff and perhaps consultants. Because of the amount of work involved and the number of people required to conduct a SISP, it is always performed as a project. The duration of such a project is typically between three and six months and requires the involvement of a team comprising between three and six members, not all of whom will usually be full time. It is important that the team should be multidisciplinary, ie individuals should be drawn from as many user departments as possible.

It is critical at the outset to establish the scope and the timescale of a SISP. A SISP may be conducted for a department or a division or the whole firm. It will normally look ahead to the activities of the IS in the firm over the next three to five years. If these parameters are not established then the focus of the study may be blurred and its impact reduced.

1.2   FACTORS LEADING TO THE CURRENT IMPORTANCE OF SISP

SISP has become a major issue for many reasons. There has been an increasing need in recent years for firms to improve both their efficiency and their effectiveness in the marketplace. This has been brought about by generally tough economic conditions, both nationally and internationally, and by severe competition from local and foreign firms especially from the Far East. This trend can be expected to continue with even more competition eventually emerging from the USSR and other Eastern European countries, particularly Hungary and Czechoslovakia.

Many industrialised countries are going through a period of extensive deregulation which has also led to a search for new ways of increasing business performance. Furthermore, a number of businesses are experiencing changes to basic economic demand which in some cases are due to shifts in fundamental socioeconomic and demographic trends (Drucker, 1985) and industry restructuring (Toffler, 1984). The effect of these factors has been collectively referred to as turbulence (Ansoff, 1984), and firms have begun to look towards innovation as a way of coping with it. In addition, many enterprises have turned to IS. The use of IS to help gain a competitive advantage has become a significant area for innovation which is available to many firms, large and small.

There have been enormous improvements to computer hardware and software. The apparently ever-improving price-performance ratio of the hardware being sold by the major vendors, with its obvious capability to handle much more than mere record-keeping activities or simple summary information for management decision making, has resulted in a drive to use these machines as tools with which to enhance the business.

The size of computer memories and disk storage offered for quite modest sums of money is now far beyond what was available only a few years ago. Furthermore, many of these new computers include substantial improvements to telecommunications hardware and software which allow much freer access to databases both nationally and internationally. In addition, standards for Electronic Data Interchange (EDI), to mention one area of recent development, are being established to allow firms to explore entirely new ways of doing business. Application tools such as computer integrated manufacturing (CIM), computer aided design/computer aided manufacturing (CAD/CAM) and artificial intelligence (AI) are now available and many firms need to incorporate new technology such as this into their planning.

The management of an ISD is becoming increasingly complex, requiring more and more funds. There is also more pressure for productivity, quality assurance, hardware performance and measurement than ever before. New tools such as computer aided system engineering (CASE), new operating environments, and various database languages have been developed which require new sets of skills, as well as very substantial investments.

The demand for end user computing has in some cases become overwhelming, which has had a substantial impact on the ISD's ability to fund new investment.

Recent research in the USA suggests that more funds are now expended by US firms on end user computing than on all other computing equipment put together. This is a relatively sudden development which needs careful management and must be incorporated in the firm's strategic planning.

The remarkable success of some users in improving their market positions by the use of IS has set a precedent for others to follow. The two most frequently cited examples are American Airlines and American Hospital Supplies. By providing travel agents with terminals, and by providing access to multiple airline timetables and reservations systems, American Airlines substantially increased their market share. Furthermore, they increased their non-flight revenue by charging a small fee for reservations on other carriers made through their computer. American Hospital Supplies, a retailer of general medical supplies, gave their customers terminals with which to enter orders. Later they allowed suppliers access to the database and thus directly connected demand to supply. There are several advantages to this situation for both parties, one of which is that these electronic connections reduce the amount of time it takes between placing an order and receiving the goods.

Systems like these have played a key role in what is sometimes described as a time-based competitive advantage (Stalk, 1988), and are examples of what has been described as a locking-in strategy which has recently developed into the broader concept of electronic markets (Malone, 1989).

The massive improvement in computer literacy and computer fluency, especially among middle and some senior and top managers, has primarily been brought about by the arrival of the personal computer. This has made non-computer trained staff realise that there is nothing intrinsically more difficult about computer issues than other business matters.

Prior to this increase in computer awareness, computer decisions including policy and planning were almost exclusively delegated to technical experts who seldom, if ever, had an overall business perspective of the firm. This computer literacy or fluency allowed business minds to look at IT/IS opportunities from a fresh perspective and not simply through the technical point of view of data processing professionals.

A new body of knowledge concerning the use of IS has been created. This has been brought about by the publishing of papers and textbooks on business strategy and information systems, at Harvard Business School, the Massachusetts Institute of Technology and other business schools. These clearly and convincingly argue that IT and IS must be considered as a key corporate resource in developing a comprehensive, credible and achievable corporate strategy. Synnott (1987) has in fact coined the expression "The Information Weapon", which he sees as a vital part of the firm's corporate assets.

The recognition that Information Systems Planning is an important part of corporate planning and must be integrated into the framework of a firm's strategic thinking. More and more firms are beginning to recognise information as one of their most valuable resources, which can be used as a competitive weapon to improve performance, reduce stock levels, improve credit control policy, reduce business risks, etc. Some of the early academic work which defined the framework for subsequent analysis included the definition of generic strategies and the specification of the value chain concept (Porter 1980 and 1985). This work encouraged firms to seek ways in which IS could be used to improve competitiveness, and also to find applications which could directly support the enterprises' attempts to pursue a generic strategy. In such cases IS would be used to help gain a competitive advantage.

1.3   THE IMPORTANCE OF SISP

Research conducted by the Society of Information Management in the USA shows that SISP is one of the most important issues facing IS managers.

In a recent survey the following were identified as key issues in Information Systems Management:

- – Strategic planning;
- – Competitive advantage;
- – Organisational learning;
- – IS's role and contribution;
- – Alignment in the organisation;
- – End user computing;
- – Data as a corporate resource;
- – Information architecture;
- – Measuring efficiency;
- – Integrating data processing, office automation and telecommunications.

In addition to this survey, the importance of SISP to IS management may be seen by the fact that there is a plethora of courses offered on the subject. Academic departments in universities are beginning to take an interest in the subject, and more and more computer consultants are developing methodologies to cope with the problems of SISP.

1.4   THE SCOPE OF A SISP

The scope of a SISP can vary considerably; sometimes it will look at the enterprise as a whole, or concentrate on a department or subsidiary. Sometimes the SISP will focus on a timeframe and concern itself with a three to five year plan. Sometimes the SISP will have a hidden agenda: for example, how to pull together two recently merged firms, or how to restructure the management and control of the ISD. Therefore the objectives, the approach, and the format of the SISP will vary considerably. A few examples are listed below:

A heavy engineering firm

Introducing top management to the need to incorporate IS issues in their strategic thinking and strategic plan formulation. Establishing how the ISD may be reoriented away from a strictly cost containment culture to a return on investment (ROI) culture, and how the firm can establish procedures for the identification, assessment and implementation of strategic and/or competitive information systems.

A firm offering professional services

Exploring more ways of automating the services that the firm offers. Establishing a programme which will reverse the advantage which several competitors may have gained through the use of end user computing. Improving the ratio of professional to support staff. Identifying stand-alone computers which can be used as workstations and be connected through a local area network in order to serve the needs within a building. Establishing standards of connectivity which will allow communications between buildings using a wide area network. Providing access to telex, facsimile and other gateway services through the system. Establishing appropriate training facilities and schedules to ensure the success of this plan.

A manufacturer of household goods

The firm is currently undergoing a period of rapid change in its business environment. The key forces of change are:

- the move away from exclusively high-value/low-volume business towards low-value/high-volume sales;
- sustained rapid business growth;
- large increase in indirect sales.

Given these industry drivers the firm believes that a revised organisational structure and the necessary systems to support it constitute an area which demands priority attention.

1.5   POSSIBLE DELIVERABLES OF SISP

The deliverables of a SISP will vary depending on its objectives and its scope, but will frequently include:

- An action programme which, if followed, will ensure that the ISD directly contributes to the business success of the firm.
- Various written reports addressing such issues as systems audit, information architecture and strategic information systems opportunities.
- Business models for the organisation as a whole, with particular emphasis on the administrative aspects of the firm. These models may include enterprise models, functional models and data models.
- A definition of the requirements for the various applications to support the administrative function.
- A list of hardware and software and a timetable for its acquisition or development. This timetable is frequently expressed using project management techniques such as Gantt charts, critical path analysis and PERT charts.
- An enthusiastic and committed senior management who are frequently prepared to spend more on the ISD than they would have without a SISP.

- A highly motivated project team which can assist in the implementation of the SISP.

An important aspect of the deliverables is the development of business indicators which may be used to measure the impact of the new systems to be developed.

The steps involved in the preparation of these deliverables are:

- Identification or determination of the firm's business objectives, corporate strategy and critical success factors.

- The definition and specification of a business model which must reflect both the business needs as they now exist as well as being able to accommodate the anticipated growth over the next five years.

- An assessment of the extent to which current systems satisfy the business model.

- The creation of a list of application software requirements showing how these programs relate to the performance of the business functions under consideration.

- The identification of appropriate statistical measures for the monitoring of the performance of the new systems to ensure that the success of the application may be measured.

- The creation of a timetable showing all resources required and expenditure for the project.

1.6   METHODOLOGY

In performing SISP studies such as the ones mentioned above, it is important to use a methodology. The methodology for the planning of information systems must inter alia provide an appropriate context for the planning effort, because users find it very difficult to respond effectively to non-contextual requests for the definition of information or systems needs. The SISP methodology may be defined as a systematic procedure for problem solving or opportunity identification. It is the dominant issue on the IS planning agenda, as well as the organisational setting in which the IS decisions are made.

Methodologies play a most important role in various aspects of IS, and have been available for a number of years for planning, systems analysis and design. Methodologies for planning are just now coming to the fore.

The methodology must incorporate some or all of the elements of strategic planning. It must identify broad-based goals for the ISD as well as the key means of achieving them. This is not an easy matter, as the difficulty in linking the strategic plan to the detailed plan is a persistent problem in all aspects of business.

There are many different methodologies available. All the major management consultancies, firms such as Andersen Consulting, Ernst & Young, James Martin Associates, Coopers & Lybrand Deloitte market their own and have proprietary approaches to SISP supported by computerised tools that assist in automating some of the paperwork.

Figures 1.1 to 1.4 show outlines of the methodologies used by Database Consultants Europe (DCE), IBM, Coopers & Lybrand Deloitte and ICL (UK).

It is interesting to see how the basic approaches to SISP offered by these proprietary methodologies are quite similar, although they differ considerably in detail. More information on the major methodologies is supplied in Appendices 3 through 12.

Finally Figure 1.5 shows a possible timetable for a medium length SISP study in a Gantt chart form. Note that it is not realistic to expect a SISP to be conducted in a period less than that suggested in this diagram.

1.7   SUMMARY

IS has been harnessed to help firms compete in an increasingly complex world. In doing this, a new body of knowledge has been created which allows firms to seek greater benefits from their computing resources, by drawing them closer to the central business issues of the firm. It is possible to produce broad-based plans for this or to simply focus on a single aspect of the business. In either event a methodology is most advantageous in formulating such plans. Not all firms will wish to undertake a SISP for a number of different reasons. A SISP is both expensive and difficult. Members of the ISD often don't want to be involved with business issues and some senior managers are still apprehensive about computers. Firms which conduct SISP typically:

- are mature, experienced users of IT;
- have a proactive attitude to helping users get the most from their IS;
- treat IS in much the same way as any other corporate services department.

It is therefore very important that every enterprise does not rush headlong into a SISP as many organisations will simply just not be ready for this type of planning. In such cases the results will be very unsatisfactory and much cost will have been incurred.

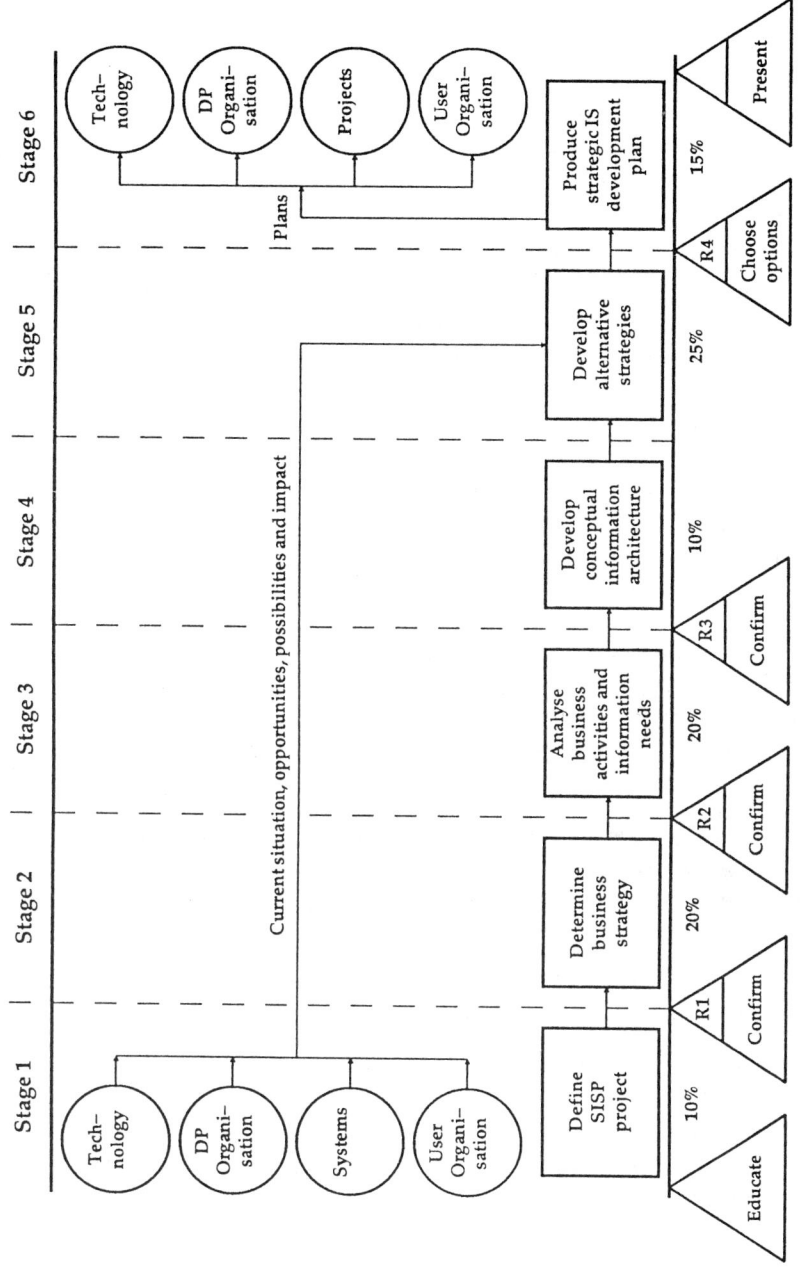

Figure 1.1 Outline of the DCE methodology

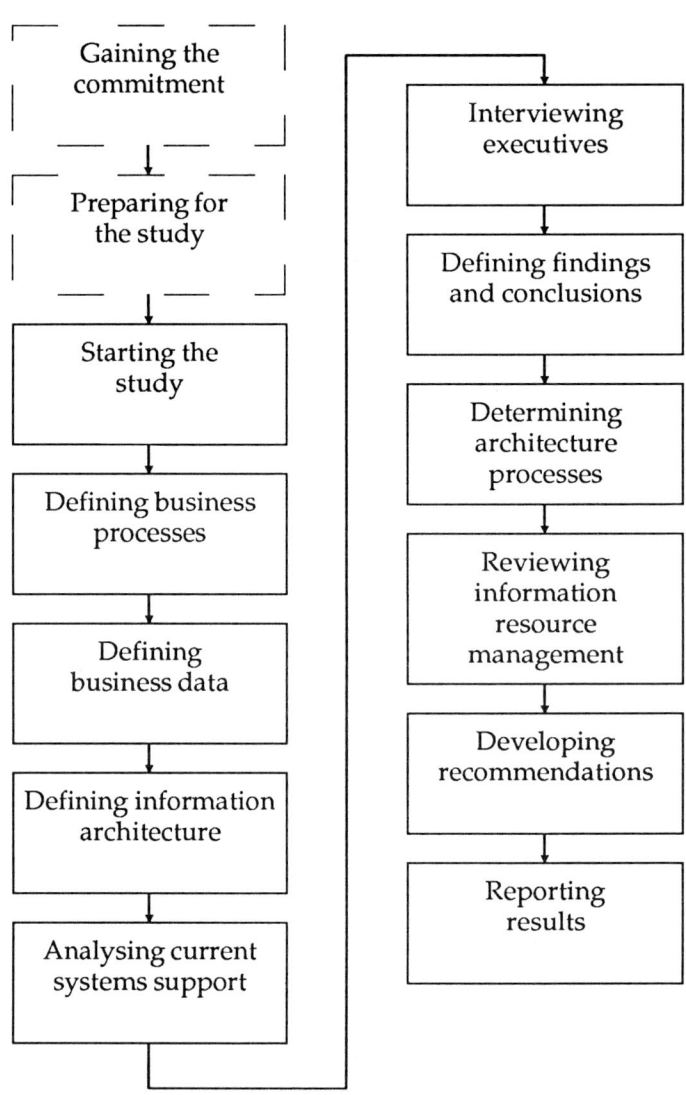

Figure 1.2   The IBM BSP methodology

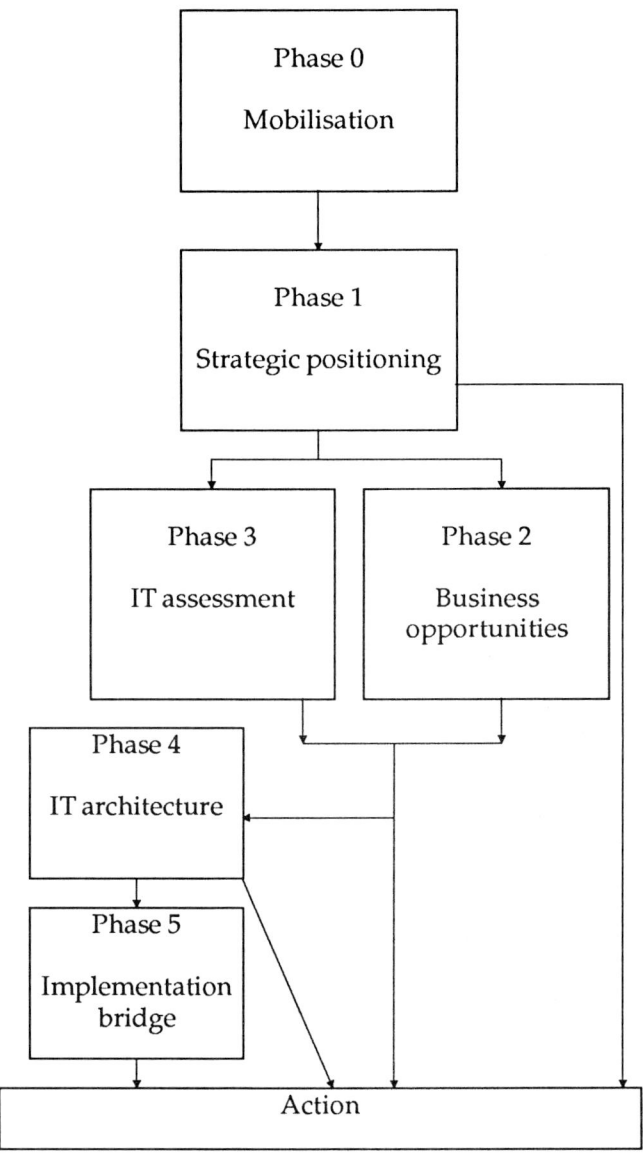

Figure 1.3   The Coopers &Lybrand Deloitte SUMMIT-S methodology

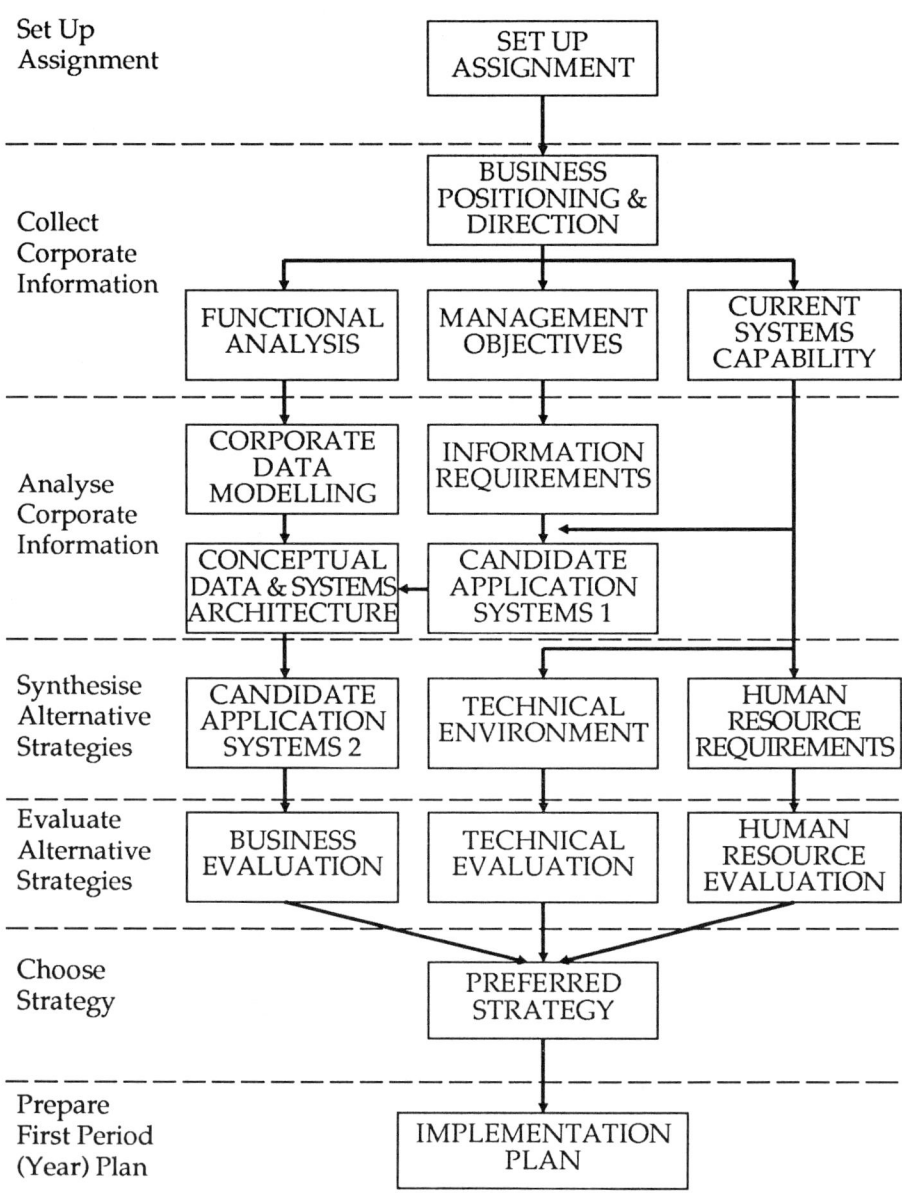

Figure 1.4 The ICL (UK) SISP methodology

Task	Preparing for BSP study		Study Execution (based on full time)					
	2 weeks before	1 week before	Week 1	Week 2	Week 3	Week 4	Week 5	Week 6
Determine scope, select team and leader, and educate	-----							
Prepare for study	----	----						
Start the study			▬					
Define processes			▬					
Define business date				▬				
Define information architecture					▬			
Analyse present systems support					▬ ----			
Conduct interviews						▬		----
Determine architectural priorities							----	▬
Review IRM								▬
Develop recommendations								--
Prepare report		----		-----------------------------------				

Figure 1.5   Possible timetable for a BSP SISP study

2 The Planning, Management and Control of the ISD

2.1 DIFFERENT PERSPECTIVES OF IS ACHIEVEMENT

From a positive perspective it can be said that most medium to large firms have computerised the bulk of their transaction processing applications. These include systems such as debtors, creditors, payroll, inventory record keeping and ledgers, as well as other more interesting applications including order processing, production planning, etc. On the whole these jobs have been done well, and although there have been problems with costs and schedules, most firms report that they are pleased with what has been achieved. The proliferation of basic systems is now so extensive that few of these firms could function for long without them. However, as it has been estimated that these basic systems represent about 50% of the total of all the business processes which will ultimately be computerised, it can clearly be seen that there is still a big job ahead for the ISD.

Taking a less positive perspective, the last ten years could be described as quite traumatic. ISDs have simply swallowed money. Research conducted by Nolan Norton Associates (Waller, 1989) states that for some large firms, the funds spent on IS during the last decade has increased seven-fold. The Butler Cox Foundation has reported that IS projects are frequently late and over budget. Some projects are so late that they are never implemented, as by the time they are ready to be used they are no longer relevant to their prospective users. Ed Yourdon (1990) has shown that in the USA 25% of large systems development projects never finish. In addition there are between three and five errors in every hundred program statements after testing. Yourdon also claims that the probability of successfully fixing an error on the first attempt is never more than 50%, and that this drops to 20% if a substantial change has to be made. The backlog of maintenance and enhancement grows ever longer, with some firms reporting delays lasting years.

The opportunities for greater profits through the use of computers has become an issue, but not as many firms as initially thought are availing themselves of this technology. In a number of industries, programming productivity has virtually remained stable and has now become a critical issue. According to Yourdon, the average programmer productivity is ten to fifteen debugged program statements per day, and that this has had a very substantial negative impact on the use of IT.

Whichever perspective is adopted there is no doubt that the ISD will always need very careful planning and control. Yet research shows that about 30% of enterprises using IS have no formal system of planning. Considering the amounts of money involved in IS this is an amazing situation. All business activities, other than the most trivial, require some degree of planning, even if it is only to ensure that essential resources are available at the appropriate time.

At another level, planning is critical to the management process because it provides a standard against which performance can be measured and without which there can be no control of the business. There are five possible approaches a firm may take to IS planning. These are shown in Figure 2.1.

Planning Type	Approach
1. No planning	No formal plans are produced for either business or information systems. A certain amount of informal planning may occur in the heads of top management.
2. Traditional IS planning	Traditional business planning and budgeting takes place. IS planning also occurs but in isolation from the business planning process.
3. Reactive IS planning	IS plans are developed to reflect changes in business policy, although they are not dependent on the business plan.
4. Linked IS planning	Corporate planning takes place, followed by IS planning. The IS plan is derived directly from the business plan. There is only one-way communication from the business plan to the IS plan.
5. SISP	Corporate planning and IS planning are combined to form a single process. Each is dependent on the other. Thus there is an extensive two-way impact on plans.

Figure 2.1   The five approaches to IS planning

2.2   NO PLANNING

The first of these options is no planning, in which the firm's management flies by the seat of its pants; as the above research showed, a surprisingly high proportion of firms – 30% – still conduct their affairs in this way.

2.3   TRADITIONAL IS PLANNING

Traditional methods of IS planning and implementing rely heavily on the skill of the IS professionals who choose the hardware and software, and decide what applications are needed. The ISD specifies the jobs, gets them approved, and schedules the systems analysis, systems design and the programming. It tests and installs the finished systems in the user department, writes the manuals and maintains the system. At least four penalties result from this approach:

–   There is a major rift between the ISD and everyone else. Only ISD personnel understand what really is happening with the firm's systems. Everyone else perceives computers and everything to do with them as some sort of black magic. This frequently results in the very inadequate use of information within the firm.

–   The applications which are computerised are not necessarily those which have the greatest impact on business performance. Payrolls, debtors, inventory, ledgers etc are computerised. The issue of how the computer could help improve business performance is hardly ever addressed.

–   The user department is kept waiting too long for new applications. The extent of delays in the preparation of systems is legendary. In some cases jobs which are quoted in months take years. On other occasions, projects are simply abandoned; for some systems, by the time the new application comes on stream it is already out of date, and no longer contributes significantly to the business.

–   Application budgets are overspent again and again. In defence of IS management, planning and budgeting for the ISD is a very difficult business. The environment, both inside and outside the firm, is volatile, suitable staff are frequently in short supply, vendors continually change equipment design and performance. Standards are still relatively underdeveloped and end users make changing demands on the ISD. In addition, until recently IS expenditure has been perceived by many, if not most, boards of directors as an expense which must be minimised.

The main characteristics of an ISDs traditional planning are:

–   Cost containment.

–   Budgets often produced as an update of last year's numbers.

–   Focus only on the next 12 months.

–   Little or no tie-in with business strategy or effectiveness issues.

The absence of planning in the ISD represents a substantial exposure to the firms in this group, for without any plans the firm cannot measure how well their ISD is performing. In addition, when planning is not done, the firm is regularly subjected to surprises, which in the IS field may be quite traumatic and very expensive. In addition, much of the planning which does take place is performed on a bottom-up basis. Bottom-up IS planning involves establishing the current system requirements, including the backlog, and developing a series of plans which will enable the majority of the resulting demands to be met within the planning cycle. Bottom-up IS planning is characterised by priority setting and resource allocation. It is considered to take a narrow view of the status quo and to try to find ways and means of coping with the firm's immediate circumstances.

Some companies are spending 2% or more of their turnover on information systems, and to utilise these funds effectively it is necessary to take a different approach to IS planning. The traditional ways of planning and running ISDs are no longer producing the required results. They have relied heavily on extrapolating last year's figures as a basis of this year's plan, and required individual applications to be defined and justified on a piecemeal or standalone basis. They have also led to new applications whose return on investment passed a set level being placed in a queue for implementation; a queue often so long it may be months or years before the application comes up for attention.

2.3.1 Developing a Traditional Financial Budget for the ISD

In virtually all ISDs, operations or production are a fixed overhead cost within which there is very little scope for manoeuvring. It is generally a very large proportion of the budget and there are very few ways to save money without drastic reductions in the service level offered.

As new applications are completed, or 'dropped down' into operations/production, there will be continuous additional cost added to the data processing fixed overhead. Research has found that each year generally 25% to 50% of the previous year's development cost should be added to the operations cost as new systems come into production. All these costs will increase with inflation, and will also increase if the transaction volumes requiring processing increase.

Maintenance has to be done on all operational systems. Programs have a lifespan. Research has found that the average suite of programs lasts between six and seven years and then need rewriting. If the program is well maintained then it will last longer and will still have useful functionality to the user departments. If a program is allowed to 'rust' then it may have to be replaced sooner.

Research has also found that many firms spend at least 38% of the operations cost on maintenance. The amount spent on the development of new applications is a discretionary figure. If it is too low then the users will be constrained; if too high then some of the money spent on new applications may be wasted. Many firms spend 25% of their operations budget on new application development.

Figures 2.2 to 2.6 show how easy it is for the ISD to consume huge sums of funds without achieving any great advances against the new applications mountain, or the maintenance lake. It is not intended that these figures should accurately represent a detailed IS budget. No attempt has been made to balance requirements for hardware, application development tools and people, to mention only a few items. Rather, the figures are presented to demonstrate the propensity of the IS cost to escalate over time at a much faster rate than might otherwise be imagined.

Assuming an operations cost of 100, and allowing 38% for maintenance, and adding a steady amount each year of, say 25 for development, then without any management effort the cost of IS will escalate from 163 to 318 during the total planning period, ie nearly double in 10 years. This is without any growth in the business, no inflation and no demand for new application systems over and above the 25 budgeted for that area per year (Figure 2.2).

```
IS DEPARTMENT COST SCENARIO OVER A TEN YEAR PERIOD

SCENARIO 1 - No Business Growth
YEAR NUMBER             1     2     3     4     5     6     7     8     9    10
New Applications       25    25    25    25    25    25    25    25    25    25
Maintenance            38    43    48    52    57    62    67    71    76    81
Production/Operations 100   113   125   138   150   163   175   188   200   213
                      -------------------------------------------------------
-
TOTAL IS EXPENDITURE  163   180   198   215   232   249   267   284   301   318

Additional Cash each year    17    17    17    17    17    17    17    17    17
```

Figure 2.2   Financial budget for IS department over ten years showing minimum physical growth

It is the above type of cost escalation profile which has caused much concern to corporate controllers who are concerned with keeping IS costs under control.

Assuming a business growth of 5% per annum, the IS department budget moves from 163 to 429 in 10 years. IS expenditure only takes seven years to double (Figure 2.3).

For many firms a 5% per annum growth is quite modest, and therefore they

```
IS DEPARTMENT COST SCENARIO OVER A TEN YEAR PERIOD

SCENARIO 2 - 5% Business Growth
YEAR NUMBER              1     2     3     4     5     6     7     8     9    10
New Applications        25    25    25    25    25    25    25    25    25    25
Maintenance             38    45    52    59    67    75    83    92   102   111
Production/Operations  100   118   136   155   175   197   219   242   267   293
                      -----------------------------------------------------------
TOTAL IS EXPENDITURE   163   187   213   239   267   296   327   360   394   429

Additional Cash each year    24    25    27    28    29    31    32    34    36

Assumptions
Business Growth             5.00%
New Systems completed p.a.  50.00%
```

Figure 2.3   Financial budget for IS department over ten years showing a 5% growth in business

are frequently faced with IS cost growths which are even greater than suggested above.

With a business growth of 10% the cost of IS escalates from 163 to 585 in 10 years and doubles in just over five years (Figure 2.4). This situation has been faced by many firms in the past decade and it has led to many organisations becoming very concerned about cost control issues in the ISD. However, in reality, there is frequently little which can be done to control these expenses and the firm simply has to face the fact that the ISD continues to require more funds.

```
IS DEPARTMENT COST SCENARIO OVER A TEN YEAR PERIOD

SCENARIO 3 - 10% Business Growth
YEAR NUMBER              1     2     3     4     5     6     7     8     9    10
New Applications        25    25    25    25    25    25    25    25    25    25
Maintenance             38    47    56    66    78    90   104   119   136   154
Production/Operations  100   123   147   174   204   237   274   313   357   406
                      -----------------------------------------------------------
TOTAL IS EXPENDITURE   163   194   228   266   307   353   403   458   518   585

Additional Cash each year    31    34    38    41    45    50    55    61    67

Assumptions
Business Growth            10.00%
New Systems completed p.a.  50.00%
```

Figure 2.4   Financial budget for IS department over ten years showing a 10% growth in business

The last three examples of the growth in the ISD budget shown in Figures 2.2 to 2.4 were somewhat unrealistic in that they made no provision for inflation. With a business growth of 10% and inflation of 5% the cost of IS escalates from 163 to 840 in 10 years and doubles in four years (Figure 2.5). An inflation rate of 5% is very modest, as although the price:performance ratio continues to improve, the absolute amount spent has continued to increase. In addition few IS staff wage settlement increases have been as low as 5%.

```
IS DEPARTMENT COST SCENARIO OVER A TEN YEAR PERIOD

SCENARIO 4 - Inflation at 5%
YEAR NUMBER                     1    2    3    4    5    6    7    8    9   10
New Applications               25   25   25   25   25   25   25   25   25   25
Maintenance                    38   49   61   76   93  112  134  160  190  225
Production/Operations         100  129  162  200  244  295  354  422  500  591
                             --------------------------------------------------
TOTAL IS EXPENDITURE          163  203  248  301  362  432  513  607  715  840

Additional Cash each year           40   46   53   61   70   81   94  108  125

Assumptions
Business Growth            10.00%
New Systems completed p.a. 50.00%
Inflation                   5.00%
```

Figure 2.5   Financial budget for the IS department over ten years show-
              ing a 10% growth in business and 5% inflation

With a business growth of 10% and inflation of 5% and an increasing demand for new applications of 10% per annum, the cost of IS escalates from 163 to 992 in 10 years, but also only doubles in four years (Figure 2.6). This scenario represents a five fold increase in expenditure in IS in a decade. These assumptions are generally rather conservative. Inflation is often higher than 5%. Many businesses are growing faster than 10% and the demand for new applications, especially with the explosion of end user computing, is much more than 10%.

```
IS DEPARTMENT COST SCENARIO OVER A TEN YEAR PERIOD

SCENARIO 5 - Inflation at 5%, new Application Growth 10% etc
YEAR NUMBER                     1    2    3    4    5    6    7    8    9   10
New Applications               25   28   30   33   37   40   44   49   54   59
Maintenance                    38   49   62   78   96  118  145  176  213  257
Production/Operations         100  129  163  204  253  312  381  464  561  676
                             --------------------------------------------------
TOTAL IS EXPENDITURE          163  205  255  315  386  470  570  688  828  992

Additional Cash each year           42   50   60   71   84  100  118  139  164

Assumptions
Business Growth            10.00%
New Systems completed p.a. 50.00%
Inflation                   5.00%
Growth in New Applications 10.00%
```

Figure 2.6   Financial budget for the IS department over ten years
showing a 10% growth in business, 5% inflation and 10% per annum
growth in demand

Accountants and financial controllers tend to worry about such rates of growth in projected expenditure. As these figures climb, almost certainly faster than those of other departments in the company, the accountants will probably impose arbitrary restrictions on department spending. For example, the ISD may not be allowed to spend 5% more than last year's budget in an effort to accommodate the business growth. As may be seen from the above expense projections, this would represent a substantial squeeze and would mean cutting back in some way.

2.3.2 Diminishing Development

The situation demonstrated in the above scenarios may also be depicted graphically, as shown in Figure 2.7. In this figure the focus is on the overwhelming non-discretionary nature of IS expenditure, which means that in most circumstances the current situation is a heavy, if not predominant, constraint and there is thus very little, if any, manoeuvrability left with which to pursue developmental expenditure.

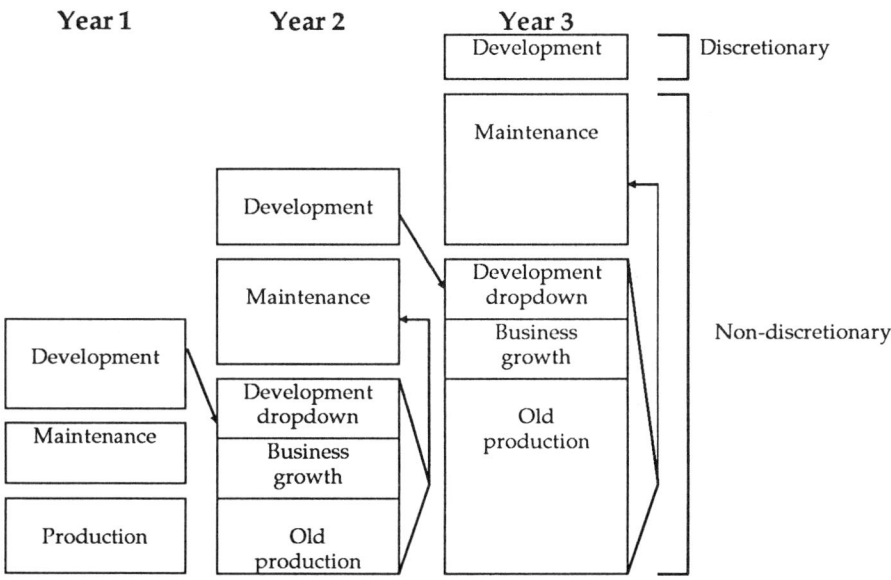

Figure 2.7   The balance of IS expenditure

Inevitably the situation depicted in Figure 2.7 leads to a re-evaluation of the ISD's financial circumstances with a resulting attempt to reduce expenditure. When the financial squeeze happens there are a number of alternatives open:

- Cut back on operations and degrade the service;
- Run certain programs less often;
- Let the terminal users suffer reduced response;
- Offer a longer lead-time for adhoc requests;
- Cut back on maintenance and let the programs rust;
- Do not enhance existing systems;
- Delay development.

Normally the main item to suffer is new development. New development is the only IS activity which is really discretionary. With cutbacks in development, many IS people migrate over the years towards maintenance. Discouragement of new work means that without new applications coming online there is little chance of gaining any new experience and developing a competitive edge through the use of IT. Although development seldom disappears entirely, in some cases it has steadily diminished until it becomes a token activity. Figure 2.8 shows how development expenditure is continually squeezed under this traditional approach.

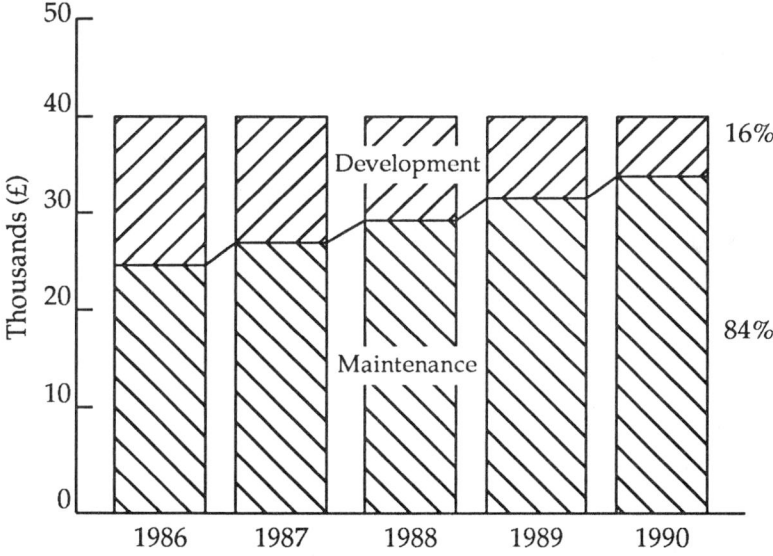

Figure 2.8   Reduction of development

This traditional view of IS led to the approach to IS planning shown in Figure 2.9. This involved an intense focus on last year's budget and backlog, combined with a strong control on staff headcount and salaries, as well as hardware costs. In this environment the traditional planning process was nothing more than an exercise in priority setting and subsequent resource allocation. The result of this was an IS plan which would not make much impact on the performance of the organisation.

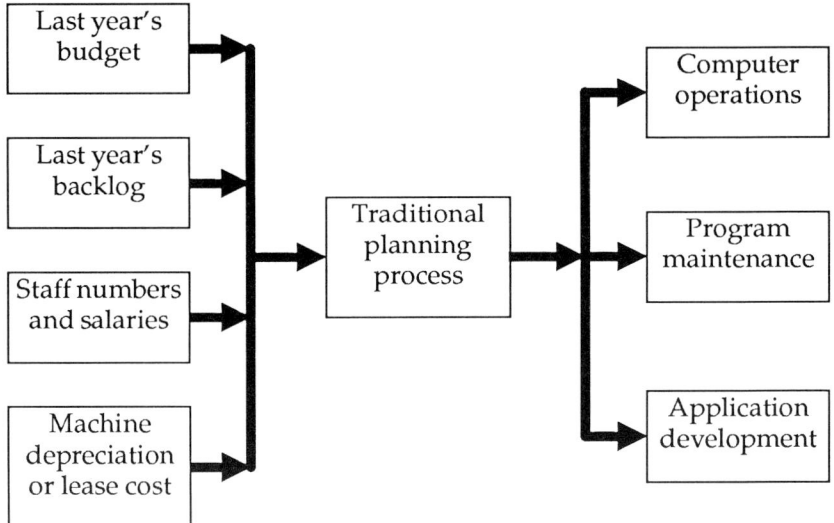

Figure 2.9 The traditional development of the IS plan

2.4 REACTIVE PLANNING

A reactive IS planning situation commences with the development of a business plan. Once this has been completed the ISD is asked to react to the business plan in terms of what hardware, software and people are required to support these business plans. The result of this request is an IS plan which attempts to follow the firm's business trend without having input into the original thinking which created the business plan.

In a reactive IS planning situation, when the business plan changes, the ISD is asked to respond to those changes as quickly as possible. Because of the long-term nature of IS investment, and the technological infrastructure required to support it, especially staff requirements, it is not always possible for the ISD to react quickly.

2.5 LINKED IS PLANNING

A linked IS plan is developed through a series of discussions and interviews between business managers and IS managers, whereby business objectives are presented and the groups identify management information systems and information systems projects which will be required in order for the firm to achieve its objectives. Linked IS planning focuses on the traditional IS project techniques of priority setting and resource allocation.

2.6   IS COSTS

In the above discussion it was assumed that it is fairly easy to identify the costs of IS. In fact, this is not very realistic. IS costs are incurred, not just in the ISD, but also in the user departments. End users have hardware, software, implementation costs, etc. They frequently work with the IS professionals to install new systems. There are a number of such costs involved, and these are seldom well recorded.

In addition there is a whole new area of computing growing up outside the ISD. In some manufacturing and distribution firms computerised factory and store-keeping equipment is being installed which gathers data for control of those functions, and this data is becoming a vital part of management decision-making. Terminals are being installed in customer premises and direct links made with suppliers and other external systems.

Research has shown that as much as 40% of IS costs are now being incurred outside the ISD. When this is taken into account, the true cost of IS as a percentage of turnover could, in many firms, be significantly higher than the 2% originally quoted.

The new approach to IS planning must find a way of assessing these costs, and then find a way of understanding how they will grow and how they can be controlled. Establishing these costs is not a trivial matter. Frameworks have been developed to help ensure that nothing is missed.

2.6.1   A Framework for Establishing IS Costs

There are many frameworks which may be used to ensure that the firm has come to terms with a full view of their IS costs. The S-curve is the technique used by Nolan Norton to analyse IS expenditure (Figure 2.10).

This S-curve shows how a company's expenditure on information technology grows slowly at the start or introduction stage, as initial learning is required. It is relatively easy to establish and monitor costs in the introduction stage. Expenditure on IT is then relatively low and has probably only been initiated by a small number of individuals in the firm. Often, each item purchased is specifically authorised. Computer usage then grows much faster in the second stage, which is referred to as the absorption or contagion stage. This is when many users within the firm begin to take advantage of the technology. It is usually not easy to either calculate or monitor costs

The S-curve of Organisational Learning

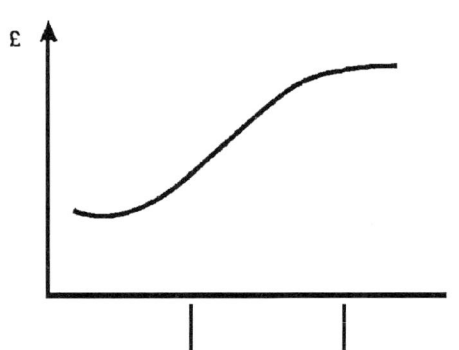

Figure 2.10   The S-curve representing the use
of computing in the firm

during this stage. There are frequently many purchasers of IT equipment. Some purchases are made centrally while others are perhaps made by end users. The rate of usage growth then tails off at the third stage during consolidation, often due to an artificially imposed accountant's limitation of expense. Therefore the first step in determining IS expenditure is to establish where the firm is on the growth curve.

In addition, the S-curve can be looked on as a learning curve. The enterprise as a whole is learning to use IT. It is very difficult to hurry people along the learning curve. All that can be done is to encourage users to grow by learning and experience. If the firm wants to move from one stage to another, considerable costs are entailed.

Growth of learning depends on four growth processes which are shown in Figure 2.11. These processes are Technology, Applications and Tools, Users and Management. These four processes should always be promoted in balance. If money is poured into new technology without the applications and tools being appropriate, it will be either ineffective or simply wasted. Users will not grow in awareness and skill if the style of management is not conducive to the use of computers. Equally, computers will not be used irrespective of the tools and management attitude if the staff are not ready to accept their application in the firm.

This analysis may be expanded to look at a number of sub-categories under each of the main headings.

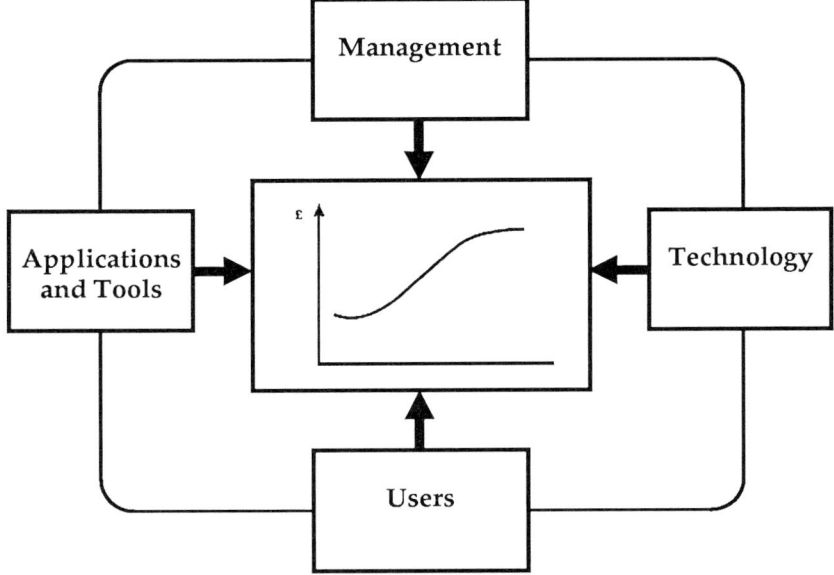

Figure 2.11   The four growth processes

Figure 2.12 shows the Nolan Norton approach to this analysis, which they refer to as the Iron Cross. This provides a more detailed way to view IS expenditure so that the money spent under the headings in each growth process may be analysed. The control of expenditure as it applies to each process may then be introduced. This makes management aware of the current position, or in their jargon the baseline status, of IS and helps them plan what should be done next in each area. It is important to note that each growth process may be divided into an arbitrary number of sub-sections or sub-processes. The number of sub-processes is a function of the size of the firm, the industrial sector in which it operates, and the style of management.

The Technology analysis is divided in this instance into five subsections, which includes the costs of PCs and workstations in user departments, and the central processor cost perhaps written off over three to five years, the network of communications, IS staff and their overheads. It also includes IS expense in user departments, analysed under the headings of networks and data storage.

The Application analysis is also conducted under five headings which shows how the total IS spending is analysed into five application types: Institutional, Professional, Physical, External and Infrastructure. Institutional applications are those which are compulsory for the organisation to

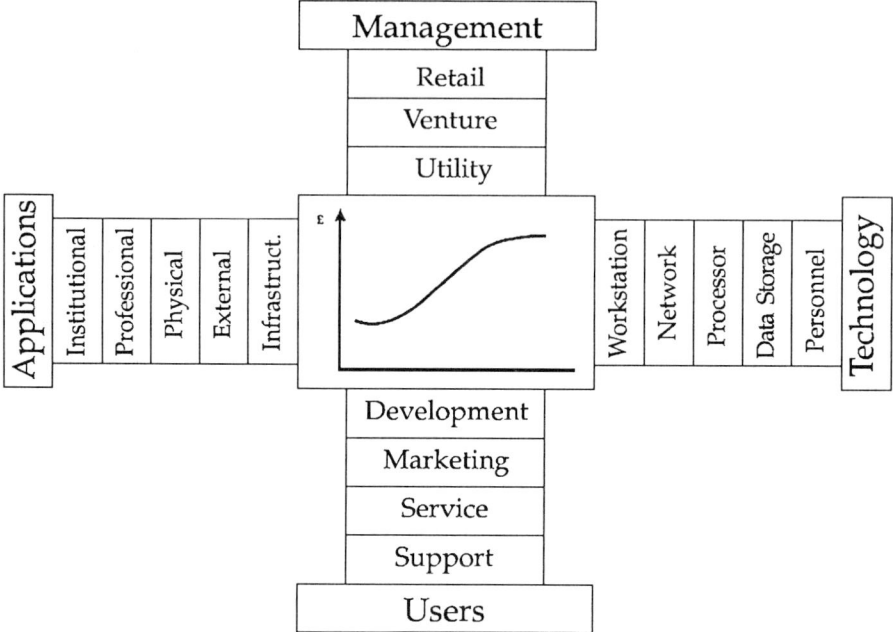

Figure 2.12   The Nolan Norton Iron Cross

perform. Examples of these are payroll, ledgers etc. Professional applications are those conducted by managers and other executives and which improve their professional effectiveness. Physical applications include the use of IT in the manufacturing process for things such as flexible manufacturing, robotics, industrial control etc. External applications involve the use of IT to connect the firm with customers or suppliers. Infrastructure applications relates to operating systems etc.

Users are particular to the organisation, but the total costs can be allocated to departments, or to functions performed by those departments. Alternatively analysis may be by type and grade of staff, such as industrial, sales, secretarial, clerical, accounting, management etc.

Management analysis considers the way in which IT is organised and may be considered under three headings. Retail applications are those which are demand driven, and which are primarily supplied to managers and executives through networks. Venture applications are high risk research and development type projects which may develop or may eventually be discontinued. Utility systems are regular reports which are needed on a daily, weekly, monthly or annual basis.

IS planning in the new age of IS is likely to be a question of balancing expenditure according to a number of different criteria. As demonstrated in Figure 2.7, there are never going to be sufficient funds to do everything required. It is essential to structure IS objectives, and to focus on the areas which will produce the most immediate benefits and prepare the ground for areas which will produce the long-term, and thus perhaps greater, benefits which may be obtained from strategic systems. It is also necessary to ensure that some of the urgent projects receive attention. In fact the plan must involve balancing between a wide range of different areas of demand.

Which areas to address is one of the critical issues of SISP. The task of senior management, including senior IS management, is to establish a SISP which should be closely integrated into the business objectives of the company.

2.7 SISP TECHNIQUES

SISP achieves this balance between the various demands made on the IS resources by applying three separate techniques to the planning process. These techniques are top-down planning, bottom-up planning and information weapon planning.

Top-down planning begins by establishing the firm's objectives, its strategies, and its critical success factors (CSFs), and then determining the systems required to support these. Bottom-up planning looks at the current situation in the ISD and establishes what is urgent, and develops a programme to tackle it. Bottom-up planning is essentially a process of priority determination and resource allocation. Information weapon planning refers to how a firm may seek opportunities with which to use its IS to gain a competitive advantage.

The format of a SISP report is normally a document produced at three to four year intervals; it should have annual updates, which will indicate what the firm intends to achieve with its ISD in the next 12 to 18 months, in the next three years and in the next five years. Thus the SISP has both short- and long-term implications for the firm. It is a direct derivative of the Corporate Strategic Plan which defines the enterprise's business objectives and how the firm intends to achieve them. The CFSs which will have been outlined as a result of the Corporate Strategic Plan are key focal points for the SISP. This is the top down aspect of the SISP. It highlights both the non-discretionary areas of IS expense as well as the discretionary areas for IS investment. The objective of the SISP is to ensure that the expenditure on IS is as effective as possible. SISP is concerned with defining the hardware, software, communications and people required to support the IS function in its endeavour to assist the enterprise achieve its business objectives. By comparing Figures 2.9

and 2.13 the differences between the old traditional approach to planning and the new SISP approach will become very clear.

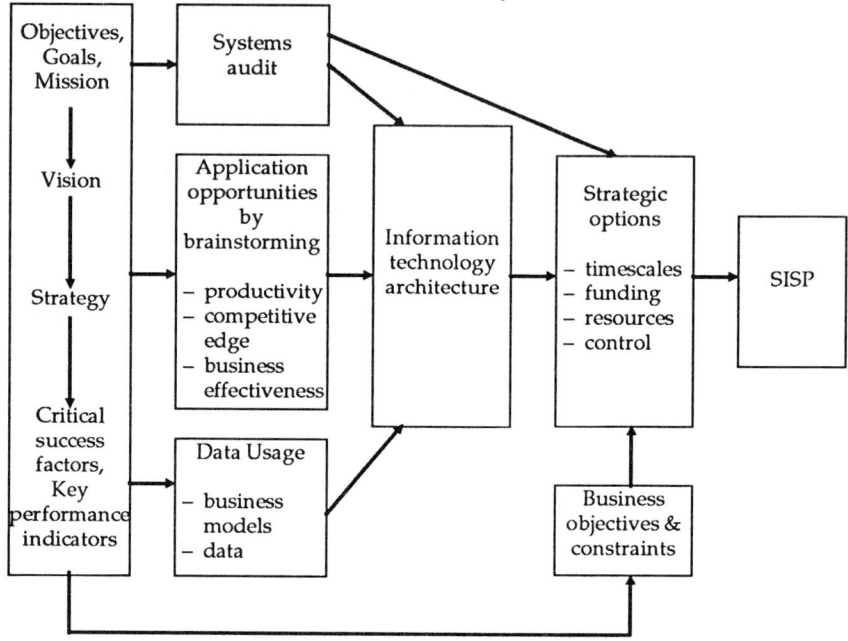

Figure 2.13   Another approach to a SISP

As previously mentioned, the traditional budgeting technique for IS was to use the previous year's figures as a basis. This is obviously a quick and easy way to prepare financial figures. But budgets to most IS people are not motivating, are requested by the accountants at inconvenient times, and are always wanted in a hurry. Neither is there much incentive for IS people to get these figures right.

However, the traditional budgeting technique has some satisfactory dimensions, in that during the budgetary process IS management can take stock of the amount of cash spent last year under the various headings. The budget offers an opportunity to consider the backlog of work and a reasonable growth rate in staff to address this, commensurate with the hiring, induction and training load imposed by new staff. The budget also allows the ISD to assess the firm's ability to afford new hardware to support these potential new staff with enough machines.

The final budget is traditionally divided into the areas discussed before, ie the operations department budget, program maintenance budget and application development budget. And as previously discussed these areas compete with each other for funds.

If the firm is to convert to using the SISP approach, there must first be a strategic plan for the business. When this is in place then IS can be re-oriented to support these strategic plans. This implies integrating the strategic planning and the IS planning processes. The integration of what were two different planning processes is in many ways circular. This is because IS opportunities will become apparent which will influence the business strategy or even the business objectives and thus affect the plans for the whole business.

Business plans require vision. When there is vision, then there can be strategy. The strategy will generate a number of CSFs – the things that have to be done well if the strategy is to happen. Some of these will be management issues, some will be human factors and organisation or training, a few will be IS-related.

A baseline or systems audit defines the current environment. It is most important to know what the current situation is and what resources, applications, skills and strengths are available as well as the ISD present weaknesses. This is the bottom-up aspect of the SISP and these details have to be matched with the top-down plans before the SISP is finished. Doing top-down or bottom-up only leaves a large gap in the firm's IS thinking.

The third dimension of information weapon planning is essentially about knowing what opportunities there are in the market to use IT competitively. These opportunities are often found through a process of creative or lateral thinking. Robert Galliers (1991) describes this as '*A synthesis of different views and visions and a process of creative thinking which needs to be incorporated into our ISPs*'. This creative thinking exercise is also sometimes described as information weapons development. These information weapons frequently come from existing systems and clients, and reinforce the firm's ability to ensure its competence with its CSFs arising from the business strategy. The idea of information weapons is expounded in detail in Chapter 4.

Finally, in producing a SISP it is important to look at the firm's long-term requirements for hardware, software and communications. This is done by undertaking information technology architecture (ITA). An architecture plan is the only way to move forward with new applications. Splintered development is what was mostly done in the past, and this can be very wasteful. There is not much that can be done about the old programs, but at least the new can be well designed and replace the old over the next few years. Effective architectures can be quite expensive. One of the options facing the firm is to spend money on the architecture now in order to save money in the future. This is not always an easy decision.

Before concluding a SISP, other strategic options have to be faced such as which applications will deliver the best return. The staffing decision is also critical, ie whether to hire more staff and develop faster, or defer important applications until next year. Also, how much capital expenditure should be committed now or over the next few years? What skills does the ISD require, and where will such people be found?

All the time the firm is constrained by what is already in place at the moment and the work currently in hand. Frequently these two issues are completely overriding and produce enormous obstacles to developing a suitable SISP for the firm.

Nonetheless at the end of the day a SISP will be produced. The plan must state clearly what is intended to be done, when it is to be done, who will do it, and how it will be done. There will also be a budget and a cash flow forecast with this plan.

2.8 SUMMARY

A new approach to IS planning has been needed for some time and SISP has quite effectively filled this need.

However, no matter how successful the firm becomes at developing Strategic Information Systems Plans, planning itself is not enough. It is essential that management continues to run the business, including training, motivating and controlling the ISD staff. Expenditure on the infrastructure is an investment in the future so that next year the firm shall be able to work more effectively and in a shorter time frame, within budget.

3 Introduction to Strategic Information Systems

3.1 INTRODUCTION

Strategic information systems (SIS) are one of the most important issues facing management today. There are several different approaches to defining an SIS and a number of these will be discussed in this chapter. However, a useful short definition of an SIS is *an IT application which directly assists the firm in achieving its corporate strategy*. In order to appreciate the importance of such systems it is necessary to understand how computer systems have developed to where they are today.

Business computing is 40 years old (Earl, 1988). It was pioneered in the UK by the food conglomerate Lyons which set about constructing its own system called LEO (Evans, 1981). This system was introduced to perform elementary and routine administrative tasks and such activities continued to be the primary function of business computers for about the next 30 years. During this period many firms experienced considerable difficulties with their computers or their data processing and executives frequently complained that they were not obtaining value for the large sums of money expended on their computer systems (Cash et al, 1988). An interesting although, perhaps, tongue in cheek description of executive attitudes towards computers is supplied by Townsend (1970):

> First get it through your head that computers are big, expensive, fast, dumb adding-machine-typewriters. Then realise that most of the computer technicians that you are likely to meet or hire are complicators, not simplifiers. They're trying to make it look tough. Not easy. They're building mystique, a priesthood, their own mumbo-jumbo ritual to keep you from knowing what they, and you, are doing.

Fortunately much of the above attitude has changed. Since the end of the 1970s computer professionals, consultants and academics have strongly emphasised that computers should no longer be thought of as administrative tools, but rather as devices which may deliver strategic advantage (Parker and Benson, 1988). These computer systems, which are either referred to as strategic information systems, or competitive edge systems, have been the subject of much research, debate and discussion in the computer industry. Some authors such as Synnott (1987) claim that there has been a fundamental shift in the way computer systems are used, and that this may be expressed as the transformation of the computer era into the information era.

During the very early years, ie the 1950s and much of the 1960s, there was really no management framework for computerisation. Firms simply computerised routine administrative tasks. Typical applications such as payroll, ledgers and inventory were all developed on a historical bookkeeping basis with little or no management utilisation other than for the purposes of maintaining statutory records.

By the end of the 1960s a theory of business computing or data processing had begun to emerge. During this period the conceptual framework, in which much of the systems development and discussion took place, was based on ideas derived from the paradigm, or model of business, developed by Robert Anthony (1965) and applied in the business computer systems field by William Zani (1970 cited in Wiseman, 1985).

According to Anthony, the enterprise may be seen in terms of a trinity consisting of the three processes of strategic planning, management control and operational control. These three processes are displayed in terms of a triangle which reveals the hierarchical nature of these activities. In this analysis strategic planning is defined as the process of setting the firm's objectives, of deciding upon the level of resources required, and of determining the policy by which these resources will be used. Management control is defined as the process by which the firm assures that the resources will be efficiently and effectively employed. Operational control refers to how the organisation ensures that the detail of the work to be performed is efficiently monitored.

The planning and control systems required are the way these processes are facilitated and by which the organisation ensures the firm is kept on course. Computer systems are excellent tools for helping management ensure that these processes are being performed.

Figure 3.1 shows the standard Anthony paradigm which illustrates the management trinity.

3.2 MANAGEMENT INFORMATION SYSTEMS

Five years after the publication of Anthony's ideas Zani developed a framework for producing management information systems (MIS) which would support the functions of the firm. These functions were defined in terms of

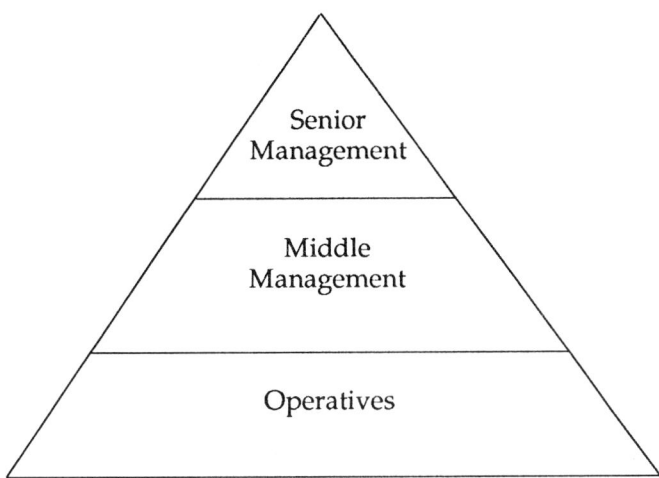

Figure 3.1   The Anthony paradigm

the Anthony triangle. Therefore Zani saw MIS as being used to support strategic planning, management control or operational control. This vision of MIS was bounded by a belief that systems developers should look only for opportunities to support managerial decision making within the confines of the Anthony trinity. This meant that the proper place for MIS was in support of how the enterprise was monitored and controlled in each of the three distinct areas defined by Anthony. Of course Zani also considered some of the labour-efficiency aspects of computers; within his analysis he recognised two types of information system, which are those automating clerical operations and those supplying decision- making information to managers.

In the information systems environment the Anthony paradigm aims to produce detailed plans for systems in each department. This is reflected in Figure 3.2. Thus financial systems may be developed for senior management, middle management and operators. This is shown in Figure 3.2.

3.3   DECISION SUPPORT & EXECUTIVE INFORMATION SYSTEMS

The next step in the conceptual or theoretical development of systems theory was the introduction of the idea of a decision support system (DSS). This work, performed by Gorry and Scott-Morton (1971), defined a DSS as an information system that supports either semi or unstructured decisions made in the area of strategic planning, management control or operations control.

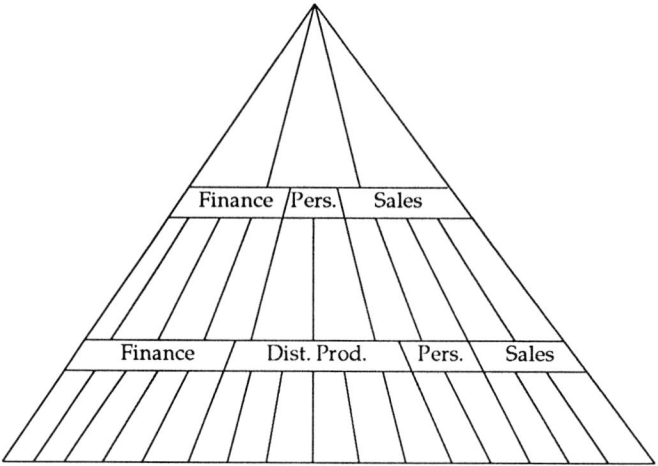

Figure 3.2   Detailed departmental systems plan

These ideas were further developed by the introduction of another concept, the executive information system (EIS), which was intended to signal a new era in the organisational use of computers (Rockart and Treacy, 1982). The definition of an EIS stated that it was a system used by top executives for the more effective use of information in the planning and control processes of their organisation. An EIS involved the use of an information warehouse or repository which might contain details of past, present and anticipated future data, at whatever degree of detail was appropriate. This would be accessed through a series of easy-to-use tools, supported by a group of consultants reporting to EIS users, that is top management. An EIS, intended to help with less structured decision making than DSS, would involve internal data as well as information supplied by such facilities as value added data services (VADS). Although this represented a new emphasis with regard to who should use information systems, there was no change in the basic structure which really still focused on the issues reflected in the Anthony paradigm. Strategic information systems had not yet been discovered.

3.4   INFORMATION SYSTEMS PLANNING METHODOLOGIES

Following on from these attempts to find suitable areas of application for information systems, thinkers in this field turned their attention to the concept of information systems planning (ISP), and in particular to the notion that a methodology could be developed for this purpose. One of the first steps in this direction was taken by the development of the idea that the data processing function within the enterprise develops through very specific stages (Nolan, 1974). Nolan initially identified four stages in the growth of all data processing (DP) facilities. These are:

- *Initiation.* This is the stage during which there is frequently emphasis on cost-reduction accounting or financial applications.

- *Contagion.* As the use of DP takes off within the firm there is the general proliferation of applications in all functional areas.

- *Formalisation/Control.* The proliferation of applications often means that DP expenditure gets out of hand, resulting in a moratorium on new applications accompanied by a strong emphasis on control.

- *Integration.* Piecemeal applications produce problems such as data redundancy and unsynchronised data. Eventually this situation becomes more and more difficult, and the organisation attempts to implement database applications.

Subsequently, Nolan added two other stages, which were data administration and maturity. These stages were used to develop Nolan's information systems planning methodology and consequently allowed Nolan Norton consultants to be able to offer advice to a range of clients from small firms to the largest and most established enterprises. By knowing where an enterprise is located in terms of these benchmark scales, and by knowing where it should move to, a planner may formulate a course of action for the ISD. Figure 3.3 shows the Nolan six stages of systems development.

Nolan identifies a transition point in the development of the firm's IS when a re-orientation occurs allowing the enterprise to progress with its IS much more rapidly and thereby reaping much greater benefits than in the early stages.

3.5 CRITICAL SUCCESS FACTORS

Another important contributor to SIS thinking is the approach referred to as critical success factors (CSFs) (Rockart, 1981). CSFs may be defined as the limited number of areas in which the enterprise must ensure success in order for the firm as a whole to have satisfactory performance. Also CSFs may be seen as those few areas which, if they are not correctly managed, will mean that the firm will not flourish, even if in all other aspects it performs well. There are normally only a few CSFs, perhaps between three and eight. CSFs are conceptually linked to the hypothesis underlying the 80/20 rule, ie only a few issues really count and it is most important to focus on these specific issues. The primary use of CSFs in the IS field was to help individual

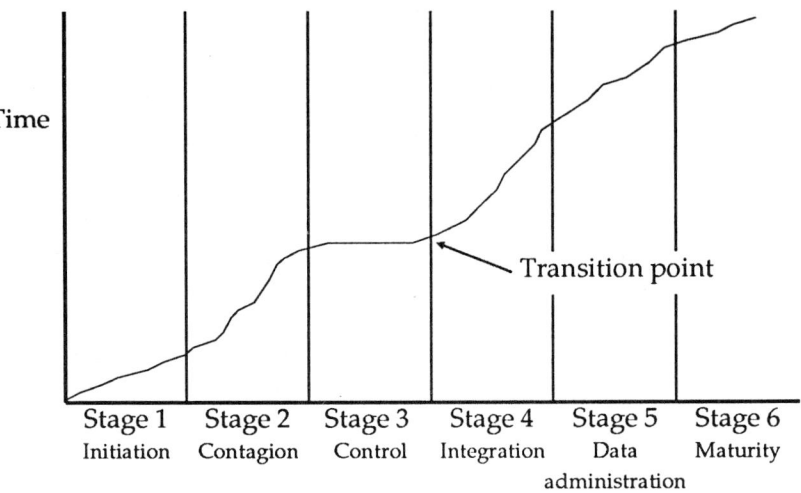

Figure 3.3 The Nolan six stages of system development

managers to determine their information needs. However, it is now considered to be another tool for assisting in the methodology of information systems planning. Looking closely at both the Nolan and the Rockart work, the Anthony paradigm is still used as the cornerstone which underpins these basic conceptual frameworks.

3.6 PLANNING METHODOLOGIES

These pioneers in the concept of information systems were followed by others including many of the international firms of management consultants such as Arthur Andersen, Ernst & Young, Coopers and Lybrand Deloitte, James Martin and Associates, and by some hardware vendors such as IBM and ICL. These methodologies incorporate additional dimensions which indicate management's concern with being able to use information systems in a much broader way than was thought of before, and this planning process is today frequently referred to as strategic information systems planning (SISP) or information systems strategic planning (ISSP).

This change, which took place during the 1980s, reflects the fact that there has been a very substantial re-orientation of business thinking about computers. The most obvious manifestation of this is a new attitude towards computing both on the part of top management and of computer profession-als. This new attitude says that computing is no longer a backroom support function (McFarlan, 1984) which might only be used to supply information to various aspects of the business, but has matured to become an integral part of the way the enterprise conducts its business.

3.7   KEY DRIVERS RESPONSIBLE FOR THE MOVE TOWARDS SIS

In fact corporate computing has now become a strategic resource (Earl, 1988). This is reflected in various ways, including the change of name given to business computing which is no longer generally referred to as electronic data processing or data processing, but rather information technology (IT) and information systems (IS). In addition this change may be seen by the fact that many firms are now actively looking to how they can utilise their IS to directly support their corporate strategy and thereby gain a competitive advantage. The aim of these new systems is to help the firm achieve superior performance and therefore have a competitive advantage in the market place.

This search for competitively advantageous applications has resulted in many IS departments changing their management approach from reactive to proactive. This proactive orientation, is, of course, interpreted as one of the prerequisites for success within the firm, ie a basis for action (Peters and Waterman, 1982).

There are many forces behind this re-orientation of thinking about compu-ters. Some of these have been discussed in Chapter 1. The following are additional factors:

- Increased internal efficiency led to most firms improving and extend-ing their use of information systems. Once these firms had mastered their IS from the point of view of internal efficiency, they began to look for other opportunities for the use of the increasingly powerful equip-ment being put at their disposal, and the search to find SIS was on. In these firms Information Systems Planning became more formal and began to be incorporated into the firms' strategic planning processes as a means of achieving a competitive advantage.

- Consumers are becoming more and more sophisticated and continue to demand more information and better service. Firms want to know, sometimes to the hour, when goods have been dispatched and have been delivered to their premises. In other cases buyers want to know when suppliers' manufacturing facilities will be able to commence production of their goods.

- Electronic markets occur when vendors supply, through the medium of a data communications network, not only details of their own product, but also information about competitive products. This new phenomenon, which has evolved out of the locking-in strategy, is said to represent the start of a major change in the way business will be structured in the future. Because of the efficiency with which markets may be tapped using this technology, electronic marketing will make it more attractive to buy certain goods and services than to manufacture them. This will eventually have the effect of making vertical integration less appealing to many enterprises. The relevant types of SIS in this application area are inter-organisational systems (IOS) and EDI.

There are now hundreds or even thousands of firms which have used IS to gain competitive advantages. It was claimed in a recent research survey conducted in the UK (Butler Cox, 1987) that there are many firms who report having obtained competitive advantage through the use of their IS. This research reinforces the views of Perry (1986) who stated:

IS now touches every business activity of a company offering a product or service, from conceptualisation, design, and production, to marketing, distribution and support. As a result, IS has become a critical component of corporate strategy planning and competitive advantage.

Thus it is now recognised that information systems planning is an important part of corporate planning and must be integrated into the framework of the firm's strategic thinking. By integrating corporate and information systems planning it is frequently said that the firm has a better chance of discovering opportunities for SIS.

Within the firm itself there are several aspects to the development and management of IS (Cash et al, 1988). These need to be considered carefully when the firm is researching SIS and deciding how to proceed with their implementation. In the first place, whether the IS activity may have strategic relevance to the firm is, of course, not a constant. It varies not only as a function of the firm's industry, but also in respect of the competition, the firm's structure, the current management attitude, etc. In fact, aspects of the corporate culture such as attitudes to corporate planning, financial control and speed of technological absorption are all keys to the firm's ability to use SIS.

Several authors including Earl, Wiseman and Synnott, have developed conceptual frameworks within which to analyse these systems. In addition, numerous firms in the UK and the USA, and also the UK Department of Trade and Industry, have commissioned studies of how such systems have been effectively introduced.

3.8 FRAMEWORKS FOR SIS

There are a number of different conceptual frameworks through which it is possible to understand the idea of SIS, superior performance and competitive edge applications.

3.8.1 Achieving Superior Performance

In general there are two distinct ways with which a computer may help a firm to achieve superior performance. The first approach is to use the computer system to help change the basic attractiveness of the industry in which the firm operates as per the Porter model shown in Figure 3.4. The second approach is to use the computer system to give direct support to the firm's generic corporate strategy.

As a firm's performance depends on the industry structure in which it competes, the possible impact that IS has on this structure is of considerable importance. A firm's industry structure may be described in terms of five major characteristics: strength of buyers/customers; strength of sellers/suppliers; ease of entry of new competitors; ability to use substitutes; and rivalry among competing firms. Figure 3.4 indicates the five competitive forces in the industry structure acting upon the firm and determining the industry profitability.

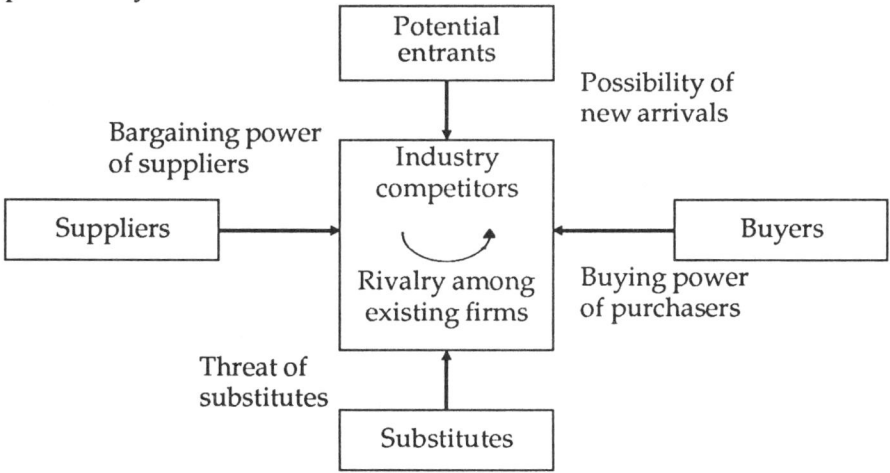

Figure 3.4 Competitive forces determining industry attractiveness

IS may be used to increase a firm's relative strength/effectiveness in each of the following areas:

- Strength of buyers/customers. In a market where there are strong buyers a firm may moderate their power by introducing a switching cost.

- Strength of sellers/suppliers. Strong sellers/suppliers may keep the price of inputs uncomfortably high.

- Ease of entry for new competitors. New firms may be discouraged from entering the market simply because of the cost of establishing a competent IS facility with which to compete with established operators.

- Ability to use substitutes. New product development may be substantially enhanced by using IS.

- Rivalry among competing firms may be, and often is, expressed in how these firms use IS to serve their clients.

3.8.2 Business Strategy

To use an IS to give direct support to a firm's generic corporate strategy the firm must in the first instance be pursuing a generic strategy. In addition it is important that appropriate systems are chosen to reinforce the strategies which have been used to create a competitive advantage.

Before discussing SIS more closely, it is important to examine what is meant by business strategy, and to establish a context in which it is possible to combine various concepts of business strategy and information systems.

It is useful to begin a discussion of strategy by considering the definition supplied by the *Shorter Oxford English Dictionary* (1983), which makes the military background of the word strategy very clear by stating:

STRATEGY. The art of a commander-in-chief; the art of projecting and directing the larger military movements and operations in a campaign. Differs materially from tactic; the latter belonging only to the mechanical movement of bodies set in motion by the former.

From the above definition it is not difficult to deduce what the business equivalent for the term strategy should be.

BUSINESS STRATEGY. The concern of the managing director or chief executive; the art of planning and directing the larger business issues of what the firm is trying to achieve, its objectives and how it tries to achieve these objectives, ie the firm's policy.

Although this definition is reasonably straightforward, many business practitioners find that they cannot easily relate to the concept of strategy, let alone translate it into effective business action.

The main difficulty which arises is that it is not always clear which business issues should properly be considered as strategic. This problem stems from several difficulties, including the fact that it is often not easy to identify what the firm is trying to achieve, except in the most general terms, such as profit maximisation or some variation on the profit theme. For a long time it was accepted and taught as a fundamental axiom in economic theory that the only objective of business was to make profit, and as much of it as possible. Profit maximisation was the guiding principle behind all business decisions. It was also considered for a long time that this profit maximisation was a useful practical concept to always be borne in mind when planning and directing the business.

In recent years, although the desire and/or need for profits has not declined, the term profit maximisation is no longer viewed as sufficiently specific to be helpful in planning or directing the firm. The result of this is that the firm's objectives have been stated in terms which more specifically relate to the type of organisation concerned and to the type of industry in which it functions. Examples of this include the firm wishing to satisfy various types of demand or to achieve a certain level of market share or a particular position in the market. Furthermore, objectives are often stated in terms of achieving high quality performance through the development of the firm's people and/or through the use of technological innovation. In other cases objectives are expressed in terms of capital acquisitions or diversifications. Of course, the profit motive has by no means disappeared and it still remains of great concern to the management of the firm. But it has now been added to.

Although this is much more helpful than simple statements about profit maximisation, it does in turn lead to difficulties when considering the strategic aspects of the business. The major problem is that there are so many different elements of the organisation which must be considered, planned and directed that it is far too easy to believe that just about every aspect of the business is strategic. However, if all aspects of the business are, or can be, strategic, then the concept of business strategy quickly becomes virtually unmanageable. One of the key elements in coming to terms with the concept of corporate strategy is to understand that strategy requires a multi-functional perspective which can cope with a wide variety of issues and which should sort out those issues which are strategic.

3.9   KEY ASPECTS OF CORPORATE STRATEGY

To come to terms with the business definition of strategy it is useful to review some of the leading writers on the subject. H. Igor Ansoff (1965) wrote one of the early textbooks on the subject of business strategy which he called simply, *Corporate Strategy*. In this book he defines strategic issues as follows:

> Strategic decisions are primarily concerned with external, rather than internal, problems of the firm and specifically with selection of the product mix which the firm will produce and the markets to which it will sell. To use an engineering term, the strategic problem is concerned with establishing an 'impedance match' between the firm and its environment, or, in more usual terms, it is the problem of deciding what business the firm is in and what kinds of business it will seek to enter.

Here we use the term strategic to mean 'pertaining to the relation between the firm and its environment'. This is more specific, and different to a more common usage in which 'strategic ' denotes 'important'. Depending on its position, the firm may find operating decisions to be more important than strategic.

Strategic decisions deal with a choice of resource commitments among alternatives. By contrast to most other business decisions, strategic decisions are not self-regenerative; they make no automatic claims on top management attention. Unless actively pursued, they may remain hidden behind the operations problems.

Although this definition takes quite a different approach to the *Shorter Oxford English Dictionary* it does re-iterate that strategy is to do with broad issues, such as what business the firm is in and which products and markets it should be exploiting. The Ansoff definition is important because it stresses two things. First, strategic issues are to do with external, rather than internal, problems or opportunities. This is emphasised by stating that the firm's relationship to its environment lies at the centre of the strategic issue. Secondly, Ansoff makes it abundantly clear that in his view the terms strategic and important are not synonymous. To use them as such creates problems.

In a subsequent work, *Implanting Strategic Management*, Ansoff (1984) develops the argument:

> All firms have a strategy. Some firms spend much time and money in reducing their strategy to writing while others simply act out their strategy and do not bother to articulate it. The former are said to have to have formulated their business strategy while the latter are said to have an implicit strategy.

This view is supported by Mintzberg (1988) who suggests that there are various distinct definitions of strategy including strategy as a plan, a pattern, a position and a perspective. Mintzberg distinguishes between deliberate and emergent strategy and points out that an emergent strategy is one which is formed in an organisation without active conscious intention.

Whether a firm will formulate a strategy or rely on an implicit strategy depends upon whether the historical dynamics of the firm allow it to continue to evolve automatically in a profitable and expanding direction (sometimes referred to as adaptive growth). If this is the case there is no need for the expensive and time consuming process of strategy formulation.

However, as firms become more complex, and as the environment, technology and competition rapidly change, so it becomes less and less easy for firms' own internal dynamics to provide automatically the re-focusing required to ensure continued development. Therefore, at some stage, many firms have to move from explicit strategies to deliberate strategic formulation. The main purpose of the strategy formulation is to provide the firm with a set of guidelines which may be used to help re-orientate the organisational thrust so that the firm can cope with new opportunities and threats. Whether the strategy is deliberate or emergent, the final result is well described by Quinn et al (1988):

> A strategy is the pattern or plan that integrates an organisation's major goals, policies, and action sequences into a cohesive whole. A well formed strategy helps to marshal and allocate an organisation's resources into a unique and viable posture based on its relative internal competencies and shortcomings, anticipated changes in the environment, and contingent moves by intelligent opponents.

According to Porter (1985), to ensure that a competitive advantage is achieved a firm must develop one of the following generic strategies:

– Differentiate its product so that the marketplace will perceive the product to be superior;
– Establish itself as a low cost leader in the market;
– Find a niche to service.

These strategies may be clearly viewed in Porter's classic 2x2 matrix as seen in Figure 3.5.

Clearly IS can substantially enhance the firm's efforts in pursuing any of these generic strategies. If the firm's strategy is that of differentiation, then IS may be used to directly add value to the product or service by improving order processing, delivery, after-sales service, etc. If its strategy is that of low cost leadership then IS may be used to directly reduce the cost of buying and servicing the product. Niche strategies will be enhanced by a combination of these two as well as using IS to monitor and select appropriate market segments for the purposes of establishing a niche.

Thus, when IS is used to achieve a competitive advantage it may be referred to as a strategic information system (SIS). However, in using the term SIS in

Competitive Advantage

		Lower Cost	Differentiation
Competitive Scope	Broad Target	Cost Leadership	Differentiation
	Narrow Target	Cost Focus	Differentiation Focus

Figure 3.5 Porter's classic generic strategy options

this way it is important to ensure that a common understanding is achieved and an appropriate definition of this term used as there is a wide range of views as to the meaning of an SIS.

3.10   CORPORATE STRATEGY AND COMPETITIVE ADVANTAGE

The process of strategic management is progressively being defined as the management of competitive advantage. The idea of competitive advantage was articulated in the 1970s by McKinsey who based the concept on what they observed from the Japanese penetration of western markets under difficult conditions. One of the leading authorities on corporate strategy today is Professor Michael Porter of Harvard Business School. Porter has written two books, *Competitive Strategy* (1980) and *Competitive Advantage* (1985).

The following quotation from *Competitive Strategy* indicates Porter's outward looking view of what constitutes strategy.

The essence of formulating competitive strategy is relating a company to its environment. Although the relevant environment is very broad, encompassing social as well as economic forces, the key aspect of the firm's environment is the industry or industries in which it competes. Industry structure has a strong influence in determining the competitive rules of the game as well as the strategies potentially available to the firm. The essence of strategic formulation is coping with competition.

3.10.1   Porter's Value Chain

The work conducted by Michael Porter actually offers several opportunities for seeking SIS opportunities at the industry attractiveness level, the generic strategy level and the value chain level. With regard to industry attractiveness issues, the classic data communication networks installed by the airlines and pharmaceutical distributors were attempts to lock-in clients and thus change the power structure the firm faced. On the question of generic strategies, Porter brought home the issues of matching systems to strategies. Thus the fact that high-cost systems should not be used by firms seeking to be cost leaders is emphasised. In addition the value chain is a most powerful concept in looking for SIS opportunities. This concept emphasises the fact that to find SIS opportunities it is necessary to look closely at the way the firm functions. Porter defines nine value chain activities which he claims exist in most industrial firms. However, service organisations will, of course, have different structures. In addition, the value chain concept is important as it offers the enterprise a chance to focus on the linkages between the different procedures a firm may be pursuing in each of its value activities and these linkages are prime areas for SIS opportunities. Figure 3.6 shows a value chain for a typical industrial organisation.

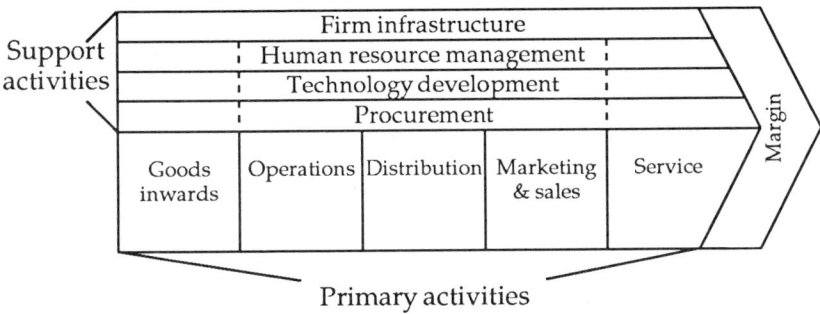

Figure 3.6   Porter's value chain

Figure 3.7 shows some of the detail of the marketing and sales value activity in a typical firm on which an analyst must focus when looking for SIS opportunities. A closer examination of the work involved in each activity within the value chain shows that all value activities rely on IT support. This is shown in Figure 3.8.

Porter's value chain concept becomes even more important when it is extended to the whole industry in which the firm operates. Thus in the industry value chain there are, in addition to the firm itself, its suppliers and its clients, referred to by Porter as buyers. The relationships between these players are shown in Figure 3.9.

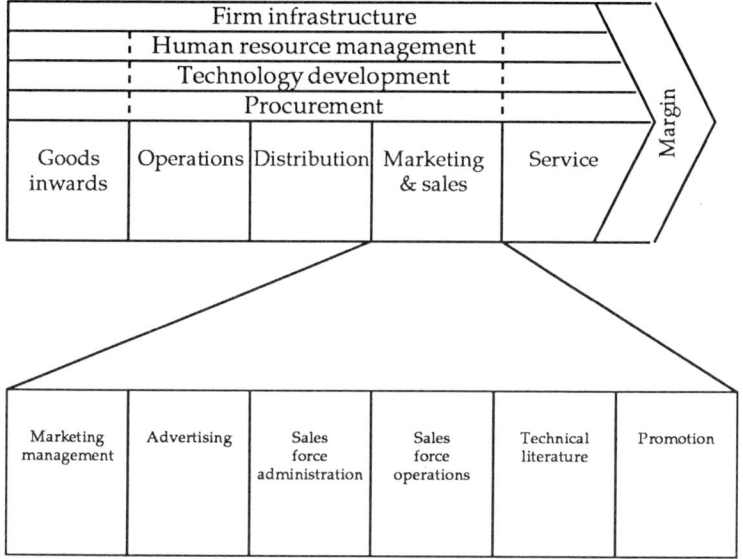

Figure 3.7   Typical marketing & sales activity

In searching for SIS, the firm should look at the linkages between the different firms in the value chain as it is in this area of linkage that most competitive advantage may be obtained. In Figure 3.10 these linkages are shown. A typical linkage is the one between the firms Outbound Logistics, and its clients Inbound Logistics. The American Hospital Supplies application is a classical example of joining the outward logistics of the supplier with the inbound logistics of its clients through an SIS.

3.10.2 Strategic Information Systems

Applying Porter's value chain concepts, the following is a usable definition of an SIS.

An SIS is an IT application which helps a firm improve its long-term performance by achieving its corporate strategy, and thereby directly increasing its value added contribution to the industry value chain. An SIS will give management an opportunity to increase the effectiveness with which a firm relates to and operates within its industry value chain.

The following elaborates on this definition by describing some of the

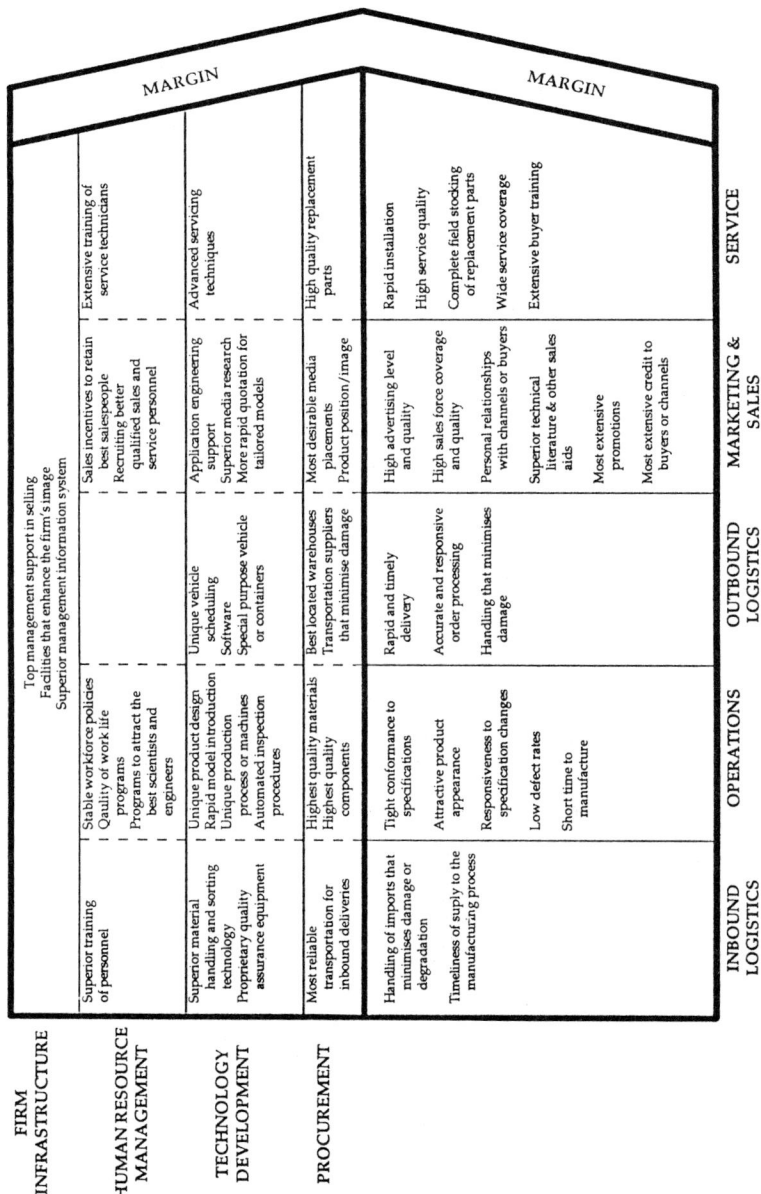

Figure 3.8 Details of work in the value chain

Figure 3.9   Porter's industry value chain

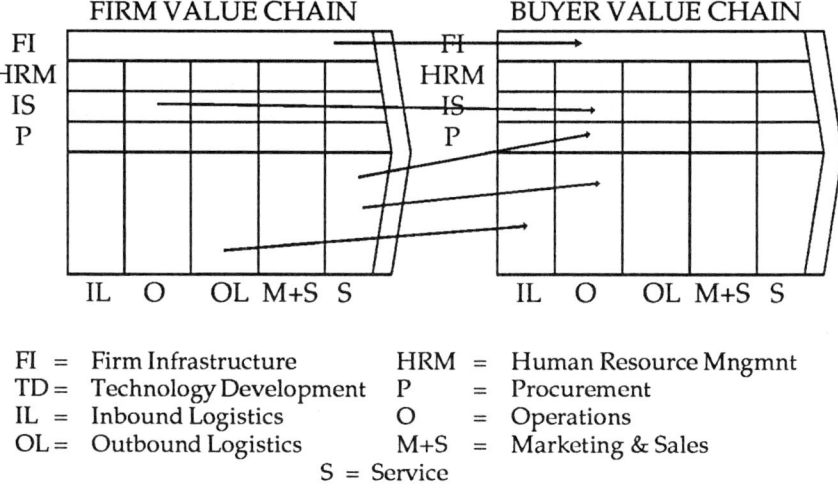

FI	=	Firm Infrastructure	HRM	=	Human Resource Mngmnt
TD	=	Technology Development	P	=	Procurement
IL	=	Inbound Logistics	O	=	Operations
OL	=	Outbound Logistics	M+S	=	Marketing & Sales
			S	=	Service

Figure 3.10   Linkages between industry value chains

characteristics of an SIS.

- It must be outward looking, ie it must be set up in order to service clients.
- It must offer real benefit to the client, and therefore must not be either trivial or fatuous.
- It must not be too easily copyable and therefore where possible should use proprietary hardware, software or data.
- It must be capable of changing the marketplace's perception of the firm.

The use of computers for IS has changed dramatically in the last few years, in that certain firms are now using their computing facilities in innovative and creative ways to achieve superior performance. This has been achieved by either changing their relative position within their industry structure or by re-enforcing their generic strategy to achieve a sustainable competitive advantage. Many of the firms who have undertaken this course of action have increased the size of their operations by increasing turnover, or by establishing new businesses. Also, many firms have reported that their new approach to IS has produced better profits. The SIS which firms are using to achieve superior performance are rapidly becoming an essential part of the firms' corporate strategic plans.

3.10.3 McFarlan's Strategic Matrix

McFarlan's strategic matrix provides another view by offering a taxonomy by which a firm can measure its IS effort in respect of strategic and non-strategic systems. The ideas behind the strategic matrix, which are similar to the famous Boston Consulting Group's 'strategic investment portfolio matrix', allow information systems to be categorised as either strategic, turn-around, factory or support. These categories are presented graphically in Figure 3.11. This analysis may also be used as a framework for resource allocation, including both staff and money, as well as for the making of buy or make decisions.

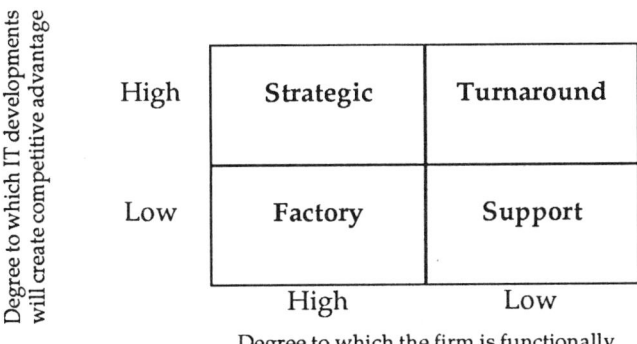

Figure 3.11 McFarlan's strategic matrix

Figure 3.12 shows how financial and investment resources may be matched to the four systems categories defined by McFarlan.

Clearly support and factory systems can be easily bought in from software or system houses while strategic and turnaround systems cannot.

In *Increase Profits with Strategic Information Systems* (Remenyi, 1988 published by the NCC) both Porter's 'value chain' and McFarlan's 'strategic matrix' are discussed in detail and directly related to the SIS issue.

Degree to which IT developments will create competitive advantage

	Strategic	Turnaround
High	**Strategic** As much investment as practical Senior staff	**Turnaround** As much expense as practical Younger staff
Low	**Factory** Sufficient investment Experienced	**Support** Minimum expense Junior staff
	High	Low

Degree to which the firm is functionally
dependent upon IS/IT today

Figure 3.12 Categorisation of resources

3.10.4 Synnott's Information Weapons (IW)

William Synnott has made a major contribution to the thinking in the SIS field in his book *The Information Weapon* (1987). However he does not use the term SIS but rather uses the name Customer Support System. Synnott's book is a very comprehensive treatise on a wide range of IS issues which he believes are necessary to support Information Resource Management (IRM). IRM for Synnott is the key to being able to develop information weapons.

Synnott argues that in moving from the Computer Era to the Information Era, IS has been revolutionised. Figure 3.13 shows some of the issues which have changed due to this transition.

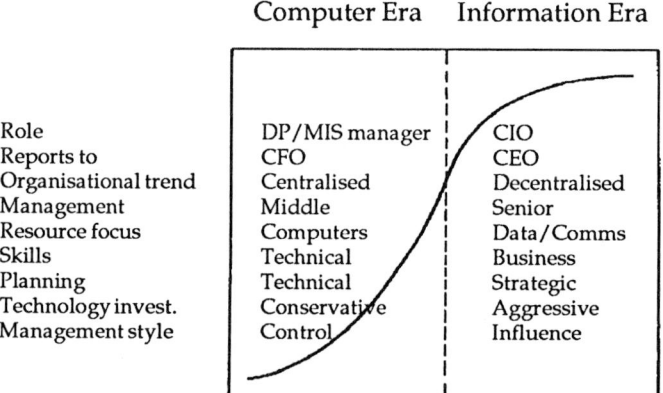

	Computer Era	Information Era
Role	DP/MIS manager	CIO
Reports to	CFO	CEO
Organisational trend	Centralised	Decentralised
Management	Middle	Senior
Resource focus	Computers	Data/Comms
Skills	Technical	Business
Planning	Technical	Strategic
Technology invest.	Conservative	Aggressive
Management style	Control	Influence

**Figure 3.13   Issues influenced by the transition from
the computer era to the information era**

Furthermore the move from the computer era to the information era has produced a re-orientation from focusing on Operations Support Systems (OSS) to Management Support Systems (MSS), and then on to Customer Support Systems (CSS). Figure 3.14 shows this diagrammatically.

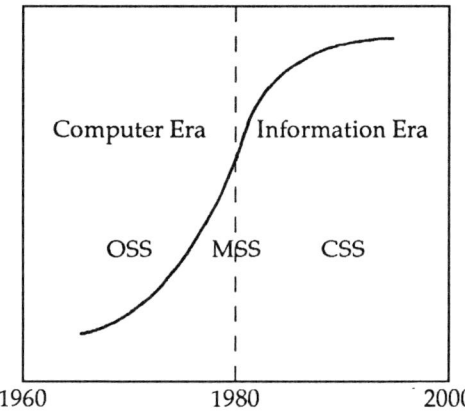

Figure 3.14 Synnott's reorientation

Synnott provides a model for developing an IW. He argues that there are three primary strategies for IWs. These are innovation, information and productivity. Each of these strategies may be viewed from two additional dimensions which are internal and external. Also the firm may be either a leader or a follower in any of these strategies. Thus according to Synnott there are 12 primary IW planning options available to the enterprise. These are shown in Figure 3.15.

Synnott's work involves a detailed analysis of the function of the ISD in which he focuses on a number of issues including business architecture, systems architecture, end user architecture, etc. The dependence and relationships of these architectures are shown in Figure 3.16.

Synnott concludes his analysis by developing 64 Information Weapons.

3.11 SUMMARY

The theory of IS has developed very rapidly over the last 25 years. During this period the emphasis on the role of IS has dramatically changed from administrative, cost-focused operations support systems, through various types of management support systems, which although important, were still primarily internally orientated, to externally focused, often aggressive, customer support systems. These latter systems are designed to give the firm a compe-

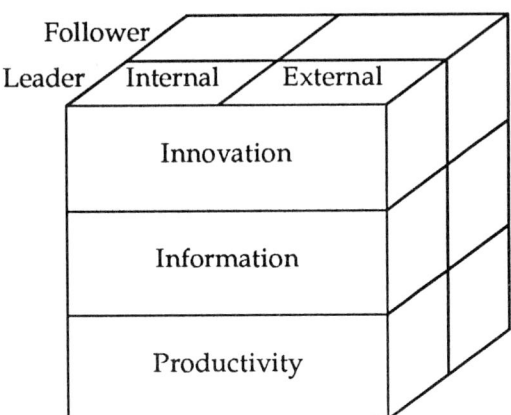

Figure 3.15   **The 12 primary information weapon planning options**

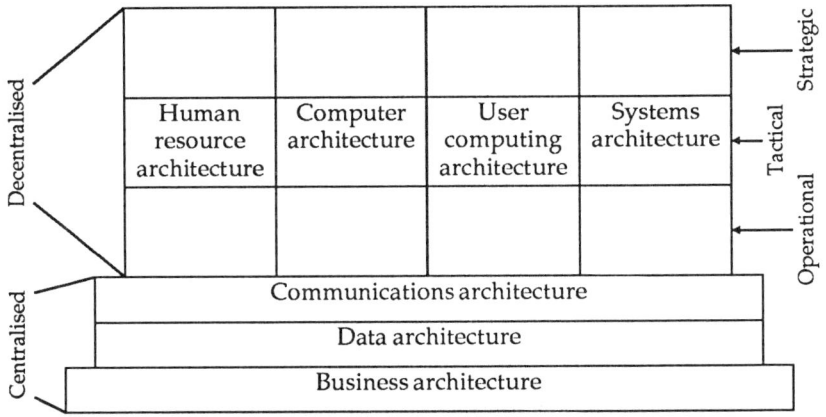

Figure 3.16   **The dependencies and relationships between the architectures described by Synnott**

titive advantage and are best described as SIS. It is important that there will be much development in the area of SIS during the next few years as more and more firms begin to use their systems in this way.

4   Conceptual Frameworks for SIS

4.1   INTRODUCTION

There are a number of different conceptual frameworks through which it is possible to understand the idea of a SIS. In the last chapter the work of Michael Porter, Warren McFarlan, William Synnott, and others was discussed. In this chapter another two conceptual frameworks will be explored. These frameworks have been developed by Charles Wiseman and are clearly described in his book *Strategy and Computers - Information Systems as Competitive Weapons* (1985), and by John Rockart (1979, 1981, 1982) who pioneered the concept of the use of Critical Success Factors in conjunction with IS. Wiseman's ideas are important as they attempt to both present a complete picture of what a SIS is and how it may be used, and provide a technique which helps the executive find SIS opportunities in the firm. He calls this the Strategic Options Generator. John Rockart is widely published, especially in the *Harvard Business Review* and the *Strategic Management Review*.

4.1.1   The New Perspective

According to Wiseman, a SIS is an information system used to support or shape the competitive strategy of the organisation. SIS represents a new kind of information system, radically different in organisational use from those countenanced by the conventional perspective.

The conventional perspective, which is described in the previous chapter, is based on the notion that IS should only focus on ways of supplying information which will support management in monitoring and controlling the firm in terms of the Anthony Triangle paradigm.

This approach is unsuitable for guiding the systematic search for SIS opportunities and is incapable of explaining the strategic significance of such applications. In terms of the conventional perspective there were only possible opportunities for IS applications. These opportunities are best expressed diagrammatically as shown in Figure 4.1. It is important to note that all these systems based on the traditional perspective are to do with either automation, basic office processes, or supplying information to management.

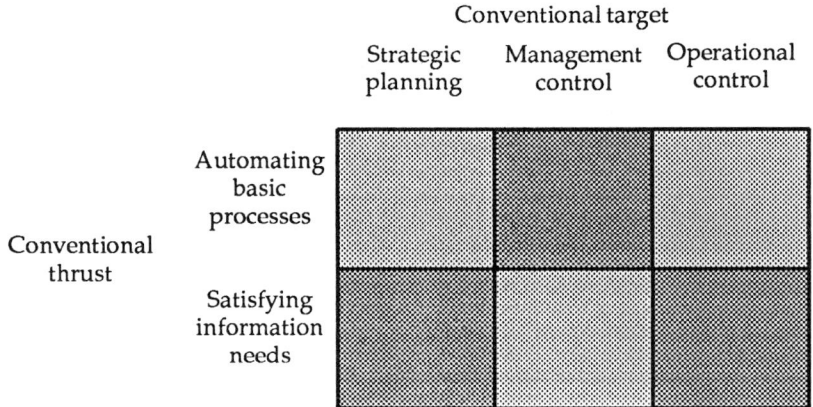

Figure 4.1 The six opportunities for IS applications

4.2   DEFINING A SIS

It is possible to distinguish between the organisational uses and the technical functions of an IS. Some of the uses to which an IS is put are conventional and some are strategic. The organisational use of an IS refers to whether it automates basic clerical processes, or satisfies informational needs, or supports and shapes competitive strategy. The technical function of an IS refers to whether it is a transaction processing system or an information processing system.

There is not much agreement as to a universal definition of the term Management Information System (MIS). Initially MIS referred to systems which delivered reports which aided management in decision making. However, in recent years, the terms DSS and EIS have respectively taken over this role. For most IS executives the term MIS is now used to refer to the activities involved with predefined transactions and producing fixed format reports on schedule. Thus the main aim of MIS is to automate basic business processes within the enterprise with the objective of cost reduction or avoidance. These systems are also referred to as Transaction Processing Systems (TPS).

In contrast to the MIS there is the Management Support System (MSS). A MSS is a system which provides end users with a query language and an analytical capability. These are aimed at assisting executives and professionals in the decision making process. These systems are also frequently referred to as DSS or EIS. The development of a MSS requires a different attitude and a different type of developer from those involved with MIS. A MSS requires much more management input and much less systems input.

A SIS may be either a MIS or a MSS. The dimension which makes a system strategic is that it directly supports or shapes the competitive strategy of the enterprise. From Figure 4.2 it can be seen that SIS straddles both these other systems categories.

Use\ \ \ \ Function	Automating Basic Processes	Satisfying Information needs	Supporting or shaping competitive strategy
Transaction Processing	MIS		SIS
Query and analysis		MSS	

Figure 4.2   A taxonomy for information systems

SIS is a new information management product line. It targets new user groups providing new benefits which are not delivered by either MIS or MSS. It links the IS effort directly to the business, gaining a competitive edge by finding, getting and keeping clients. SIS frequently requires the activities of the ISD to be extended. It may require new hardware and software as well as additional personnel and an organisation and culture change. It is a major addition to the way the firm does business. A SIS will generally change the focus of the ISD from the function of applications to the use of applications which may be seen as a shift from a features orientation to a benefits orientation.

Of course it is possible to have a certain amount of overlap among these systems. A MIS may have MSS dimensions which in turn may have influence on the way the systems could be developed into a SIS. For example a MIS may have SIS potential, as in the case of the airline reservation systems, and a MSS may be developed into a SIS, such as the treasury systems now marketed by the banks, etc. These overlaps are clearly seen in Figure 4.3.

Identifying potential SIS depends upon the organisation's conceptual

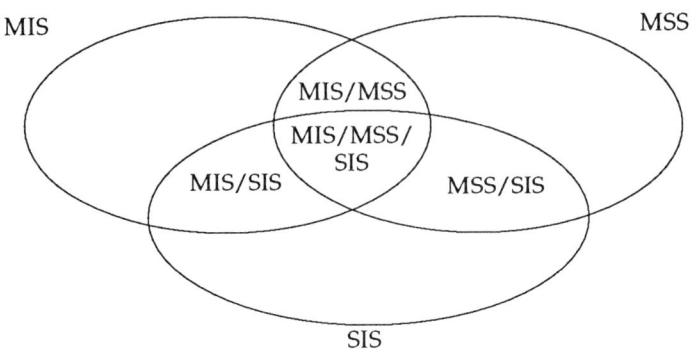

Figure 4.3   Overlap between MSS, MIS and SIS

framework. If a suitable conceptual framework is not used then it will not be possible to perceive SIS opportunities. However, if the method by which a firm's information system may be used to support or shape its competitive strategy is understood, then the firm is said to have developed strategic information system vision. Firms with this vision have a perspective of how IS can constitute a competitive advantage. Firms with such a vision encourage the search for SIS, and when such a system is discovered the firm ensures that sufficient resources are made available to support them.

4.2.1   Strategic Thrusts

Strategic perspective may be seen in terms of strategic thrust. A strategic thrust is a major move which an enterprise undertakes in its search for advantage. By supporting or shaping a strategic thrust a SIS supports or shapes the firm's effort to obtain a competitive advantage. Thus a strategic thrust is a critical interface joining competitive strategy with information systems.

According to Wiseman there are five generic strategic thrusts which are:

−   differentiation;
−   cost;
−   innovation;
−   growth;
−   alliances.

These generic strategic thrusts manifest strategic polarities, ie they are capable of assuming opposing sets of attributes depending upon their strategic use. For example, some firms will use differentiation offensively while other will use it defensively. Using differentiation offensively a firm will attempt to gain a competitive edge and thus increase its market share, while using it defensively the firm will simply be attempting to protect its share from some attack from a competitor. The same is true for each of the other strategic thrusts.

Generic strategic thrusts frequently occur in combination. For example, a growth thrust may be combined with a cost reduction thrust, or an innovation thrust may be part of a differentiation thrust. Generic strategic thrusts are subject to a variety of ordering and degree relations. For example, it is possible to have a major, or a medium, or a minor cost thrust and it might also be feasible for the firm to have a long term or medium term differentiation thrust. Generic strategic thrusts are often related by dialectical processes. This means that the process of selecting one or more thrusts frequently leads the planner to realise that other considerations should be taken into account. Thus new ideas are generated.

4.3   STRATEGIC OPTION GENERATOR

A strategic option generator is an instrument designed to help identify SIS opportunities. The strategic thrusts serve as the engine which power the generator. The generator directs attention towards strategic targets and then the thrust is used to hit them.

There are three basic classes of strategic targets:

(1) suppliers;

(2) customers;

(3) competitors.

In this context suppliers are companies which supply goods or services – raw materials and finished products, intangibles such as insurance and banking – to the firm.

Customers include organisations and individuals which purchase the firm's products. These may be end users or various sorts of intermediaries.

Competitors are those firms selling products or services judged by the enterprise to be the same as, or similar to, or could serve as a substitute for, the firm's product. Competitor targets may include direct competitors, potential competitors and substitute or indirect competitors.

A firm's suppliers may also be its customer and competitor, and there may be several sub-categories of targets producing a polarity of thrusts.

With five generic strategic thrusts and three generic strategic target classes there is a potential to strike in one of 15 different ways. Figure 4.4 shows these 15 areas of opportunity for SIS.

Strategic target

	Supplier	Customer	Competitor
Differentiation			
Cost			
Innovation			
Growth			
Alliance			

Strategic thrust

Figure 4.4   Areas of opportunity for SIS

This number may be dramatically increased by having sub-classes of targets and by introducing the polarity or mode of the generic strategic thrusts. The mode of a strategic thrust refers to whether it is used offensively or defensively and the direction of a strategic thrust refers to whether the IS support or shaping of the thrust is used by the firm, or whether it is provided to help reach its target. The distinction between supporting or shaping the strategic thrust is important. If the SIS is supporting the thrust then it is functioning as a facilitator, but is not the main issue itself, whereas if it is shaping the thrust then the SIS itself delivers the strategic advantage.

The strategic options generator is essentially a checklist which guides the executive in a systematic way through all the parameters which must be considered in seeking a SIS opportunity. By promoting a series of thoughts and questions which relate to strategic thrusts and targets the strategic option generator encourages its users to search scientifically for SIS opportunities. Figure 4.5 is a list of the issues to be addressed.

According to Wiseman, no firm which has tried to identify SIS opportunities through the use of a strategic option generator has failed to do so.

Wiseman's ideas are useful because they offer a complete framework with which to search for and also evaluate SIS opportunities. They also offer a concise language structure which may be used to discuss potential SIS. Wiseman is one of the few authors who make a very strong claim for the universality of SIS. However, the argument in his book, that if a firm uses his

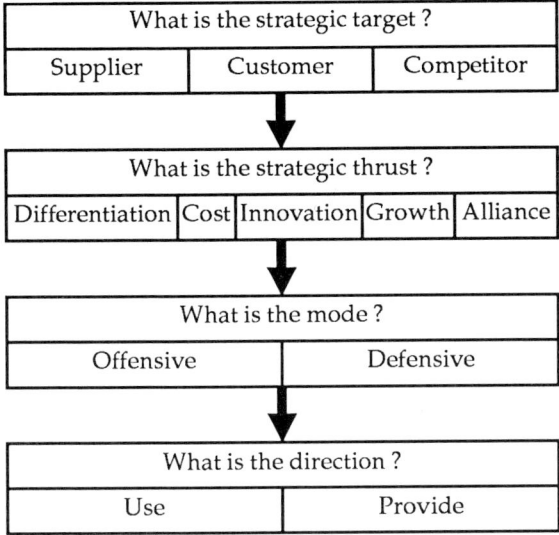

Figure 4.5   Strategic option generator

strategic options generator approach they will definitely identify opportunities for SIS, is perhaps somewhat simplistic, even to the point of naivete and over-optimism (Remenyi, 1988).

4.4   CRITICAL SUCCESS FACTORS

Another important approach to establishing the possibility of using information as a competitive weapon is the critical success factors technique. Critical Success Factors (CSF) may be defined as the few important areas where things must go right for the business to flourish, or those few areas in which if things do not go right, although all other aspects of the firm are well, the business will not prosper.

The technique is derived from the same thinking as the 80/20 rule. It has two main functions, which are the encouragement of individual executives to focus on those issues which are the most important and then to help them think through their information needs in these areas. CSF analysis often forces executives to make explicit the unconscious or implicit CSF which they have been using for some time.

For every CSF identified there should be a key performance indicator (KPI). A KPI is a business measure which will inform management how adequately the firm is performing in its efforts to achieve the CSF.

Research conducted at the Massachusetts Institute of Technology (MIT) by John Rockart and others has demonstrated that the CSF technique in IS planning is an effective way to approach this subject. The technique was originally developed as a means of identifying the information requirements of a firm's chief executive but was subsequently expanded to embrace a much wider range of executives throughout the enterprise as a whole. The critical success factor technique has become the cornerstone of several SISP methodologies including those offered by Index Systems, Ernst & Young, James Martin & Associates and McKinsey and Co. Thus the CSF technique has attained a high degree of acceptance amongst IS planners.

CSFs are derived directly from the goals or objectives of management. When management goals are linked to the business strategy then the CSF method may be used to identify how to match IS investment with business objectives and strategies.

In using CSF the first steps are to establish the objectives of the enterprise as a whole. From this point the firm's business strategy must be derived. The next move is to generate the CSFs required to realise the strategy and thus achieve the stated objectives. This is done by eliciting the critical information set from the key staff. A very broad view of the firm is required and thus a sizable sample of management must be interviewed. An interview could easily extend for half a day and the time taken for preparation and writing up the findings from an interview could be as much as two days. The CSF method involves a series of personal interviews which are sometimes followed by a number of group brainstorming and planning sessions. The data obtained from the interviews is further refined and prioritised during these group sessions during which the KPIs are agreed. To be able to calculate KPIs such as stock turnover, asset utilisation, waste factors or staff turnover the organisation's ISD must have access to appropriate data. This data is then used to develop the firm's strategic data model (SDM) or architecture as well as define higher return IS opportunities.

Sometimes there is confusion about what constitutes an objective, a strategy and a CSF. An objective is a condition which the firm intends to achieve. Examples of objectives include an ROI of 10%, a positive cash flow of a million per quarter, a market share of 20%. Objectives should be clear, unambiguous and measurable. They should be realistic, and all employees who can aid their attainment should be aware of them. Although there may be some small differences of emphasis, objectives, goals and missions may be considered as synonyms. Strategies which have been discussed in some detail in Chapter 3 refer to how the firm intends to achieve its objectives. There are essentially only two generic strategies, ie cost leadership and differentiation.

CSFs include issues such as increasing average value per invoice, increasing the number of sales calls per day, decreasing the number of days debtors, reducing the percentage of waste materials in the manufacturing process.

This method of information collection and analysis has a top down planning orientation. There may be considerable debate and interaction between the evaluation of the CSF and the data needs which these suggest must be included in the SDM. The CSF exercise helps to influence and prioritise the elements which constitute the SDM. The information requirement identified by the CSF exercise frequently exists in different incompatible systems or media and sometimes requires the combination of hard and soft data. Hard data refers to the facts and figures produced by the accounting system, whereas soft data refers to information from less formal sources.

CSFs may be determined for the enterprise as a whole, and for individual departments or functions. CSFs for parts of the firm are sometimes referred to as lower level CSFs. In Figure 4.6, these different types of CSFs are shown.

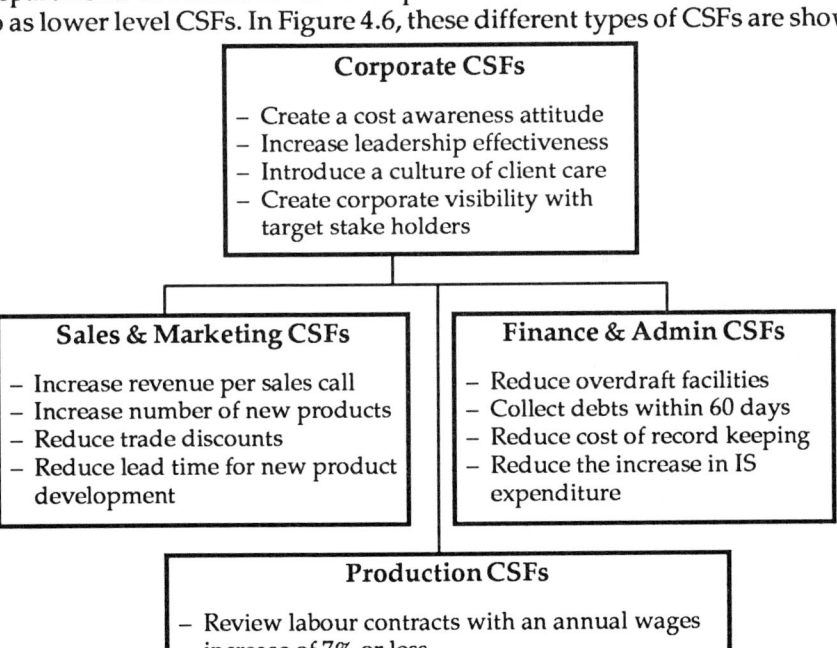

Corporate CSFs

 – Create a cost awareness attitude
 – Increase leadership effectiveness
 – Introduce a culture of client care
 – Create corporate visibility with
   target stake holders

Sales & Marketing CSFs

 – Increase revenue per sales call
 – Increase number of new products
 – Reduce trade discounts
 – Reduce lead time for new product
   development

Finance & Admin CSFs

 – Reduce overdraft facilities
 – Collect debts within 60 days
 – Reduce cost of record keeping
 – Reduce the increase in IS
   expenditure

Production CSFs

 – Review labour contracts with an annual wages
   increase of 7% or less
 – Obtain raw materials at no increased cost
 – Reduce wastage costs by 10%
 – Ensure that capital in work in progress does not
   increase

Figure 4.6   Different types of CSF

In the same way as CSFs may be used to define the requirements of general systems the technique may also be employed with a specific focus. Therefore the CSF technique may be used to obtain a critical decision set which would be used to plan for the development of a Decision Support System (DSS) and a Critical Assumption Set which could be used to plan the development of an Executive Information System (EIS). In the same way as already described these findings would impact the Strategic Data Model (SDM) and feature in the list of high return IS opportunities.

The SDM is an entity relational model showing how different data entities interrelate to each other. These models may be large and complex. It is beyond the scope of this introductory text to discuss data modelling in any detail. However in Figure 4.7 there is reproduced a simplified version of such a model.

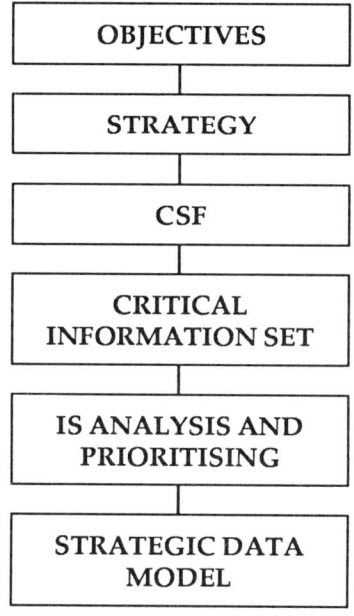

Figure 4.7   The steps for CSF

The model provides an opportunity to examine and communicate strategic data requirements. For example, a vendor's records need to be available to examine equipment, expense, purchase order and accounts payable modules.

4.5 SUMMARY

Wiseman's SOG is a very important concept because it provides a comprehensive taxonomy for thinking about SIS. Furthermore the SOG is also a mechanism for an SIS search which may be used as part of the SISP effort.

Critical success factors are even more important as they underpin most of the proprietary SISP methodologies offered in the market. This technique is seen as a way of directly accessing the IS issues of major importance to the firm, and thus to the SISP.

5 Information Technology Architecture

5.1 INTRODUCTION

An overall architectural strategy is needed to deliver SIS because such systems require effective corporate-wide policies which optimise capabilities and minimise redundancy and systems inconsistency.

An information technology architecture (ITA) plan has as its primary objective the establishment of the firm's long-term technology infrastructure which will allow systems to be designed and implemented in an effective and efficient way. ITA seeks to avoid fragmentation, redundancy and inconsistency. It defines components, formats, structure, etc, including interfaces. It may be seen as a measure of the firm's IT status, direction and strategy. An ITA plan shows where the firm is headed and what structures need to be in place before it can achieve its long-term objectives. Without such a plan, as decentralisation proceeds, the technical environments become diverse, uncontrolled and inefficient. An ITA puts into place policies and standards so that hardware functions effectively and software allows access for system management and control. ITA planning is one of the most important roles of the chief information officer (CIO). It is too important to be left to the technologists.

5.2 WHAT CAN AN ITA PLAN DO FOR THE FIRM?

It is not easy to precisely define the term information technology architecture. An ITA has been described as the structure of IT within the enterprise, which has been developed with the specific purpose of facilitating the firm's business objectives. It refers to all the different aspects of IT within the enterprise and not just the centralised information systems. The meaning of an ITA may be better understood by looking at the *Shorter Oxford English Dictionary* definition of architecture which states inter alia that architecture is the art and science of developing plans for any building, structure or system.

The ITA deals with the structure in which the different aspects of the firm's information technology exist. Its aim is to enable the enterprise to carry out its business in new ways which have strategic potential far beyond the traditional role of simple administrative systems. An ITA differs from a SISP in that it takes a much longer view of the IT function in the firm, usually looking ahead between five and ten years. Also an ITA focuses on the IT infrastructure and the policies and standards which the firm must have in place to allow IS to develop efficiently and effectively.

For almost 40 years a large number of companies have been installing computers. Each year more applications are implemented. Each one is justified according to the criteria imposed by management, designed and implemented using the most up-to-date, state-of-the-art technology and tools, and installed with great care and attention and put into use by the departments concerned. There may be many groups of application writers, or even outside contractors who may have little or no contact with each other, and each of which may have their own specific ideas about how systems should be developed and implemented.

Many systems have provision for management information to serve the decision making process. In some cases statistical reports are generated for measuring departmental or corporate performance and also for assessing strategy. Better systems will have these reports incorporated at the design stage while in other cases these requests for reports have to be bolted on at a later stage.

However, as many of these systems are generally introduced piecemeal without an overall architectural design or plan, they sometimes do not fit or integrate well. Typically what happens is that as experience grows, separate departments begin to share information. For example, sales affect warehousing, which in turn affects production, which then has an effect on buying, and so on, through all stages of the process. Bridging programs are built at considerable cost to bring data from one disparate set of programs to another. However, even with bridges, the data may not be in suitably compatible forms and thus may cause a considerable amount of operational difficulty.

Figure 5.1 shows how such a system would typically look.

Systems built in the way described above are very cumbersome and inefficient as well as being very expensive to maintain. Maintenance and enhancement of such programs is very difficult because they will tend to have been written as separate, standalone programs in their own right and not as part of a system. Furthermore they may have been written in previous generation languages, for machines now no longer in use, coded by programmers now long departed or promoted, who have left very little documentation behind.

Some organisations have decided that this way of 'growing like Topsy' is not a desirable approach. They have produced a new departmental or cor-

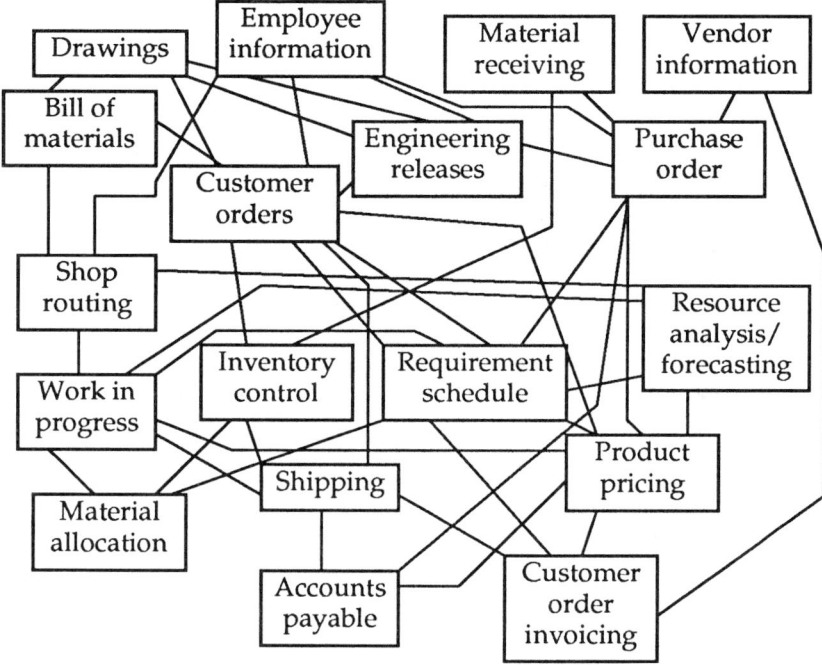

Figure 5.1 **A typical out-of-control piecemeal system**

porate plan which attempts to integrate all their information needs as well as specify IT policies and standards. To do this an ITA plan is required. Of course, an ITA plan in turn grows and develops as changes of requirement are incorporated, or design mistakes are corrected. Therefore the architectural plan must be broad, flexible and logical so that new developments may be added without disrupting the entire structure. The details of the firm's physical computer architecture constantly change as new equipment is acquired, and the plan must be broad and flexible enough to accommodate such changes. Systems developed in terms of an ITA are generally much easier to integrate and can be maintained with much less difficulty. Such systems often grow in clusters as displayed in Figure 5.2 and then the clusters are sometimes bridged as described in Figure 5.3.

5.3 ITA AND SIS

An overall architectural strategy is especially needed to deliver SIS because such systems require effective corporate-wide policies which optimise compatibility and minimise redundancy and systems inconsistencies. Thus an

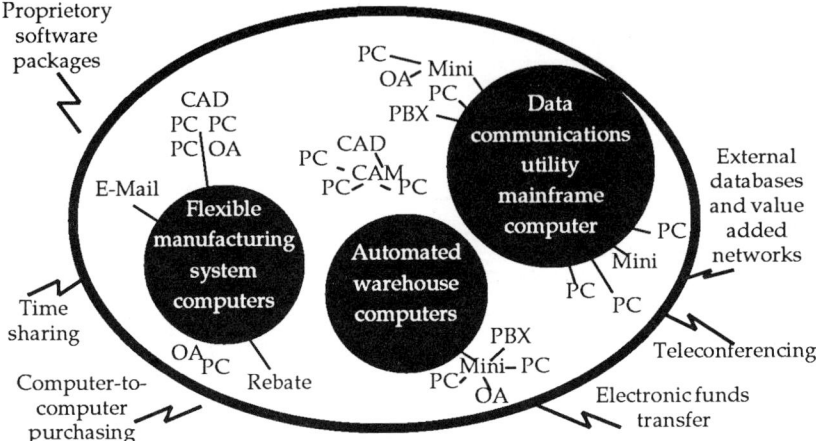

Figure 5.2 Clustered systems without any attempt at integration

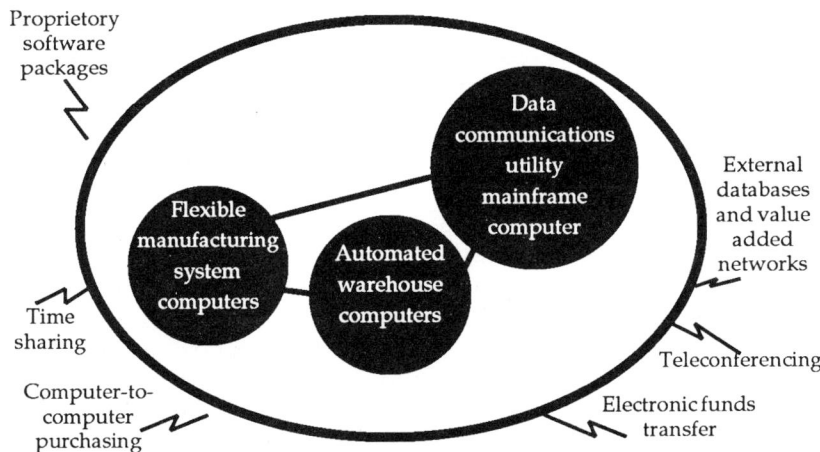

**Figure 5.3 Systems connected through the use of bridges to produce
some integration**

ITA is critical as a device to support the use of IS to gain a competitive advantage.

An ITA plan has as its primary objective the establishment of the firm's long term technology infrastructure, which will allow IS to be designed and implemented in an efficient and effective way. ITA seeks to avoid fragmentation, incompatibility, redundancy and inconsistency. It defines the firm's use of systems components, functions, structures, etc, including hardware and software interfaces. The ITA may be seen as a measure of the firm's IT status, a statement of its direction and its migration strategy. It not only shows where the firm is going but also what infrastructure needs to be in place if the firm's plans are to be achieved in the long term. Without an ITA, as decentralisation and end user computing proceeds, the firm's technological environment becomes diverse, uncontrolled and incompatible. An ITA puts into place policies and standards so that hardware purchases are compatible and software acquisitions allows access to data manipulation and consolidation. ITA planning is one of the most important roles which the CIO must fulfil. It is not merely a technical exercise, but requires extensive input from management.

5.4 ITA PLANNING

As an ITA plan is essentially a top-down exercise, the key ingredients are clear business vision, an integrated approach to business issues, and leadership. It is essential that the ITA be built on a clear understanding of the firm's objectives. These objectives must be easily understood by all the senior staff who need also to be able to relate to what they personally have to achieve if these objectives are to be realised. Staff must also be made aware of what data they need in order to achieve their objectives. Although the ITA plan is a top-down process, the ITA design and implementation is developed on a bottom-up basis. This simply means that from the ITA plan the corporate database is specified, then the applications are decided and this in turn leads to hardware and communications as shown in Figure 5.4.

Each component of the ITA must be separately reviewed and defined from both a logical and physical perspective. A logical perspective requires an examination of how data flows in and out of each business function and how these functions are related. A physical perspective examines the location and make up of the actual physical components which constitute the system such as the processors, peripherals, networks, and applications. Logical design concerns itself with integration whereas physical design looks at interfaces.

5.5 BUSINESS POLICY ISSUES

There are a number of different approaches to developing an ITA. The method described below incorporates some of the elements of a number of the popular approaches which may be modified to suit the circumstances in any particular firm.

Figure 5.5 shows the basic phases in the groundwork which need to be undertaken in developing an ITA plan.

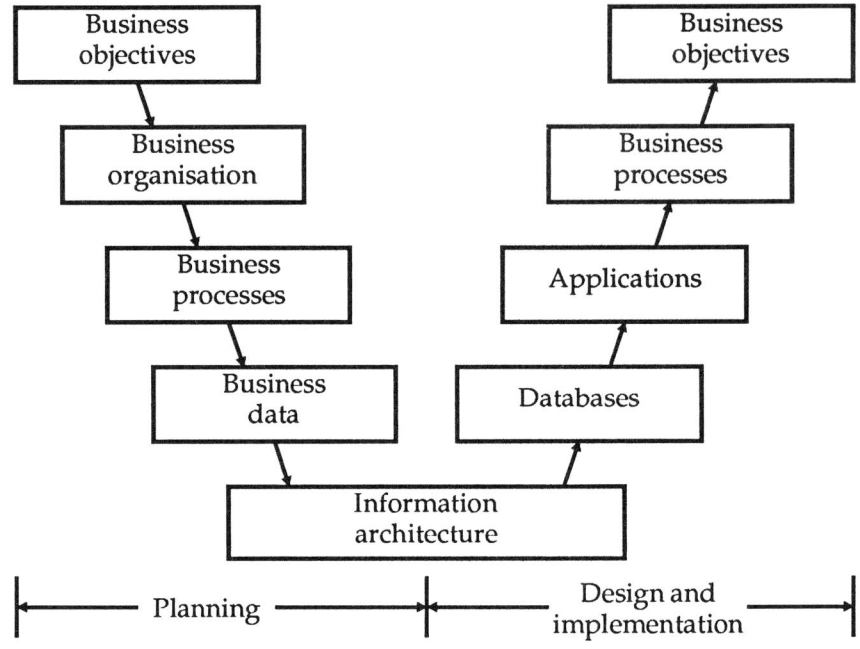

Figure 5.4   Top-down analysis with bottom-up implementation used by IBM's BSP

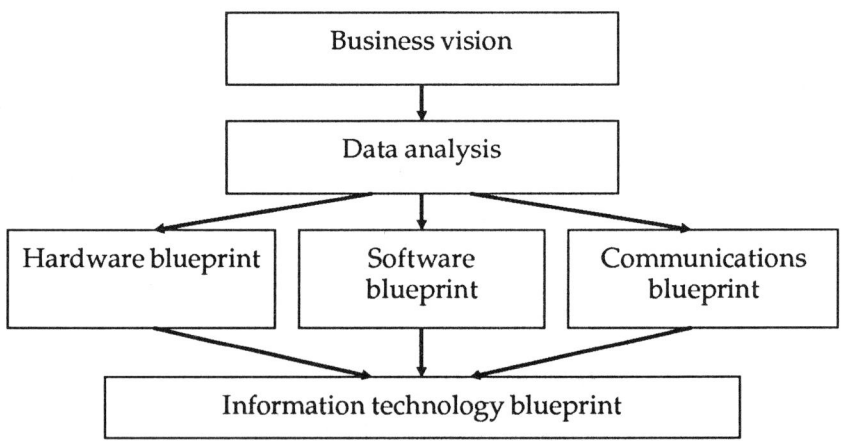

Figure 5.5   The phases of ITA plan development

As may be seen from Figure 5.5 there are four phases in the development of an ITA plan. The first phase concerns the business planning issues and

Figure 5.4 shows the importance of these business elements in the ITA plan by spelling out the different planning steps. A business vision, corporate goals, strategies and CSFs must first be developed and clearly understood by all levels of management concerned. If these procedures are not a regular part of business practice in the firm, then the CIO will have to attempt to acquire this information directly. This may be done by discussions or interviews with appropriate members of the management team. The result of this phase is the identification of the firm's mainline business activities and establishing the policies which govern these business areas. An organisation chart with supporting detailed descriptions of how the different key elements in the chart relate will often be the deliverable at this stage of the ITA plan. This phase is sometimes referred to as the business architecture.

5.5.1   Function, Entity and Data Modelling

Phase two addresses the issue of developing a data blueprint. A data blueprint spells out in detail the data which the firm requires and will require during the suggested timescale in order to achieve its objectives. The development of a data blueprint requires the involvement of a number of steps and should be conducted by a team consisting of both line managers and data professionals such as a database administrator. The development of this data blueprint is part of the firm's data resource management. This work should be conducted using a top-down process but in fact this does not always occur as it is difficult to find management time available for the detailed work required in the development of a data blueprint. This is a major weakness in this type of planning which may lead to difficulties, especially in establishing data requirements in the future.

There are several tools available to the analyst in developing the data blueprint. Some of the more popular tools are association analysis, property matrices, decomposition analysis, and function, entity and data modelling.

Step one in using these tools is to have a clear idea of the business functions required to operate the enterprise. It is important to have a fresh look at the firm's business process and functions etc., and not to assume that the way things have always been done is the optimal way.

5.5.2   An Association Matrix

An association matrix as shown in Figure 5.6 is quick and easy to document and modify the information requirements for the firm. It shows the complexities and interrelationships between the sources and uses of information. Figure 5.6 represents one of the screens available in Ernst & Young's Planning Workstation.

	Process customer orders	Receive customer orders	Fill customer orders	Ship customer orders	Validate vendor invoices	Pay vendor invoices
Product	✓	✓	✓			
Product inventory	✓		✓		✓	
Location	✓		✓			
Customer	✓	✓	✓		✓	
PO	✓	✓	✓			
Shipping vendor				✓		
PO line item		✓		✓		
Customer agreement		✓		✓	✓	✓
Order				✓	✓	
Salesperson				✓	✓	
Sales region					✓	✓

Figure 5.6 An example of an association matrix

Sometimes the business functions established by this analysis may not match very precisely with the existing organisational practice and structure which may be an accident of history, or depend on the personalities of the specific managers concerned. Function modelling is the technique used to establish requirements in the firm. Figure 5.7 shows a function model diagram for some aspects of an order entry system.

Because there may be different views about the actual functions performed a cross-reference is necessary to relate the ideal business functions with the existing procedures in the departments who currently carry out those functions. As an indication there could be up to several hundred business functions in a large complex organisation.

Step two is to establish the data that is used and which could be used to operate these functions. This is not easy, because some of the data will already be on the computer in a form which is transparent to the user, and the user departments then tend to forget that it exists. The computer deals with that and it is therefore not a problem and so not in their immediate conscious mind. In addition there are always new data elements not yet on any computer which should now be incorporated. All this data must be documented and cross-referenced to the functions that use it. The data will have to be named, and it will be convenient if the names of the data are exactly what they are called in the organisation, not just as decided by an analyst or

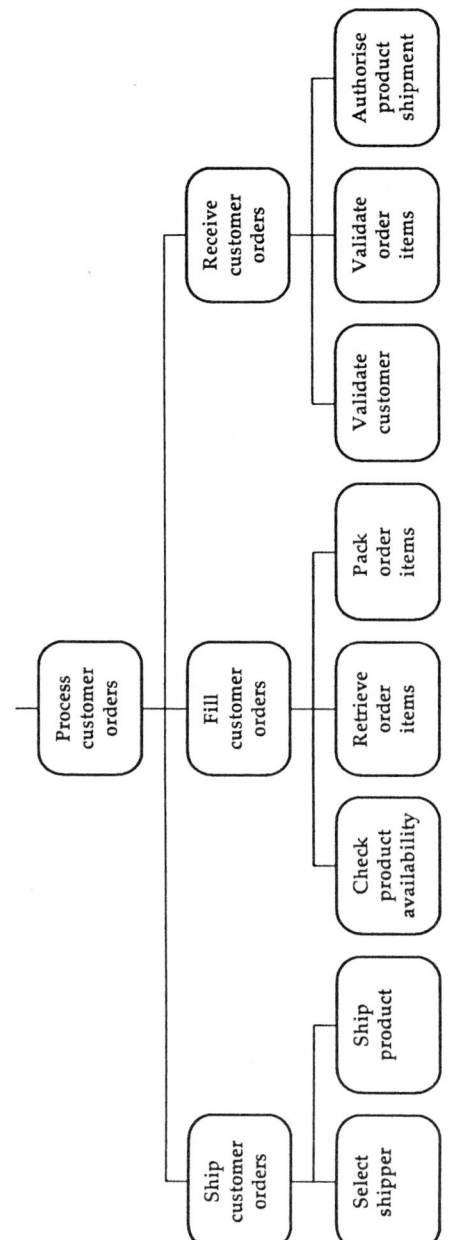

Figure 5.7   A function model, detailing aspects of an order entry system

outside consultant. These names will have to be unique, or cross-referencing will not be possible. There should not be too many data items, perhaps 180 in all.

5.5.3 Data Entity Modelling

Data Entity Diagrams show how the different data elements and items relate to each other. Figure 5.8 shows a typical data entity diagram. Note the use of the connecting lines. Data entities can be connected by a single line which denotes a one to one relationship. In addition it is possible to have more complex relationships such as one to many, or many to one. These relationships are shown by the use of diagrammatic conventions such as appropriate 'crow's feet'.

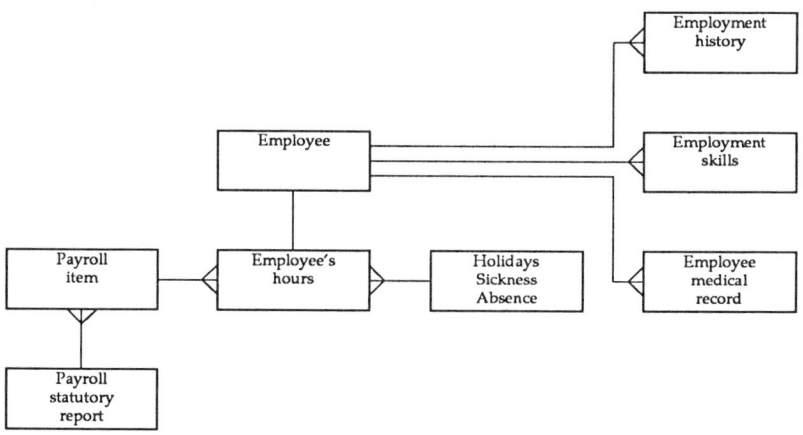

Figure 5.8 A data entity diagram

The consultancy industry has a number of different ways of presenting entity diagrams; sometimes within one consultancy there will be different conventions. Some use squares, others circles or oblongs. Some use straight lines or curves. Some use sheets with pre-ruled boxes like computer programming block diagrams. In addition some consultants use a single piece of paper to show a wallpaper size diagram, while others will use multiple sheets of A4.

Having drawn up the diagrams, the next stage is to ascribe precise attributes to each data entity. This is referred to as data modelling. It requires a lot of work and results in very detailed documentation. Figure 5.9 shows a data model diagram.

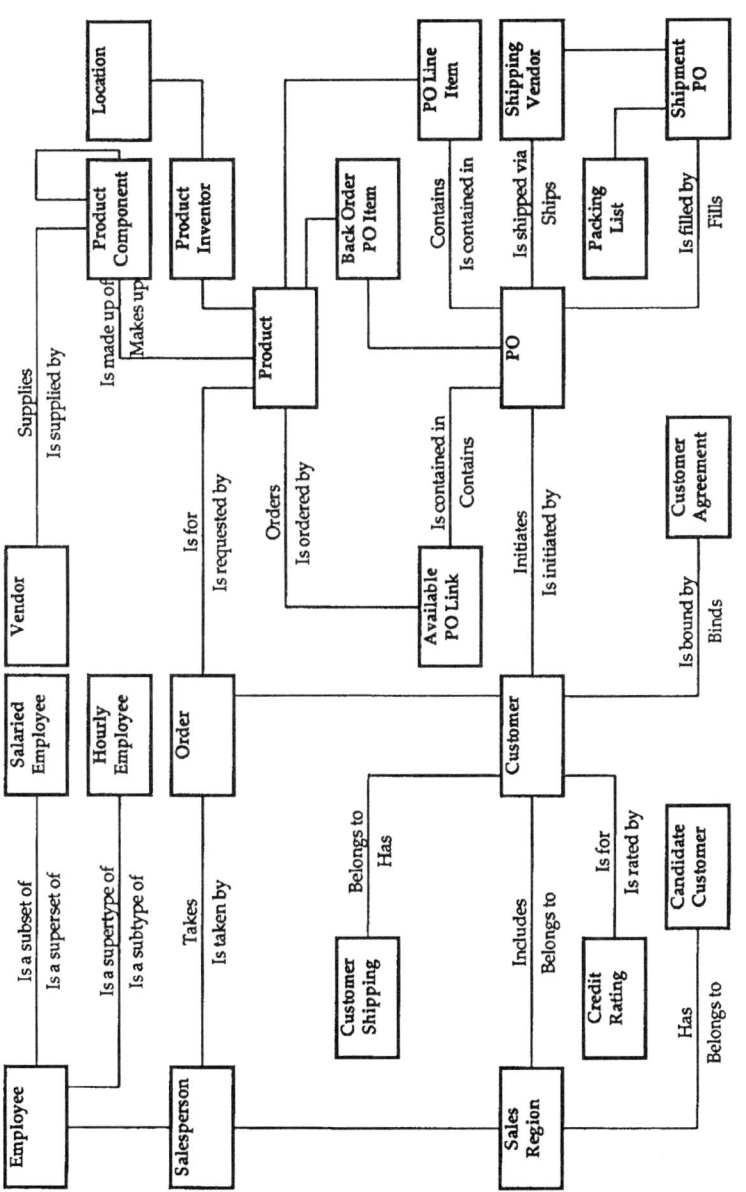

Figure 5.9   A model of the entire business operation

As far as the architecture is concerned, the diagrams give a very clear indication of how the data can be gathered into clusters. Usually a very large matrix is generated on the computer showing how all the data entities are used by functions. In forming clusters Create is the senior criterion, Update is next, Delete is third and Read is last. There are programs for forming clusters according to rules. Most users do it by inspection and produce good results. There could end up being about 70 clusters of data items each of which is created and updated by a small group of business functions. These data items can now be regarded as candidates for handling in a separate database, either on a separate computer or as a sub-database in a larger computer.

The technique is usually to draw data entity diagrams. Each item of data will be identified as to who creates, updates, deletes and reads it. This makes sure nothing is missing and helps to see how each item of data can be clustered into convenient sub-databases. It quickly becomes apparent that there are going to be perhaps 70 different clusters of data and that database architecture is a major undertaking. Figure 5.10 shows an association matrix with data clusters.

	Process customer orders	Receive customer orders	Fill customer orders	Ship customer orders	Validate vendor invoices	Pay vendor invoices	Bill customer	Identify potential customer
Product	CR	D	C					
Product inventory	C		C					
Location	D		UD					
Customer	D	RU	C					
PO	U	D	CR					
Shipping vendor								
PO line item		CD						
Customer agreement		CDR				D	UR	C
Order						CDU		CU
Salesperson						R		RD
Sales region						D	C	DR
Shipping PO						CU	DR	CU
Packing list								
Product component								
Vendor								
Employee								
Hourly employee								

**Figure 5.10   An association matrix showing how
each process affects each entity**

5.6 APPLICATIONS ARCHITECTURE AND COMMUNICATIONS ARCHITECTURE

In step three attention is given to the applications and communications requirements of the firm.

The first step in this exercise is to assemble an applications inventory. This will produce a current up-to-date picture of where the firm currently stands. This is not as simple a task as it may first appear, as it is necessary to include in the inventory not only the central systems but also the applications which have been developed by end users.

In addition to a simple list of systems, each application should be evaluated in terms of its strengths and weaknesses. Application programs may be less than satisfactory in that they no longer provide the functions that users require, or they are difficult to maintain, or the data or reports are not quite right. This can be a substantial job as there may be a thousand or more programs to assess in as many as 30 major applications. This information is required so that the firm will obtain a comprehensive picture of the health of the application portfolio and that decisions may subsequently be made as to whether to retain systems, enhance them or to rewrite them.

From the information collected during the business architectural stage it is now possible to establish a list of applications which will be required over the time frame of the ITA plan. This list may now be matched to the current inventory and analysis may be performed to identify what is required to bring the current applications up to the required level. This will result in a clear picture of where the firm wants to be and what must be done if the organisation is to achieve this level of application.

5.7 COMMUNICATIONS ISSUES

In many organisations there will be more than one large computer. If the computers are at different physical locations then data communication will be in use or will need to be provided. Because of the ease with which incompatible systems are frequently acquired by firms it is essential that communications issues are handled centrally and that a clear set of standards and policies are laid down.

Strategic communications planning is primarily concerned with network planning which may be viewed as either local area networks (LANS) or wide area networks (WANS). There are various different options as to how communications facilities may be structured and these are discussed in Chapter 9 on communications.

5.7.1   LANs and WANs

The need for LANs and WANs is a function of the firm's data sharing requirements. As recently as a few years ago it was believed that LANs should be purchased for the purpose of facilities sharing. However, with the continued drop in the price of hardware this is no longer the case. Data sharing is now the key. Many firms are now using some sort of LAN technology and it is expected that within the next few years most firms will be taking advantage of this technology. In order to avoid chaos, standards and policies must be set for LANs as early in the experience cycle of the firm as possible.

With regards to WANs, the firm must decide upon a network configuration based upon its current and projected internal needs. Again data sharing is the key to the size and power of the network. However, as more and more firms are using their WANs as a critical component in the way that they gain a competitive advantage, it is vital for organisations to look outwardly and assess the possible business potential of their WANs. As communications compatibility is an important issue, and as open systems interconnection (OSI) appears to be growing in popularity, this should be considered as well as any proprietary network system.

Communications can be especially expensive. Connections can be provided at speeds like 10 MBit (10 million bits per second) or even 13.4 Gbit (13.4 billion bits per second) and can provide transparent access to the data wherever it is required. However, such links, together with the necessary computer hardware at each end, are very expensive and quickly get overloaded. As a result, local processing wherever possible is desirable, which means that parts of the database may well be located at remote areas. If this is done then there will have to be computers at the remote areas, and no decision on what computers are relevant at each location can be made before an assessment of the data, applications and communication requirements. This analysis may be quite complex, and indeed it could require the use of some expert people for several months before it is all tied down and agreed.

5.8   ITA AND DBMS

The fourth phase in the exercise brings together the requirements of the first three phases and develops a set of standards and policies which is defined as the ITA.

Figure 5.11 shows the ITA hierarchy.

Because of the need to have a broad-based and flexible set of standards and policies many firms have decided that Database Management Systems (DBMS) are the answer. In fact most industry observers would agree that a

Figure 5.11   The ITA hierarchy

database has become a required tool in all new techniques of program development. More and more firms are moving to a situation where ITA policy demands that all new programs be written using database techniques, so that the data will then always be available in consistent and accessible format for use in all subsequent programs, and for any requests for management information.

This database policy must be controlled centrally because, left to their own devices, departmental managers may want to generate and control their own data, possibly to the exclusion of other departments. In such circumstances other departments can either ask for permission and find that the data was created for a slightly different purpose or over slightly different timescales from their requirement, or they can set up a rival database with some common data which is then seen to be different from the original for good and valid reasons. If this is allowed to happen then the new databases will "grow like Topsy", and after a few years it will be apparent that more time assigned to designing the architecture of the database with an eye to possible future requirements will have been well spent.

Thus data is clearly a key business resource, which is so important that management must focus directly on its control. For this reason some firms practice data resource management (DRM) which involves strategic data planning, data administration and data dictionary development. The main objective of such activities is that the data should be structured to support corporate objectives. It frequently takes quite a long time for a firm to re-organise its data, with many organisations having a five to ten year plan for this. Therefore DRM must focus not only on the present situation but on prospective as well as existing applications.

5.9 RULES FOR THE CORPORATE DATABASE

The corporate database must avoid the above problems. To do this, clear and unambiguous rules must be laid down. The following is an indication of what some of these database rules could be.

– Each item of data must have one nominated owner who can create, update and delete it. Other users may read it but not change it.

– Data shall be processed at the location of the owner and will normally be optimised for the use of that owner.

– The location of the data shall be such that it is accessible by all who require to use it. This may mean that it is located at a central computer even if the owner is not at that location.

– Duplicate data shall not exist, or at least be strongly avoided.

Each firm will have its own rules, governed by the objectives of the enterprise. The net result will be that the new database will be found to be segmented into a number of related sub-files. One of the better tools for this is a relational database. Those sub-databases can then be the responsibility of specific departments. What is crucial is that specific individuals are appointed data owners and that they are accountable for its accuracy and also its security.

For example:

Customer Name and Number	Corporate Marketing at Corporate level
Customer Address etc	Sales Office held at Corporate level
Credit Rating	Finance held at Corporate level
Sales History	Operations held at Corporate level
Sales Ledger	Accounting
Customer Contact Names	Sales Office

If all these departments are sharing the same location and the same computers, then the data could be held as sub-databases of the main system using the same general structure. If not, then there is merit in having the first four held at the central computer, and processed or accessed from remote locations as required. Sales ledger and the sales contact names can be remote.

Sales history may need to be updated by sales, marketing, buying, production, stores and distribution and generally is better held centrally. However, as mentioned above, where the data is eventually held is a function of the firm's objectives and to some extent its corporate culture.

Figure 5.12 shows how different data groups may be arranged in the one database.

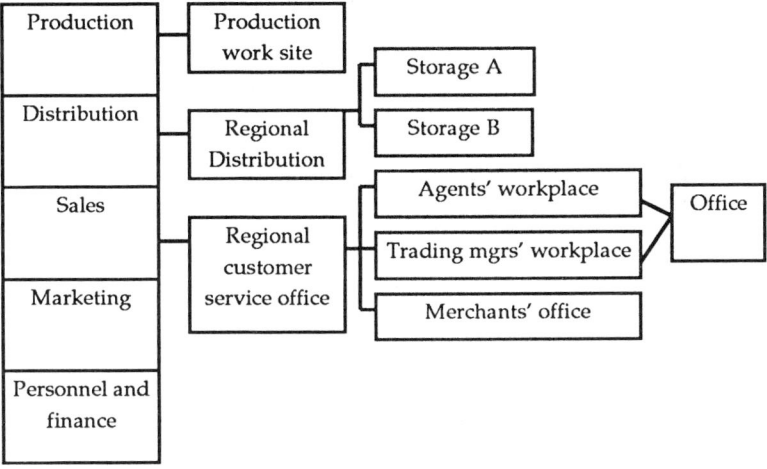

Figure 5.12 Database divided into groups

5.10 DATA ANALYSIS

Analysis of this data is not a trivial task. Some form of computer assistance seems to be indicated to cross-reference the uses of each item of data to the function that creates it, reads it, updates it and in due course deletes it. At the end there will be an ITA which may be good for a number of years and under which new applications can be developed quickly and easily. Use of a database has been shown to speed up the development of new application programs. It is not necessary to worry about most of the data; that is defined already. All that is required is to design the processing.

5.11 COMPUTER AIDED SYSTEMS ENGINEERING

There are Application Development Workbenches which are also referred to as Computer Aided Systems Engineering (CASE) tools available for the larger installations which help with systems analysis and design, as well as integrating specific database systems into the application development area.

Some of these tools can also be interfaced with code generators to produce compiled applications systems.

Perhaps better still, users can develop some of their own programs, at least for report extraction, summarising and graphics. In addition 4th generation languages can speed up the production of reports such that the user no longer has to ask for professional support for the whole range of straightforward requirements, leaving the professionals free to concentrate on the difficult issues and problems.

5.12　GUIDELINES FOR DEVELOPING AN ITA PLAN

As has been discussed, different firms produce their ITA Plan in distinctly different ways. As a guideline to developing an ITA Plan, below are listed the typical steps that most firms would need to undertake.

- Establish the enterprise's mission. It is important to note that at this stage it is essential to discuss not only the present corporate mission but also what management might want to incorporate in the near future. Thus emphasis should be placed on top management's business vision.

- Establish goals. These goals or objectives must be as specific as possible. Goals should be achievable and easily measurable.

- Decide on the organisation's strategy. Where possible a generic strategy should be chosen.

- Establish the firm's CSFs.

- Establish the functions which must be carried out by the company. Produce a comprehensive list showing how these activities fit together. Identify where each of these functions is best performed.

- Establish the data entities required.

- Establish the data flow patterns in the firm. Establish the logical and physical geographic spread of applications for the purposes of deciding on database location and communications requirement.

- Relate the existing applications to those functions and see how good they are. Functional quality is assessed by the users. Technical quality is assessed by the IS professionals. From this it is possible to identify new applications for computers or enhancement of existing applications. Establish from where the different application programs are best run to minimise operating cost and to maximise control.

- Decide where the sub-databases or data clusters have to fit into the physical locations of the company. It may be that, for example, it is the current practice for the stores and distribution functions to be at the same location as production, but it need not be, since the data clusters are not necessarily common.

– Synthesise the above to produce an ITA Plan by:

- identifying where data should be held;
- identifying the applications systems requirements;
- choosing a database management system;
- identifying the scale of computers needed at each physical location;
- designing a communications structure to serve the physical locations.

At this stage the systems architecture will have been defined and will appear as in Figure 5.13.

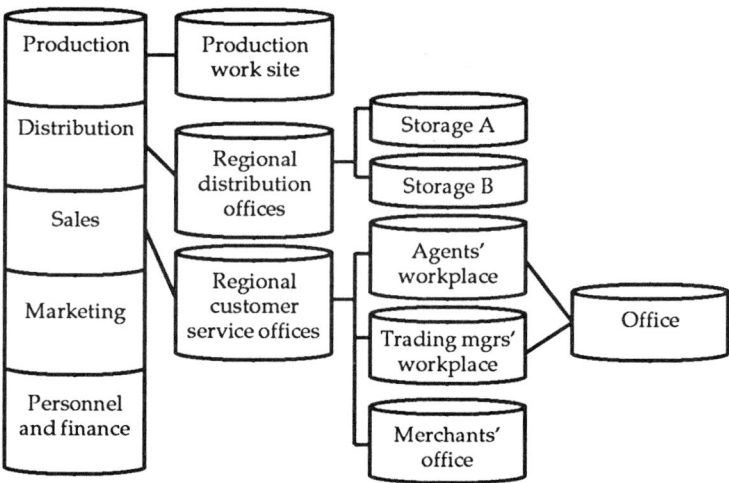

Figure 5.13 The systems architecture defined
using the above procedure

Present the ITA to senior management and obtain commitment to this long term plan. Then the next step is to proceed with the SISP.

5.13 SUMMARY

Before it is possible to obtain any real business benefits from the firm's IS it is essential to have performed a thorough information technology architecture study and have commenced its implementation. An ITA addresses the questions of Where is the firm? Where does it want to be? What does it need to do to get there? How long will it take? What are the benefits of going there? What will it cost?

An architectural plan is a lengthy exercise which may take several months to produce a first blueprint. It is a long-term ongoing process, which requires both continual work towards achieving the plan and continual updating of the plan itself. Changes to the plan are needed to reflect new business initiatives, new products and services, competitive action, changes in technology, etc.

An ITA is not the same as a SISP. These are the main differences between an ITA plan and a SISP.

-   An ITA focuses on a five to ten year time frame; a SISP may consider issues twelve months away.
-   A SISP generally addresses strategic business units (SBU) grouped by similar strategies while an ITA addresses the entire corporation.
-   A SISP contains a description of system priorities for development while an ITA will simply list them.
-   A SISP will address staffing issues, cost-benefit analysis, organisational structure, etc. An ITA will not.

An ITA and a SISP may be seen as independent issues. However if a SISP is undertaken without the prior benefit of an ITA, it may well lead to future difficulties of incompatibilities and redundant systems. Thus an ITA should be seen as an important prerequisite for a successful SISP.

With an architectural plan as a guide the firm can feel confident that it is following a consistent policy which will allow it to produce efficient and effective systems. Without an architectural plan the firm will expend much of its IS capacity in ways which will not optimise the use of its information resources.

6   Analysing the Organisation's Current IS Strategy

6.1   INTRODUCTION

An important step in conducting a SISP is to analyse the firm's current IS strategy. This is part of the bottom up planning process because once the current strategy has been determined it may then be decided whether changes should be made to the established approach. Also it is possible to categorise the firm's information systems using a portfolio analysis technique similar to the Boston Box classification system. This allows the firm to establish the relative importance of its systems and to match IS strategy with different types of systems. This is particularly important in establishing the final direction which the SISP will take.

6.2   GENERIC IS STRATEGIES

With the increasing power and reducing costs of IS there are more and more opportunities to take advantage of ways this technology may be used to achieve superior performance. However, not many firms seem capable of capitalising on these opportunities. Although there are many reasons for this, an important one is that to achieve superior performance through the use of IS, it is necessary for management to master a complex series of issues including the technology itself, the impact of it on the organisation and the field of corporate strategy. Furthermore, not only are these issues complex, but they are also dynamic, with new developments occurring regularly, requiring continual adjustment from management. In order to be successful in developing SIS, management must ensure that there is a high degree of fit between the firm's generic corporate strategy, and specifically the need for IS within this strategy, and the firm's overall management framework in respect of IS. Firms which do not achieve this high degree of matching will not achieve many of the potential benefits to be derived from their IS.

In considering how to match generic corporate strategy with the firm's information systems, it is possible to discern a number of quite different general approaches to the management of the ISD in the firm. These are referred to as generic strategies for the ISD. There are at least six different generic strategies which are:

- centrally planned;
- leading edge;
- free market;
- monopoly;
- scarce resource;
- necessary evil.

Each of these distinctly different generic strategies for the firm's IS requirements needs entirely different management approaches (Parsons, 1983). Some firms will require the implementation of more than one strategy at a time, particular strategies being implemented in different departments or functions. However, where these strategies are deliberately and consistently introduced the firm's performance will be significantly better than in firms where there is only an implicit or erratic strategy.

These IS strategies may be assessed in terms of the effort required by management to plan the amount of control provided, the strategic potential, the cost, and both the user and ISD satisfaction. This will be done at the end of the description of each strategy.

6.2.1   Centrally Planned

The major characteristic of a centrally planned ISD is that the firm has attempted to integrate its corporate strategy and its information systems strategy. Under these circumstances the latter has been derived from, and is supportive of, the former. The firm will have focused on integrated systems so that maximum utilisation is made of computer processing power. A centrally planned ISD will obviously have used a top down planning approach.

A centrally planned ISD requires top management to have a sound understanding of information technology. They will be aware of the opportunities which IS provide to achieve superior performance in the marketplace, both by affecting the industry structure and by creating a sustainable competitive advantage. Top management will also have to be familiar with what is required in terms of hardware, software and people. This is sometimes referred to as being computer literate or computer fluent.

A centrally planned generic IS strategy attempts to deploy human and physical resources to best advantage so that the firm can achieve a suitable return on investment. It is usually understood in firms applying this strategy that IS requires large sums of money in order to derive the appropriate benefits, and management is normally prepared to spend these amounts of money.

A centrally planned generic IS strategy may be appropriate for firms pursuing any of the three generic corporate strategies. If the firm is following a cost leadership strategy then this approach could be used to find ways of improving productivity, whereas if a differentiation strategy is followed the central planning activity would seek ways of using IS to innovate. The niche strategy can also be enhanced in a similar way.

Centrally planned ISDs are sometimes bureaucratic, sluggish and unresponsive. This is because of the centralised nature of the management of this type of strategy. There are often long lead-times required for decisions, and as such it is possible to miss opportunities in the market place.

Whether a centrally planned strategy is appropriate is largely dependent on the firm's culture. If the firm is generally decentralised and management style participative, then it will be highly inappropriate for a centrally planned strategy to be implemented.

Figure 6.1 is an assessment of the centrally planned strategy.

CENTRALLY PLANNED IS STRATEGY	
Planning	VH*
Control	H
Strategic potential	VH
Cost	H
User satisfaction	H
ISD satisfaction	H

Figure 6.1 Assessment of a centrally planned strategy

* VH = Very high, H = High, M = Medium, L = Low, VL = Very low

6.2.2   Leading Edge

The generic strategy of leading edge requires that the firm continually update its hardware and software with the latest developments available in the market. In such a department state-of-the-art technology is continually purchased. Experimentation is encouraged in the hope and expectation that new discoveries will be made which will lead to superior performance and a sustainable competitive advantage. However, as leading edge strategy is nearly always very expensive, it is usually not appropriate to employ this strategy in the context of a low cost leadership generic strategy. Leading edge is thus better utilised in firms where the major driving force is differentiation or innovation.

A leading edge ISD requires very little involvement from senior management other than the original commitment to the value of research and development. Of course it is very important for this strategy that the ISD management keep the senior managers up-to- date with the latest developments in the marketplace and fully aware as to how these could impact the firm's generic corporate strategy.

A leading edge strategy is normally not excessively bureaucratic and is thus quite responsive to new opportunities for superior performance or competitive advantage. Decisions are often made fairly quickly and courses of action undertaken with quite short lead-times. Firms pursuing this strategy are very popular from the point of view of prospective employees who perceive them as good institutions in which to develop their skills.

To implement a leading edge strategy ISD management must have strong entrepreneurial attitudes. This is required because much of the development in a leading edge department will not have immediate user application. In addition it can reasonably be expected that only about 50% of the development work undertaken will produce any usable results. However, when successful, leading edge developments usually provide considerable competitive advantage for the firm. Nonetheless, as this strategy is very expensive, only firms who are already profitable can really afford a leading edge approach to their IS. Therefore it is important that the general corporate culture, as well as the culture of the ISD, strongly ensues the values of risk taking and the long term benefits to be derived from learning.

Figure 6.2 is an assessment of the leading edge strategy.

LEADING EDGE IS STRATEGY	
Planning	M
Control	M
Strategic potential	VH
Cost	VH
User satisfaction	M
ISD satisfaction	VH

Figure 6.2   Assessment of a leading edge strategy

6.2.3   Free Market

A free market generic strategy assumes that the individual user is best qualified to determine his own needs. In such circumstances the user is entitled to acquire hardware, software and services, either from the ISD or from any outside vendors. The only rule which is strictly applied is that the user obtain his information systems services at a reasonable price. Therefore a free market strategy may be used in an attempt to constrain IS costs.

In a free market situation, senior management are generally not involved beyond the decision to establish the free market strategy. There is by definition no central policy and thus each user seeks out his own opportunities and attends to his own requirements.

Except in the smallest firms, it would not be possible to have a completely free market approach to information systems. It is necessary for the major accounting systems to be operated on large computers which require some degree of integration and central control. However, besides these core record keeping activities, many firms have adopted a high degree of free market strategy with regard to end user computing.

The major problem with the free market is that of duplication and the lack of compatibility between different systems. As equipment and software may only be required by certain managers for short periods per day, if it is bought without reference to the overall corporate need, it may easily be unnecessarily duplicated many times and not be used to anywhere near its potential. This strategy may also lead to false starts where individual managers acquire systems without fully understanding exactly how they will function and find that they are unable to achieve their objectives. Sometimes such systems are simply abandoned and the hardware and software lies idle in the firm. To add to these problems many computers are incapable of easily transferring data from one machine to another and thus if central planning is not applied to hardware and software selection it may not be possible to interchange information between one office and the next. Excessive amounts of money can be spent training different people on different systems, whereas if one appropriate system is chosen this cost can be minimised. Also, systems may quickly come in and out of fashion and thus be changed for no justifiable reason. It is hard to evaluate the cost of the lack of standards across an organisation but it is certain that it accounts for a very substantial amount of money.

The ISD can play a very important role in a free market strategy by establishing a microcomputer centre of competence to which end users may go for help and advice. Some firms who have set up these centres refer to them as Information Centres (ICs) and use them as the equivalent of an internal microcomputer store from which users may acquire hardware, software, training or consultancy. Of course, as this is done in terms of a free market situation, there is no obligation on the end users to buy from the Information Centre.

In a free market strategy the ISD will normally be allowed to sell its services outside. This is necessary in order to compensate for the ability of the in-company users to buy information systems services from whichever source they wish. Furthermore the ability to sell outside will help the ISD develop realistic market rates and will demonstrate to in-house users that these rates are achievable.

The appropriateness of a free market strategy depends on the degree of data communication which is required, especially between the different functioning entities or strategic business units (SBUs) within the firm. Also it would be inappropriate to implement a free market strategy if the rest of the corporate culture relied on highly centralised attitudes or autocratic styles of management. Free market strategy is often highly responsive to change and thus allows entrepreneurial managers to make the most of new IS developments to achieve superior performance or a substantial competitive advantage in the market place.

Figure 6.3 shows an assessment of the free market strategy.

FREE MARKET IS STRATEGY	
Planning	L
Control	VL
Strategic potential	H
Cost	H
User satisfaction	VH
ISD satisfaction	VL

Figure 6.3   Assessment of a free market strategy

6.2.4   Monopoly Strategy

The generic IS strategy of monopoly rests on the premise that there should be one single source of computer services in the organisation. This source is set up to meet end user demand within a reasonable cost structure and within reasonable time frames. The primary criterion for the success of a monopoly strategy is the satisfaction of the users. In order to ensure that the user satisfaction is reasonably high, a monopoly strategy requires that there be considerable excess capacity in the ISD in order to be able to cope with peaks in demand. Of course, one of the major difficulties facing a firm attempting to implement a monopoly strategy is the measurement of user satisfaction. This is often extremely subjective with, for example, two users of an identical service obtaining entirely different levels of satisfaction.

A monopoly strategy is usually seen as the exact opposite of a free market. End users are simply not allowed to purchase hardware or software, training or consultancy from anyone other than the centralised ISD. Of course the ISD itself must purchase these resources and services and may in fact have to acquire the services of outside trainers or consultants. However, this is all taken care of for the user, as it is generally considered that he is not sufficiently knowledgeable to appropriately buy these services for himself.

With a monopoly strategy the ISD is not highly involved in any long term planning of the use of IS in the firm. The ISD is simply commissioned to supply enough services to be able to achieve the objectives which are set down by a top management group. Thus a monopoly strategy assumes that top management is aware of the strategic potential of IS. This is often not the case as IS management may have greater insight into IS's strategic potential. As a result, a monopoly strategy often leads to slowness of innovation and to an inability to recognise changing roles or functions for IS within the firm.

To function successfully, monopoly systems must have considerably more resources available than are absolutely necessary. This is because if they are unresponsive to end user requirements, considerable pressure is built up for the end users to satisfy their needs by purchasing services directly from the outside. A classical indicator of a failed monopoly strategy is when there are delays for the maintenance or enhancement of systems.

Figure 6.4 is an assessment of the monopoly strategy.

MONOPOLY IS STRATEGY	
Planning	H
Control	H
Strategic potential	M
Cost	H
User satisfaction	H
ISD satisfaction	H

Figure 6.4   Assessment of a monopoly strategy

6.2.5   Scarce Resource

The generic strategy referred to as scarce resource relies on the intensive control of money being spent on the ISD. Very strict budgets are set and the ISD is often simply not permitted under any circumstances to exceed the amounts laid down. In some cases these budgets are set before the true demand for IS is known and the result is that many appropriate projects are not undertaken due to the lack of funds. A scarce resource strategy is based on the concept that administration is an unproductive cost and thus management must minimise all expenditure in this direction.

Under a scarce resource regime, only projects which indicate a very good payback or ROI are permitted. All projects are carefully costed in advance of authorisation using conservative (high) estimates of cost and conservative (low) estimates of the benefits to be derived. This is a strategy of control which is sometimes used when a firm first acquires a computer, or may also be used when the firm has reached the contagion phase of the computer utilisation cycle.

With a scarce resource strategy, the ISD will almost certainly be under the direction of the financial controller and will be seen primarily as an administrative facility. It will be bureaucratic and very unresponsive to both changes in its own technology and to opportunities which exist for using IS to achieve superior performance, and a sustainable competitive advantage. A scarce resource strategy implies long delays for both development and systems maintenance.

Firms applying scarce resource strategies are not considered good employers and often have difficulty in recruiting the right number and calibre of staff for their IS departments. Scarce resource strategies sometimes use a universal yardstick with which to evaluate the amount of funds which should be spent on data processing. One such yardstick is the 1% of revenue approach. This approach states that effectively managed organisations should be spending about 1% of their turnover on the data processing department. Such a rule as this is, in reality, very difficult to validate as the nature of the firm's industry, as well as its strategic posture, should dictate the level of expenditure on IS.

Figure 6.5 is an assessment of the scarce resource strategy.

SCARCE RESOURCE IS STRATEGY	
Planning	M
Control	H
Strategic potential	VL
Cost	L
User satisfaction	L
ISD satisfaction	L

Figure 6.5   Assessment of a scarce resource strategy

6.2.6   Necessary Evil

The generic IS strategy referred to as Necessary Evil is based on the belief that the use of computers should be curtailed as much as possible. Only applications which cannot be performed without the use of a computer and which are very well cost justified are entertained. In some environments, firms will only computerise statutory records as part of a necessary evil strategy. A minimum amount is spent on hardware, software and people. As a result firms pursuing this strategy often encounter a high turnover of their programmers, analysts and operators.

The necessary evil approach is sometimes referred to as a scarce resource strategy gone mad. When this is applied the IS function in the firm is grossly neglected. The IS management becomes extremely defensive as it is often not able to offer an adequate service. This is reflected in long lead times for new systems development and excessive delays for system modifications and enhancements. Certainly there is no prospect of it being able to use IS to enhance the firm's performance or to establish a competitive advantage.

Necessary evil strategies are sometimes difficult to break out of as they require a complete rethink of the role of IS in the firm. Also to move away from this strategy will require very large expenditures on hardware, software and people. Figure 6.6 is an assessment of the necessary evil strategy.

NECESSARY EVIL IS STRATEGY	
Planning	VL
Control	VH
Strategic potential	VL
Cost	VL
User satisfaction	VL
ISD satisfaction	VL

Figure 6.6   Assessment of a necessary evil strategy

Some of the key issues which the IS director must address are the expense and the degree of control which the firm exercises on IS activities. The generic IS strategy analysis may be used to position different IS policies with respect to their expense and control profiles. Therefore these generic IS strategies may also be represented in a 2x2 matrix using Expense and Control axes, as shown in Figure 6.7.

From this matrix it may be seen that low control strategies/policies are expensive, whilst with high control the firm has a choice of being either a high spender or a low spender.

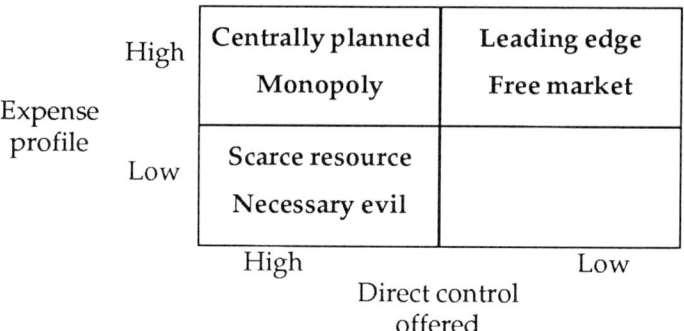

Figure 6.7   Matrix representation of the generic IS strategies

6.3   LINKING OR MATCHING IS AND CORPORATE STRATEGIES

Having described the various generic IS strategies it is important to establish how these strategies should be linked to the firm's generic corporate strategy to obtain a sustainable competitive advantage. The firm's generic corporate strategy defines the possible strategic impact of IS and it is this strategic impact that must be matched with the firm's generic IS strategy.

The reason for this matching or linking strategy is that it is absolutely essential to have a general framework to help identify IS opportunities, allocate resources to IS projects and to control any new changes which result from these strategies. It would clearly not be appropriate for a firm pursuing a generic IS strategy of scarce resources to attempt to use its IS to support a generic corporate strategy of differentiation. To achieve a a generic corporate strategy of differentiation through the IS function a considerable amount of funds must be expended on the ISD and a generic IS strategy of scarce resources would not permit this. Similarly if the firm is pursuing a strategy of cost leadership the generic IS strategy of leading edge would simply be a drain on the profits of the firm. Thus the IS strategy will, in effect, control the types of opportunities which the firm will be able to pursue in the IS field. And if the firm wishes to look at changing the basis on which it competes it may well have to change its generic IS strategy.

Firms that do not establish effective linking strategies will not achieve many of the potential benefits to be derived from SIS and will experience technical, organisational and strategic problems which are often indicators of an underlying mismatch.

6.4   CLASSIFICATION OF INFORMATION SYSTEMS

In analysing the impact of the IS strategy on the firm's ability to use IS strategically, it is useful to categorise the firm's IS activities in terms of the strategic importance of existing operational systems and the strategic impact of future IS. This classification reveals four groups or classes of IS activities which may be defined as follows:-

6.4.1   Strategic Systems

Strategic systems are those where both the current operation and the future competitiveness of the organisation are significantly dependent on the firm's IS. Systems which give the firm a competitive advantage will be in this group. These systems will be considered very important and considerable funds will be spent on maintaining and enhancing them.

6.4.2   Turnaround/Leading Edge Systems

These existing systems are not a critical part of the firm's current IS structure. The firm is not yet dependent on such systems. These may currently be high risk research and development projects, which if successful the firm will develop into strategic systems. It is expected that the work performed in this area will eventually lead to significant competitive advantage. Depending on their attitude towards using IS to support their generic corporate strategy, some firms will be prepared to spend considerable sums developing these types of systems.

6.4.3   Factory Systems

These systems are those on which the firm relies for its day to day business operation. Firms are highly dependent on their factory systems for their day to day activities, especially in so far as factory systems make a large contribution to how effectively and efficiently the firm is managed. Order processing, inventory control, airline reservations, etc are typical examples of factory systems. There is little significant competitive advantage, if any, to be derived from these systems. Further development is not seen as critical to the systems and thus they will only have very limited time and money spent on them.

6.4.4   Support Systems

Support systems provide the firm with no significant advantage in the present, nor are these systems likely to have any strategic impact in the future. Furthermore, support systems will not generally contribute to the firm's effectiveness or efficiency. They are, however critically, required for the existence of the firm in that they usually involve record keeping activities and the presentation of financial accounts. Support systems are simply there to help management to operate the business more smoothly. Therefore payroll, debtors and ledgers are typical support systems.

It is useful to display these four alternative categories of Information Systems on a 2 x 2 grid as shown in Figure 6.8. The vertical or Y axis indicates the degree to which the IT developments produced by the strategy will create a competitive advantage for the firm, and the horizontal or X axis indicates the degree to which the firm is functionally dependent upon IS at present. These axes are simply scaled as HIGH and LOW. From the previously described definitions, the four system classifications may now be placed in the appropriate boxes, as shown in Figure 6.9.

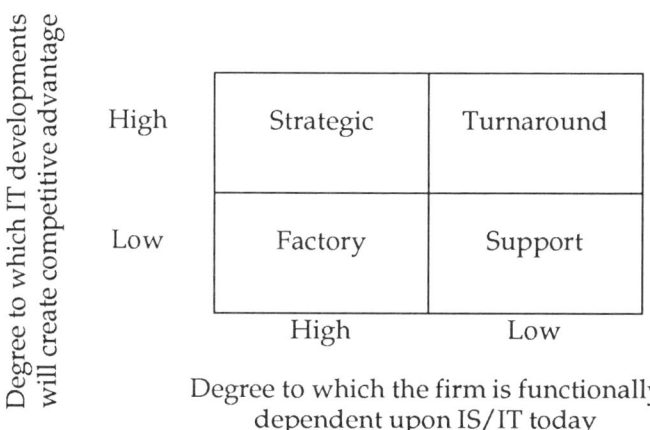

Figure 6.8   Categories of information systems

6.5   STRATEGIC INVESTMENT ANALYSIS

There is a similarity between this analysis and the Strategic Investment Analysis popularised by the Boston Consulting Group (BCG) and referred to under various names, including the Boston Box. In the Boston Box firms are also categorised under four main headings – Stars, Wild Cats, Cash Cows and Dogs. These are described as follows:

6.5.1   Stars

Stars are high performing investments requiring much attention and considerable investment and are critical to business success. Because they have a larger market share and are in the high end of a growing market, they are

		High	**Low**
High		**Strategic** Centrally planned	**Turnaround** Leading edge Free market
Low		**Factory** Monopoly	**Support** Scarce resource Necessary evil

(Left vertical axis: Degree to which IT developments will create competitive advantage)

(Bottom axis, High on left and Low on right)

Degree to which the firm is functionally
dependent upon IS/IT today

**Figure 6.9   Categorised information systems
and supporting policies**

producing a good return and are expected to continue performing for some time. They should be cherished and reinforced through the application of as much investment as the firm can afford.

6.5.2   Wild Cats

Wild Cats are investments which have a low market share but have a high growth rate potential. Thus they may be seen as investments which have yet to show their worth. They may become Stars by capturing a high market share, but on the other hand they may not. Wild Cats must be carefully analysed to see if their conversion into Stars is possible and worthwhile. They usually require considerable attention and not insignificant investment. In fact they often gobble cash. If their Star potential is not realised in a reasonable period they must be discarded.

6.5.3   Cash Cows

Cash Cows are investments which have a high market share but whose growth potential is low. A Cash Cow investment, as the name implies, produces regular and substantial quantities of cash. Because of the low growth rate, they require comparatively little attention or investment. They may not last a very long time. Cash Cows should be controlled and their cash sent to Stars or Wild Cats.

6.5.4 Dogs

Dogs are investments which have a low market share and a low potential growth. Therefore a Dog investment has no particular attractiveness. They should be divested unless there are compelling reasons for keeping them.

Figure 6.10 shows the BCG categorisation of firms and investments. Firms and investments change over time. Note that it is hoped that Wild Cats will move to the high-high quadrant and thus become Stars. Also Stars will usually, in the end, become Cash Cows. Of course it is possible for both Wild Cats and Stars to become Dogs.

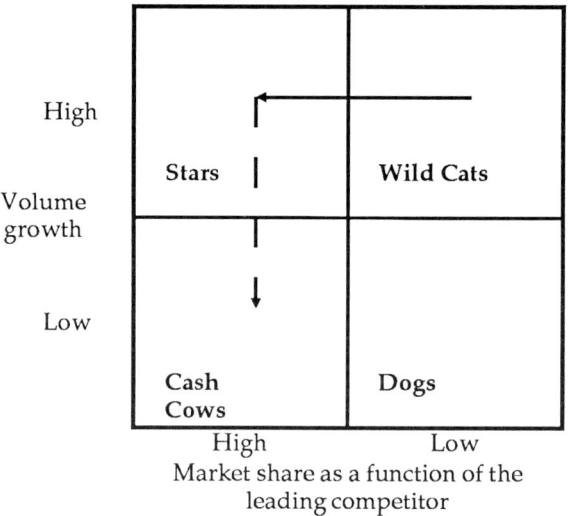

Figure 6.10   BCG Categorisation of firms and investments

The analogy between the Boston Box and the Information System Strategic Classification System rests on the following:

- Strategic Systems observe many of the characteristics of Star Investments. They contribute directly to the business' success. They are expensive to establish and maintain but are essential for the present and future prosperity of the firm. Management should focus much of its attention on strategic systems as they give the firm a competitive advantage from which it generates much of its profit.

- Turnaround Systems are similar to Wild Cat investments. Their exact contribution to the firm is not yet known. They are experimental and will normally only remain in the turnaround quadrant for six to twelve months by which time their future will be clear. They might become Stars, ie strategic systems, or they might flop. They are therefore tricky to manage, in that they can cost a lot of money, but if they develop into strategic systems they will become very important to the prosperity of the organisation.

– Factory Systems are the workhorses of the firm's systems portfolio. They supply the main mechanism by which the firm does its business, by processing orders, planning production, collecting cash, etc. They also often produce good information by which Strategic and Turnaround systems may be assessed. Without them the firm could not function effectively. Factory systems may transpire to be platforms from which they may be developed to become either a turnaround system as in the case of a pilot system which is used to test the feasibility of inter organisation system (IOS), or they may simply move directly to the strategic category. Of course most factory systems simply remain in that category throughout their lives.

– Support Systems. There is no direct parallel between Support systems and Dog type investments. The payroll, ledgers and general record keeping are support systems without which the firm would collapse and therefore there is no question of the firm wishing to get rid of these systems. However, like Dog investments, firms wish to minimise the time and money spent on support systems as they will generally not directly contribute to the firm's ability to enhance its ROI.

6.6   MATCHING GENERIC IS STRATEGIES AND THE IMPACT OF IS

Nearly all firms will have several systems in all four different classes concurrently. The classification of a particular system will depend upon the impact of IT on the firm or organisation at the time. In most firms and many organisations the payroll and accounting system will be in the support class; the inventory control system will be in the factory class; the order processing system integrated with transportation and production planning may be in the strategic class; and finally, supplying customers with direct links to the firm's database could be undergoing trial and thus it would be considered to be in the turnaround class.

Each of these four classes of IS represent very different corporate needs. Further, these categories and needs can be directly related to generic IS strategies. For example strategic systems will be best developed in an environment of either central planning or leading edge. The reason for this is that the centrally planned framework provides the ability to integrate business strategy with IS strategy, and leading edge is also beneficial because in such a strategy the ISD is continually looking for new opportunities for competitive advantage. Turnaround systems will develop best if developed in an environment of leading edge or free market. A leading edge strategy would mean that there was lots of money and new ideas available and free market would mean that there were few delays in acquiring the appropriate hardware and software, etc. In like manner it can be seen that it makes sense to use a strategy of either monopoly or scarce resources for factory systems. Support systems would be the same, or could even be controlled by a necessary evil strategy.

Firms whose IS is primarily in the Factory class generally find that the most appropriate generic strategy is that of monopoly. The next best strategy for such firms is to employ a scarce resource strategy. For those firms in which IS is simply used as a support function the scarce resource strategy is usually most appropriate. If these systems represent very low support then the necessary evil strategy may be the best to employ.

Figure 6.9 shows the IS strategies matched with systems classification on a 2 by 2 grid. The same grid may also be used to indicate funding requirements as shown in Figure 6.11, staffing requirements as in Figure 6.12, equipment requirements as in Figure 6.13, and decision making requirements as in Figure 6.14.

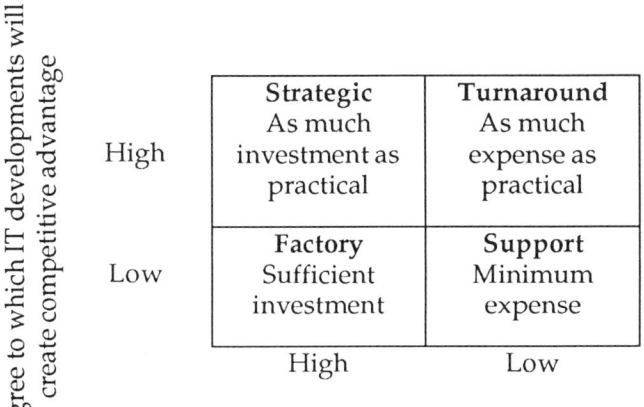

Figure 6.11   Funding requirements

Degree to which IT developments will create competitive advantage

	Strategic Senior staff	Turnaround Younger staff
High	Strategic Senior staff	Turnaround Younger staff
Low	Factory Experienced	Support Junior staff

High   Low

Degree to which the firm is functionally
dependent upon IS/IT today

Figure 6.12   Staffing requirements

Degree to which IT developments will create competitive advantage

	Strategic State of the art	Turnaround Extending the hi-tech frontier
High	Strategic State of the art	Turnaround Extending the hi-tech frontier
Low	Factory Well established technology	Support Yesterday's technology

High   Low

Degree to which the firm is functionally
dependent upon IS/IT today

Figure 6.13   Equipment requirements

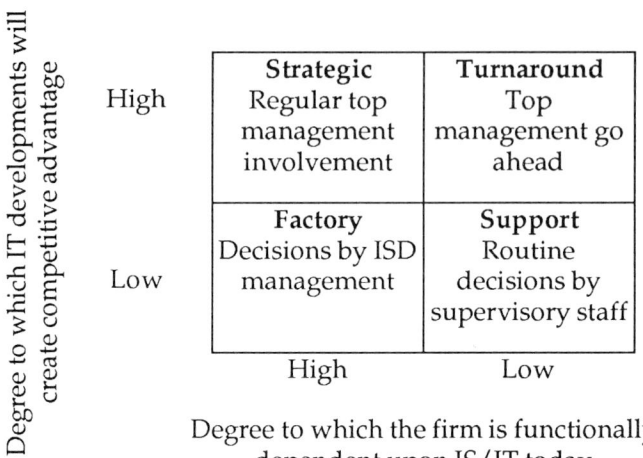

Degree to which IT developments will create competitive advantage

	Strategic Regular top management involvement	Turnaround Top management go ahead
High		
Low	Factory Decisions by ISD management	Support Routine decisions by supervisory staff

High   Low

Degree to which the firm is functionally
dependent upon IS/IT today

Figure 6.14   Decision-making requirements

It is important to note the two-way nature of the relationship between the impact of IT on the firm and the type of generic IS strategy being pursued. Not only is a centrally planned IS strategy suitable for firms with a strategic IS need, but the strategy itself pushes the firm to identify and create strategic information systems. Not only does a leading edge approach suit turnaround systems, but following a leading edge strategy will inevitably result in the firm finding turnaround systems opportunities. Similarly a scarce resource strategy will all but guarantee that IS will not be used for competitive advantage. Thus, as can be seen, matching the two strategies is essential.

6.7   SUMMARY

In order to orient the SISP effectively, it is very important for the planners to assess the firm's generic information system strategy. It is also necessary to perform an analysis of the firm's present information system portfolio. This is done during the system audit stage of the SISP and the strategic matrix is a useful way of categorising current systems. At a later stage in the SISP, during the filtering process, it is an important tool to assist in the allocation of resources to systems, and the matching of these systems to appropriate strategies and policies. The McFarlan analysis described in this chapter is very useful in this respect.

Finally, raising the issue of the firm's generic IS strategy allows the aims and objectives of the SISP to be put into context.

7   Research into the Ease of Use and Effectiveness of SIS

7.1 INTRODUCTION

There has been in the last few years a marked upsurge in research undertaken into the issues surrounding SIS. More than a dozen research projects have been undertaken in the UK. This research has been done by the major consultancy firms and professional institutes as well as being commissioned by the government. In the USA dozens of academic articles have been published, some of them appearing in MIS Quarterly.

In this chapter the results of five research projects are described. Four of them were conducted in the UK and one of them in the USA. The UK research was conducted by OASIS, Butler Cox, the Oxford Institute of Information Management and Henley – The Management College; in the USA it was conducted by PRISM.

7.2 DTI/OASIS LTD

The Department of Trade and Industry in the UK commissioned an independent consultancy firm named Organisation and Systems Innovation Ltd (OASIS) based in Maidenhead to investigate the criteria for the successful implementation of SIS. OASIS approached eleven firms which had successfully implemented such systems. The firms which were chosen were believed by OASIS to represent the most progressive users of IT in the UK. A number of different consultants were used. These people were chosen for their past experience and knowledge of the industry in which they were researching. With each firm OASIS conducted in-depth discussions with several executives from both top management and from the ISD, on how they achieved the successful implementation of these SIS. A semi-structured interview technique was used and the result of the research was presented in a standard way.

The firms chosen for this research were:

–   The Automobile Association;

- ABC International Ltd;
- British Aerospace plc;
- British Gas plc (South Eastern Region);
- Imperial Chemical Industry plc (Plant Protection Division);
- International Credit Insurance Network;
- Midland News Association Ltd;
- Patons and Baldwins Ltd;
- Rank Hovis McDougall plc (Grocery Division);
- Rossdale and Partners;
- Sinclair Research Ltd.

A detailed report was written as well as a short video produced in which four of the cases were explained. This research showed that the key issue is the use of IT investment to gain a competitive edge by making IT a central issue in the firm's strategy.

In the conclusions to the research the consultants summarised the factors which lead to success as follows:

- It is essential for management to have a clear strategic aim, which establishes the objectives to be reached and the benefits to be gained by the SISP.
- Successful schemes have a champion at a high level in the organisation.
- The use of IT provides an opportunity for, and even forces, major policy decisions.
- It is vital that new systems are fully compatible with existing equipment and software, so that information can flow freely throughout the network.
- High quality advice, based on experience as well as expertise, is required at all stages of development and implementation.
- The role of data processing departments, where they exist, is being transformed by the move to distributed processing and by the drive to align IT more closely to business goals.
- Thorough analysis of the existing position and detailed planning of the proposed system of IT is extremely important.
- Implementation of IT needs to be planned with care and managed sensitively to overcome the fear that unfamiliar technology often engenders.

– Traditional management skills and project management techniques can, with value, be applied to IT.

The general conclusion of this research is that IT can be used effectively in any business of any size in any industry.

As this research was paid for by the Department of Trade and Industry, copies of the detailed results of this research and the video are available from OASIS for a nominal charge.

7.3   BUTLER COX FOUNDATION

Butler Cox is a large firm of independent management consultants and researchers based in London conducting research assignments which are undertaken for the benefit of the Foundation's members. Butler Cox is one of the largest independent research organisations working in the field of SIS, which it has been doing for the last twelve years.

The Butler Cox Foundation offers its research services to its members who also provide the input to the research. The study on competitive information systems described below was based on postal questionnaires which were sent to approximately 100 members. These questionnaires were followed up by interviews with a cross section of members.

The Butler Cox research has revealed the following:

– Competitive edge applications are more widespread than originally thought. For a long time IS was regarded as being synonymous with administration. However, this is rapidly changing as SIS are being implemented. This has brought IS into the view of top management.

– Although these have genuine strategic consequences, few stem from strategic concepts. They are opportunistic in nature, the imaginative extension of systems put in for more prosaic purposes, and are the result of a flash of commercial insight. They may have been suggested by a change in the market or a change in a customer's needs.

– Competitive edge applications are the natural and inevitable consequence of the development of IT over the last few years. There are several reasons why IT has evolved this way, one of which has been the progressive computerisation of the sharp end of the business.

– There are six main ways in which IT may be used to provide a competitive edge in a business:

   • Create a new product or service to compete with an existing offering by selling databases.

   • Change the size and scope of the market using telecommunications.

- Reduce the life cycle cost of goods by reducing development time.
- Help produce more complex products by producing sophisticated financial services.
- Help with a rapid response to a competitive move.
- Help redistribute value-added processes within an industry using electronic links between manufacturers, retailers and suppliers.

- There is nothing special about IT systems themselves. The same systems are used as those in data processing. It is the way they are deployed that counts.

- Competitive edge applications cannot be bought off the shelf.

- Competitive edge systems may be referred to as third stage systems. First stage systems meet widespread operating needs. Second stage systems provide external parties with access to the database. The third stage adds a further dimension which builds a permanent relationship which locks in the third party, ie makes it difficult for the buyer to change to another supplier.

- Virtually all SIS stem from an idea which originated outside the IS department. Most have never appeared in the planned applications portfolio or the formal five year plan. Competitive edge application systems have not resulted from a strategic review. The fault lies partly in today's approach to planning which mostly omits a systematic review of technology trends and the uses which competitors are making of technology.

- In almost every case there has been a project champion.

- The decision to proceed is not based on cost-benefit analysis but is highly judgmental. It involves assessment of competitors and customers and risk.

- The computer equipment investment can be quite low because the infrastructure may already be in place, but training and changing the working style may be high.

- There are several keys to the successful implementation of these systems:

  - As most competitive edge application systems are inter- organisational it is most important to understand the other side's processes and needs.
  - Speed of delivery and quality of the user interface are paramount. Technical elegance and efficiency are secondary.

- Several things must be done to ensure that the opportunity of competitive edge application systems is exploited. These include:

- Changing attitudes so that competitive edge application systems become part of top management's regular agenda.

- Changing systems planning and project authorisation procedures so that there is more focus on competitive issues and competitive edge application systems to by-pass the development backlog.

Details of this research are only available to members of the Butler Cox Foundation in London. Firms may become a member of this Foundation. Membership costs £12,000 per annum.

7.4 OXFORD INSTITUTE OF INFORMATION MANAGEMENT

The Oxford Institute of Information Management is part of Templeton College, Oxford University. It has a mission to research and teach in the IT field. Between 1985 and 1988 case study research was conducted into six firms, and in a paper published in the *Journal for Multinational Business*, Michael Earl, Director of the Institute, stated that their research into competitive information systems found some surprising results. Instead of being a result of systematic planning and control these systems are more often the result of entrepreneurial activities. This case study research looked at Thompson Holidays, British Steel's Strip Products Division, Frentel, BHS and two other (unnamed) companies.

The paper written by Michael Earl, David Feeny, Martin Lockett and David Runge is 'Competitive Advantage through Information Technology: Eight Maxims for Senior Managers'.

This research revealed that:

- IT-based activities were proposed and promoted by commercial executives rather than IS executives.

- Firms experienced an evolutionary transition to IT as a competitive weapon.

- Development of SIS depends on project champions from within the business instead of IS experts.

- Competitive information systems are developed in association with users and customers, and are not guided by textbook prescriptions.

- SIS are promoted and approved outside the formal planning and control procedures.

- Sometimes competitive information systems are user developed with DIY-type tools.

The eight maxims for senior managers derived from Earl et al's research are:

- User management should be encouraged to take the lead. Encouragement may take the form of education and training as well as placing known project champions in critical user areas.

- Strategic IT issues should be uncoupled from IT strategy. The identification and development of strategic IT goes on outside the formal planning process. Young managers should be encouraged to seek such applications as a matter of course in their jobs. The creation of an environment which is IT aware is an important objective.

- Firms should invest in and build upon their IT infrastructure. As most competitive advantage systems are extensions of already existing systems it is important to have established a competent IT infrastructure.

- Devolve IT activities to actual users wherever possible. Users should be able to engage in innovative experiments and consider specialist technologies for their own needs. This means the devolution of IT activities which do not need to be centralised.

- Partnerships should be built between the ISD and users. To achieve a degree of devolution there must be a close relationship between the user departments and the ISD. It is important that this relationship be seen as a partnership in which both sides are symmetrical and working for the benefit of the company.

- Firms should work towards creating a hi-tech culture. The activities described above should help promote a hi-tech culture. This should be reinforced by having funds available for developing radical ideas as well as having new criteria for promotion, etc.

- Start the organisation development (OD) with user managers. The first step is to educate user managers. This should be continually reinforced with the objective of making all managers into information managers. In fact the whole process of creating a hi-tech culture is a task for OD.

- Apply loose-tight management. In the early stages of competitive systems formulation loose management should be applied. During the later stages the more formal and tight procedures are more appropriate. It appears that in order to innovate, loose procedures are required.

These principles have emerged as a result of interpretive and inductive research undertaken by the Oxford Institute of Information Management over a three year period.

7.5 HENLEY – THE MANAGEMENT COLLEGE

In order to conduct a research project which would add to the body of knowledge concerning SIS, it was decided to empirically explore in considerable detail actual management practice in the formulation and implementation of SIS. A case study research strategy was chosen as the best approach to this. Ten firms were approached and all agreed to allow the author to interview executives concerning their work towards the formulation and implementation of SIS. The firms chosen are large-scale operators in their industry. They are household names with a reputation for high quality products and services. It was expected that they would show the way to others not only in the marketplace but also in terms of their management practices and their use of technology.

7.5.1 The Question of Confidentiality

Before these firms would talk to the author, it was necessary to agree that nothing said in the interviews could be published without the written consent of the firms. In the event it proved quite difficult to obtain these written consents. Although individuals were prepared to speak freely about their experiences with SIS, on the corporate level the secrecy ethos so prevalent in the UK made it most difficult to obtain corporate approval to publish the material.

7.5.2 The Main Participants

It was decided to conduct in-depth research on four of the ten firms. Four was considered an appropriate number in terms of the time and resources available for a PhD. The four case studies chosen for this research represent quite different enterprises. The firms concerned are:

- Associated Commodities plc;
- Peat Marwick McLintock: Management Consultants;
- IBM (UK) Ltd;
- The English Banking Company (Trust) plc.

In the end two of the four firms did not wish to have their names mentioned in this research study for fear of their attempts to gain a competitive advantage becoming known prematurely to their competitors. Thus Associated Commodities plc and The English Banking Company plc are fictitious names and the firms are disguised in such a way that they will not be easily recognised except by members of their own personnel. In light of the difficulty in obtaining permission to publish the details of the case studies of the four main contributors the author felt that it would present unnecessary difficulties and delays to obtain written permission from the other six firms.

7.5.3   Collecting the Case Study Evidence

In conducting the four in-depth case studies the author visited each firm at least three times. These visits were to collect evidence by means of structured and semi-structured interviews or discussions. The author met with an average of five executives from each firm. Different executives were deliberately sought in order to obtain a degree of triangulation which assists in the corroboration of the facts supplied. The average length of the interviews was 90 minutes. Wherever possible documentary evidence was sought to support the information supplied by these executives. The interviews were recorded using a tape recorder. These tapes were subsequently transcribed, edited and combined with various diagrams etc into the documents in Appendix A. The firms then reviewed these case studies to clarify any misunderstandings which may have inadvertently arisen.

The interviews with the six other firms were also recorded and subsequently transcribed but not reviewed by the participating firms.

7.5.4   A Synopsis of the Case Studies

7.5.4.1   *Associated Commodities plc*

Associated Commodities plc is a large firm, employing 7500 staff, producing various products which are commodities. It is in a mature market and there is little or no opportunity for the firm to differentiate its products. Although it believes itself to be very efficient its profit record is very chequered.

Associated Commodities is a firm with a clearly articulated generic strategy which has worked for the business for many years. This strategy is that of cost leadership, and to this end it has used IT very successfully. The firm is highly computerised both from a manufacturing process control point of view as well as with more traditional data processing applications. However the law of diminishing marginal returns set in with respect to its cost reduction efforts using IT and as a result IS management started to look to other, non-cost reduction, IS opportunities from which the firm might benefit.

The interest in SIS in Associated Commodities was initiated by the IS manager who has had a long and distinguished career with the firm. In his 20 years with the organisation he has built a very successful ISD which is driven by a powerful cost containment culture. This is reflected in a highly structured financial approach to system approval. This manager became aware of what some competitors were doing with their IS and he believed that Associated Commodities must follow suit if it were not to fall behind. In addition it was felt that if it used SIS it might obtain some protection from the increasing phenomenon of foreign competitors who periodically dump products in the UK market. Therefore competition activities was the primary driver making Associated Commodities look for SIS opportunities.

At the time of the case study Associated Commodities plc had recently completed exploring the possibility of identifying opportunities for SIS. It achieved this by implementing a SISP study. During the study the firm realised that if it were to succeed with SIS it would have to effect at least a partial strategy and culture change. Because the field of SIS was new to Associated Commodities, it chose to use a firm of international consultants to guide the way during the initial stages of the SISP.

Unfortunately there was no concurrence of views as to the objective of the SISP among the top management, the IS manager and the consultants. In addition, confusion set in with regard to the firm's objectives, which were its strategy and its critical success factors. As a result much of the focus of the study was lost. Nonetheless a number of potential SIS opportunities were identified and the firm felt that the SISP had been beneficial and that its ISD was in a stronger position as a result of it.

Four systems were initially earmarked for implementation. These included a Customer Service Pilot System which would allow clients to have direct access to a database compiled by Associated Commodities containing information about the optimal use of the product range. A pilot was considered important because this system was considered a high risk one. No other special arrangements were made concerning the implementation of these proposed SIS.

This case study focuses on a number of the issues which must be addressed when formulating a strategy which will lead to the use of SIS. It primarily highlights a number of mistakes which may easily be made on the way.

7.5.4.2   *Peat Marwick McLintock: Management Consultants (PMM:MC)*

Peat Marwick McLintock is one of the largest firms of Chartered Accountants in the UK. Like all large firms of Chartered Accountants it has a management consulting group, employing some 540 professional staff. In London these consultants are located in seven separate office buildings in the City.

As the management consulting wing of one of the largest firms of chartered accountants in the UK, PMM:MC has a highly refined corporate strategy of differentiation. The firm supplies high quality services for which it charges a premium price. In pursuit of this strategy it decided to implement an office automation/end user computing system which would significantly improve its ability to quickly and effectively respond to its clients' needs. PMM:MC planned to achieve this primarily through two applications which were:

- word processing combined with E-Mail;
- a Staff Curriculum Vitae Database.

PMM:MC has been using various sorts of office automation/end user computing for several years. It had a wide variety of hardware and software installed, much of which was incompatible. These systems were used in a relatively uncoordinated way as it was only recently that PMM:MC decided that office automation and end user computing are strategic issues. The two main events which brought about this change in thinking were the considerable rate of growth of the consulting practice in the previous few years and the development of similar office automation/end user computing systems in competitive firms. The large growth rate of staff meant that it had become more and more difficult to find the most qualified consultant for any particular assignment. Competitive firms using automation/end user computing systems were able to produce higher quality proposals and reports in much shorter time frames. As a result of these industry drivers PMM:MC committed a substantial amount of resources to a project for the installation of a large network of mini and personal computers.

One of the key features of PMM:MC's attempt to implement an SIS was the fact that the systems formulation and implementation was performed concurrently. The systems plans were not fully formulated before the firm began to implement the system. This resulted in a high degree of flexibility.

The reason why PMM:MC was able to combine the activities of formulation and implementation was that it had a clear vision of exactly what it wanted to achieve. Further, it immediately established an implementation team consisting of a number of highly experienced consultants who were able to closely manage the vendor as well as the other resources required from within the firm itself. The work on the implementation was broken down into various phases with appropriate objectives and timetables, and project management software was used to monitor and control these phases.

The case study addresses the rationale for the system, the choice of hardware and software, and also the way the firm approached the implementation of the system. It also looks at how PMM:MC measured the user satisfaction with the system.

7.5.4.3   IBM (UK) Ltd

IBM (UK) Ltd is the United Kingdom subsidiary of the largest manufacturer of computers, IBM Inc. IBM (UK) Ltd employs 19,000 staff and has a turnover of £4 billion. Worldwide IBM has always pursued a strategy of differentia-tion. In addition IBM has traditionally held itself aloof, being a market leader and standard setter rather than a market responder. However the last ten years have seen dramatic changes in the computer industry with the fun-damental economics of computer manufacture and marketing radically shift-ing. This has resulted in many more computer manufacturers than ever before supplying computer power for a fraction of what it cost only a few years ago. These industry drivers have resulted in major cultural changes in IBM which are directly reflected in the way IBM uses its own internal IS resources. Thus for over ten years IBM (UK) Ltd has made very extensive use of IT to support its business strategy. This is reflected in its manufacturing systems, its data processing systems, its productivity tools systems as well as various strategic networks both for the support of product sales and for the maintenance of its larger systems.

There are many SIS in IBM (UK) Ltd and the author realised that only a very small cross section of SIS issues could be examined. For the case study the author chose two main areas to focus on. The first is how the company develops its strategy for the ISD and the second is the use of a new electronic trading opportunity (ETO) which IBM believes is one of the most exciting developments this decade. This is electronic data interchange (EDI).

In IBM the ISD has three strategic issues to focus on. The first of these relates to how the department acts as a technology partner by helping independent departments to implement IT in order to gain a competitive advantage. The second aspect of the ISD strategy is how it develops strategies or policies for its own survival within the firm. Thus it has a hardware and software strategy as well as personnel strategies, recruiting strategies, training strategies, etc. The third is how it acts as a general technology champion for corporate-wide systems which do not necessarily provide an immediate payback or compe-titive advantage.

The approach to SIS formulation in IBM depends upon whether the system has been proposed by a user department or whether it is an infrastructure system which is proposed by the ISD. A user-proposed SIS is formulated with assistance from the ISD but the user department is strongly encouraged to perceive the system as its own. This is done to achieve maximum user involvement. The proposed SIS will be reviewed by the appropriate finance and investment committee and if it meets the necessary ROI requirements it will be implemented in the usual way. Systems which do not meet the necessary ROI may be presented for consideration to a higher level of management and this process can be repeated up to the chief executive. Occasionally systems are given the go-ahead despite the lack of an adequate ROI because it is felt that they are essential.

Systems proposed by the ISD are treated in exactly the same way except that the ISD are the systems' owners.

IBM has recently begun to perceive ETO as a significant strategic opportunity. IBM have been using ETO for some time. However this has been through networks which dealers can use to obtain information on products and place orders for certain items. Only recently have they decided to implement a large scale EDI system. This system has been triggered by the firm's desire to move its Greenock plant onto a Just-In-Time (JIT) manufacturing basis in order to reduce its costs. IBM believes that although EDI may be seen as strategic today, within a few years it will become a prerequisite for being in business at all. Thus the main driver for this system was IBM's need to keep its use of IT as up-to-date as possible.

The EDI project is interesting for several reasons. Firstly the normal ROI criteria were suspended as the project was thought too important not to be implemented. Secondly a special implementation team was set up and this team worked closely with a similar team from Texas Instruments, which was the first IBM supplier to be connected to the system.

7.5.4.4   *The English Banking Company (Trust) plc*

The English Banking Company (Trust) plc is a wholly owned subsidiary of The English Banking Company Group plc. The Trust Company was set up in 1967 in order to extend the range of services which the Bank offered its clients.

The EBC (Trust) Ltd operates as an independent subsidiary of the EBC Group plc with its own board of directors and, within profitability guidelines, its own policy.

The Trust Company's turnover as reflected in the consolidated profit and loss account in its Annual Report & Accounts for 1988 was £721 million. The firm employs 1800 people. It has a salesforce of more than 500 salespeople and managers. EBC (Trust) has half a million unit trust clients, 1.1 million life and pension clients and 1.2 million general insurance clients. There are 25 unit trust products, 165 life and pension products and 65 general insurance products.

The Trust Company's activities incorporate Investment Trusts, General Short Term Insurance, and Pensions and Life Assurance. The firm has recently undergone a major re-organisation and is now composed of four business units which handle unit trust investments, insurance broking, life assurance and pensions as well as general insurance. These business units are organised as four separate companies with four chief executives, four general management teams, etc. The main objective of this re-organisation was to ensure that the business units would improve their performance by focusing directly on issues of their own profitability and accountability. Some central services such as personnel, finance and some IS activities have been retained in service organisations in the head office function of the Trust company, but the intention is to decentralise all of these in time.

The English Banking Company (Trust) plc has traditionally not articulated its corporate strategy. However over the years its emergent strategy has clearly been one of cost leadership focused on a niche of small business and individual accounts.

Computing is well established in The EBC Trust Company with a Unisys 1100/73/74 and an Amdahl 5890, which is approximately equivalent to an IBM 3090, operated by the central group. Most applications are developed using Mapper and Focus. In addition there are some 800 personal computers in use in the firm. It is believed that these will play an important role in developing SIS. The ISD has developed a list of standard software packages which the IS staff will support. These packages are:

-   Smart;
-   PMW;
-   PC Focus;
-   SideKick;
-   XTree;
-   Ventura;
-   Samna.

The ISD function is highly decentralised with there being only a small central group. The majority of the IS staff are actually employed in the operating divisions. Thus there are only 75 people in this central ISD. However the life and pensions department employs about 100 IS staff of its own, the general insurance department has 40, unit trusts about 30. There are about 30 people in the strategic group. In addition there is a 2:1 ratio of permanent to contract staff.

With the Big Bang and the IT developments which have forced rapid change in the finance industry, the Trust Company has had to reassess its attitude towards corporate strategy and the role played by its IT resources. Thus the drivers for the development of SIS in the firm have been deregulation and technological advancement. These drivers have also triggered changes in the structure of the firm. In addition the ISD has found a few SIS opportunities which were developed using current systems as a platform from which to develop.

The few SIS opportunities identified by the Trust Company were not formulated in any formal way. They resulted from managers perceiving an opportunity by extending the functionality of a current system and convincing management, including the IS management, of the value of the project. When these systems were implemented they were not treated in a different way from any other IS project, except that a stronger emphasis was given to the issue of ease of use and training the end user.

7.5.5 Learning Points from These Case Studies

The ten most important messages for management which can be derived from this case study research concerning how to successfully approach the formulation and implementation of SIS are:

  − It is not easy to formulate and implement SIS. It is necessary to adopt a new perspective to manage SIS. Success in managing a traditional ISD does not ensure success with SIS. In fact in some ways, traditional success may hinder the formulation and implementation of SIS, especially where a culture change is required. However a successful and well-regarded ISD is helpful in obtaining authorisation for an SIS.

  − A strategic vision is critical to the success of SIS. Searching around in a pool of dozens of applications opportunities will very likely simply confuse the issue. A strategic vision may be, but is not necessarily, initiated by a top manager and it should be carefully focused on a very limited number of important issues or opportunities.

  − Industry drivers play an important role in determining where the firm should look for SIS. An understanding of the industry drivers is a key starting point for thinking about SIS. Changes in industry drivers frequently indicate or suggest where to look for SIS opportunities.

  − SIS extend beyond the confines of normal cost-benefit analysis. They are systems which management believes must be done and therefore the short-term cost-benefit is not as important as for MIS or MSS. Nonetheless the enterprise must keep its eye on the financial ball. In the medium to long term SIS should produce higher than average benefits which will translate into improved financial performance.

  − If consultants are used to help with SIS they must be very carefully selected, prepared for and managed. It is difficult for consultants to establish the firm's strategic vision or strategy formulation. Consultants may help with these issues, but they will definitely require substantial input from the firm's management.

  − Formulation and implementation issues should be considered together as SIS will benefit from a seamless approach from start to finish. If formulation and implementation are treated as separate issues, an SIS may be formulated which cannot be implemented, or implementation may be far more complex, time consuming, and expensive than envisaged.

– The ISD may need to think of strategy in several quite different ways. There is the application of IS to directly support the firm's strategy by providing competitive information systems to individual managers. There is the strategy of the ISD itself, and then there is the issue of the ISD being a technology champion which will help the firm in a composite way to be more strategically effective.

– Training is a very important issue for the successful implementation of SIS and its expense is normally quite a considerable portion of the total investment. However, without appropriate training SIS will probably not succeed. Therefore training is a central issue, and the training requirement must be addressed early in the SIS formulation stage.

– Placing the emphasis on users to find and promote SIS, and then to make these end users systems owners, is a key to successful system implementation.

– Decentralisation of MIS/SIS may be a risky business especially in a firm where the general culture is predominantly centralised. A free market approach may be wasteful, especially in a firm which has reached a level of mature usage. A centrally planned approach seems to be important if the firm's efforts are to be coordinated to achieve successful SIS implementation.

– Project champions are critical to the success of an SIS. It is possible to have multiple champions. In fact, projects may substantially benefit from having several important managers fully committed to the success of the system. This is especially true for large complex systems which have strategic potential.

The above are just a few of the main points which were revealed by the case study research into the three firms. In reading the messages for management, it is important to appreciate that the subject of SIS is still in its infancy. Whereas computers have been in use in business for approximately 40 years, SIS have only been a separate computing issue for about seven years. Therefore there is much more to learn about this subject which will hopefully come to light as more and more research is undertaken in this field.

7.6 THE PARTNERSHIP IN INFORMATION SYSTEMS MANAGEMENT

In 1987 the Partnership in Information Systems Management (PRISM), which is a service offered by the Index Group and Hammer & Company, conducted research into the use of competitive information systems among its sponsors. More than 70 firms participated. Interviews were conducted with senior IS executives and other managers within the ISD. The results of the research were presented to the sponsors.

The result of this research suggest that although the idea of competitive information systems has captured the imagination of many senior IS managers, and also top corporate executives, in many cases the results of these systems have been presented in a grossly over- simplified and fundamentally mistaken way. In fact some of the success stories circulating have even been fabricated. In some cases although progress has been made towards what could become competitive systems, success has been declared too early – before it is possible to determine who will emerge a victor.

According to PRISM the reality of competitive information systems is far more complex than many of the current reports suggest. Furthermore, many firms who have attempted to introduce these systems have failed and the result has been very costly.

In fact PRISM goes so far as to say that there are fundamental misunderstandings and misapprehensions about the nature of strategic or competitive edge systems. As a result of the research PRISM argues that systems should not themselves be considered strategic or competitive as they are not usually entities in their own right. A better way of looking at these systems is to see them as capable of supporting or enabling important business change, and in as far as they do this they may acquire a strategic status. Thus a strategic or competitive system is only a component of a much larger business issue, and it is not the implementation of the system per se, but rather the greater business change question which delivers the competitive advantage. PRISM argues that the term SIS should be replaced by the expression *Systems Intensive Business Change*.

The research identified six critical issues which must be addressed if an enterprise is to succeed with systems intensive business change. These are described as follows:

- *Magnitude of the change.* For the firm to benefit the systems intensive business change must be substantial. A minor change will bring little added value to the enterprise.
- *Sustainability.* To really obtain a competitive advantage the systems intensive business change must be to some extent sustainable. This is

one of the most difficult things to achieve. Competitors may easily find out what is happening and to some extent copy the change. The following are some of the issues to be considered in looking for sustainability.

- In some circumstances the first mover has definite built-in advantages. However this is not always the case and in some case the reverse is true.

- By using proprietary hardware and software, competitors may be kept at bay for some time, but this approach is often difficult and expensive.

- If the change is on a big scale it may deter imitation as there is just too much to be done or the risk is too high.

- When the systems intensive business change particularly suits the firm's organisation or structure, and does not suit that of a competitor then the advantage may be sustainable.

In most cases the type of competitive advantage obtained from IS is not sustainable. What is provided is an environment for ongoing innovation which creates a moving target for the competitors. Thus competitive advantage can be maintained by continuous enhancement and development. This of course may end up by simply raising the cost level for all the players in the market, and it is not necessarily the case that these costs may be passed on to the client.

- *Platforms.* Many of the systems which have become central to competitive advantage were developed from already established systems. Invariably these already established systems were developed for much simpler applications which evolved into a SIS. This is referred to as the Platform Effect. Stated simply, a SIS is seldom developed from scratch. It is usually built on top of an already existing system built for traditional purposes of automation or MIS or DSS. There are several reasons why this platform effect should exist, including the fact that management is more easily persuaded if it can already see some benefit from this type of application, and if the cost of the SIS is not so great because some of the basic ground work will have been done.

There are a number of implications of the platform effect.

- Platform considerations should be included in the justification of any appropriate systems.

- Systems should be built in such a way that they may be subsequently used for platforms.

- In looking for systems intensive business change opportunities, systems should be inspected for their platform ability.

  - *Industry Structure.* It is important to really understand the industry structure in which the firm functions. Competitive advantage normally implies a winner and in most cases this implies a loser. However sometimes the wrong firms lose and this can produce an undesirable effect. For example a successful direct customer order entry system might not hurt the major players who either have one or will acquire one quickly, but it could have other victims and might wipe out smaller players. This could lead to a monopoly enquiry or just more intense rivalry between the remaining players.

  - *Customer Concerns.* Many of the systems credited with being competitive or strategic have at their roots the notion of locking in clients or suppliers. Many individuals and enterprises find this to be unacceptable. It is frequently contrary to the interest of the client, but in any case it is only possible in relatively few circumstances.

    This has been recognised and now some firms are using their system to offer electronic trading which incorporates the facility to purchase not only their products, but also products from other sources.

  - *Risk.* Not all attempts at SIS or competitive edge systems are successful. Some simply fail, costing hundreds of thousands of pounds. This can do considerable harm to the firm in its market. Even when they are successful there is the risk of imitation requiring continual improvements which are very costly. The basis of competition may shift as the power structure in the industry changes. For example, the airline industry has now almost become an efficient market for airline fares which it was not before the arrival of the major reservation and sales systems. And of course there are the standard technology risks of the hardware, software, the implementation, etc.

From the PRISM research, two conditions which are essential for the success of systems intensive business change projects have emerged.

- There is a need for a project champion who will be a senior business manager who can fight for the system. The champion must be able to see the true value which the system will have for the firm and be in a position to counter the resistance and inertia the project may face.

- There is a need to have a strong ISD, and the ISD must be a true partner if SIS are to succeed. The ISD must be good at the rapid development of robust systems using new technologies and which have platform potential. It must have the respect of top management as well as the respect of key users, and should be a stimulant for new ideas. To do that ISD personnel must have a sound understanding of business issues as well as the new technology. With these skills they will be able to build SIS that match the enterprise's unique needs and thus obtain competitive advantages.

7.7   ANALYSIS OF THE RESEARCH

It is useful to analyse the above research in terms of the frequency with which various issues or concepts are identified by the researchers. Content analysis has been performed on these research reports and the results of this are displayed in Figure 7.1. It is important to note that the issue of project champion is the most important as it has featured in all research sources. The second issue, strategic vision, is the second most popular choice, after which a number of the other issues share third place.

Issues/Research Source	1	2	3	4	5	
Strategic Vision	X	X		X	X	4
Champion	X	X	X	X	X	5
Platform	X		X	X		3
Partnership			X	X		2
Risk Evaluation		X		X	X	3
Education		X	X	X		3
Entrepreneurial		X	X			2
Approval not in IS Plan, but based on Competition		X	X	X		3
Good Advice	X			X		2
Business Change				X	X	2
Rapid Development	X		X	X		3
Bespoke		X	X		X	3

1 OASIS-DTI,   2 BUTLER COX,   3 OXFORD,
4 HENLEY,   5 PRISM

Figure 7.1   Content analysis of the research data

7.8   SUMMARY

The first three of these research studies are based on what has already become an established view of SIS, ie that there are specific information system opportunities which if properly exploited will afford the firm a competitive advantage.

The fourth research study very substantially challenges this view by suggesting that a search for so-called hot systems is a non-productive exercise and that competitive advantage will best be achieved through systems-intensive change. This puts quite a different emphasis on the firm's attitude to SIS and opens many opportunities for further research. In addition the research from the USA also suggests that the claims made for SIS are exagerrated and should be viewed with a considerable amount of suspicion. This may be one of the reasons why SISP have not generated many SIS opportunities.

8   Case Histories of Competitive Advantage

8.1   INTRODUCTION

It is now estimated that there are thousands of firms which have gained a competitive advantage through the use of SIS. In some instances the advantage has been relatively minor while in others the use of an information weapon has actually revolutionised the industry by changing the whole basis on which firms in that industry compete.

In order to appreciate the exceptionally wide range of opportunities to support generic corporate strategies through the use of SIS, a number of short case histories have been selected which will give the reader a quick impression of how these systems were applied. It is not the intention that all, or for that matter any, of these case histories will specifically relate to the readers' business, but rather that they will give an indication as to the type of applications which may emerge or may be converted into SIS.

Readers are asked to indulge in a little lateral thinking in order to convert the concepts illustrated in these case histories into practical ideas which will be helpful in their own business.

In addition to the generic strategies of cost leadership, differentiation and niche development, some of these case histories describe an additional dimension which can be offered by IT. This dimension is the development of a new product or service, or in fact a new business which the user of IT is led into by the availability of the technology and a readily definable market.

After each case history title a one letter code has been used to indicate the type of competitive advantage which the company obtained through the use of SIS. The key to the codes is as follows:

- (C) represents a Cost Leadership strategy;
- (D) represents a Differentiation strategy;
- (N) represents a Niche strategy;
- (P) represents a completely new product or service or business which the firm undertook as a result of the opportunities available through IS.

Where a firm has been able to differentiate itself in a niche using its IS then both (D) and (N) have been used.

8.2   INDIVIDUAL CASE HISTORIES

8.2.1   American Hospital Supply (AHS) (D)

American Hospital Supply manufactures and distributes a broad line of products for doctors, laboratories and hospitals.

Since 1976 it has used an order entry distribution system which directly links the majority of its customers to AHS computers. Over 5,000 terminals have now been installed at various locations.

The system also allows customers to perform their own forecasting, planning and inventory control which in turn generates incremental revenues for AHS.

The success of the system has been primarily due to the simplified order processing procedures for customers, leading to reduced costs for both parties and the ability for AHS to develop and manage price incentives to customers across all products.

This system, which is considered a classic of its type, started by a terminal being lent to a client for a fixed period of time on an experimental basis. When the time period ended the client was asked for the terminal back and AHS was asked how much it wanted to leave the terminal in place.

The result is high customer loyalty and an increasing market share for AHS. The presence of AHS's terminals on the premises of its clients represents a switching cost for the client if they change supplier.

AHS also stays ahead of competitors by analysing the industry data it collects to spot other trends and customer needs more quickly.

AHS has now been incorporated into the Baxter Travenol Group.

8.2.2   Digital Equipment Corporation (DEC) (C)

DEC utilised recently developed software technology for expert systems to significantly improve a hardware configuration problem. The problem was a large variety of equipment configuration possibilities which regularly led to necessary rework of manufactured configurations at the time of installation. This was expensive and resulted in deferral of invoicing, and therefore income, and customer complaints.

In conjunction with Carnegie-Mellon University, DEC put all the expert rules used by the design and field service engineers into a computer program

(XCON). This expert system then ensured that the appropriate configurations were developed prior to field installation.

The result is quicker field installations and customer satisfaction leading to quicker issuing of invoices and therefore quicker payment. This in turn has helped reduce costs at DEC.

Due to the success of the project, sales personnel are now using the technique for their order generating process. This ensures that customers' orders are appropriately and fully specified at the time they are entered. This prevents subsequent ambiguities and contradictions between the sales department and the client.

8.2.3 USA Today (D) (C)

USA Today was the first national newspaper to use a satellite to transmit the contents to 17 geographically dispersed printing plants. The system was introduced in 1982 and one year later was selling 1.1 million copies a day in 19 metropolitan areas.

An example of the productivity that can be achieved by the use of satellites and other IT is that the paper was able to create and transmit a 36 page, full colour edition in eight hours. The result is that the company used new technology to run more efficiently and thus more productively than the competition and became a market leader. Numerous other publishing organisations have subsequently followed this route.

8.2.4 Xerox (C) (D)

Between 1979-82 Xerox implemented a fieldwork support system to provide better and more cost effective service to the worldwide customer base of office equipment.

The system operates on more than 50 distributed minicomputers in the US, Canada and Europe and provides support representatives with computerised access to information about customers, previous call histories, workloads of technical staff, etc. Information about fault calls is put in the system so that representatives can see in advance what the problem is and the parts most likely required. It has transpired that more problems have been diagnosed, and in some cases rectified, over the phone, reducing the total number of calls made and thus reducing costs.

The result is a strategically important system to Xerox as customer satisfaction is improved by faster, high quality response time to queries. Furthermore, the productivity of the large technical workforce is improved by the ability to increase the number of calls each can make, and therefore the cost of the service operation has been substantially reduced. This represents an enhancement of the traditional process of technical service support by introducing an effective communication-computer system to the standard process.

8.2.5   United Airlines (N)(C)

United Airlines began using a teleconferencing service more than ten years ago for emergency situations and daily executive briefings. This service, which dramatically reduces the cost of bringing people together, is considered to be critical to the success of the airline's operation. It can be defined as a refinement of a current internal process through the use of IT. The system was so successful that it is now being used in more delicate areas such as labour negotiations.

Telemarketing was then introduced to qualify leads for the airline's AIRPASS – a ticket costing US$ 20,000 which gave up to 25,000 miles worldwide travel per year for five years. It was discovered that telemarketing was actually selling the product as well as qualifying leads. As a result of this the business plan was re-drafted to make telemarketing the primary channel of distribution.

The result is decreased staff costs through niche marketing using telephone selling. In addition, costs are significantly reduced by teleconferencing.

8.2.6   Toyota (C) (D)

Toyota established a system to support its widespread dealer network. The system provides Toyota with timely order and inventory control data as well as providing dealers with on-sight systems which they can use to run their own businesses. The main feature of the system is The Toyota Data Centre which is linked by a telecommunications network to the dealers' premises. The dealers then use microcomputers of varying capacities and functionality geared to their specific business needs. The system is externally focused and combines traditional processes such as order inventory, which is provided by all the other major motor vehicle manufacturers, with the new additional power of being able to support the dealer in managing their business.

The result is that Toyota benefits from more accurate sales and inventory data and the dealers can manage their own business more effectively whilst at the same time being linked more closely to Toyota. Also Toyota has differentiated itself, even if not on a permanent basis, from the other major motor vehicle manufacturers by helping dealers run their business.

Today all major motor manufacturers have strategic Data Communications and Networks (DC&N) to support their dealer and distributor chains.

8.2.7 J C Penney (C) (P)

Donald Siebert, Chairman of J C Penney, said that in the 1980s and 1990s leaders in retailing need not necessarily be the best merchandisers, but will be those companies who capitalise on the advantages IT provides.

Penney is now a leader in point of sale systems, providing:

- optimal inventory;
- cash controls;
- instant credit authorisation.

In addition to servicing its own opportunities, J C Penney is marketing its strategic DC&N services to outside parties. Its credit authorisation system has been so successful that it now markets credit card authorisation and verification to other companies including Shell and Gulf Oil.

The result is that through the point of sales systems much time has been saved leading to cost leadership. Furthermore through strategic DC&N a new product line was developed in the form of the credit authorisation business which has generated additional income.

8.2.8 Singer (C) (D)

Singer put terminals into customer locations in order that the customer would have more control over their orders, whilst at the same time reducing its own costs. It is now contemplating possible incentive schemes for users of the system.

The result is that Singer achieved differentiation in the operations area by providing better customer information and more efficient order processing for its national accounts.

8.2.9 Pitney Bowes (C)

Pitney Bowes found a strategic application of IT in the way service staff are dispatched. The company has over 3500 customer engineers who are dispatched from 99 US branch locations. They have installed a central database which is fed by 20 dispatch centres using a strategic DC&N.

A customer calls the local dispatch centre on a toll free call and the problem is first keyed into a diagnostic system to see if it can be solved over the phone. If not, the database is scanned to find the engineer, not only in closest proximity to the customer, but also the one who can handle the problem most effectively and therefore at the least cost. Previously, every service engineer had to be trained to deal with all the machinery in his area – now engineers are specially training on selected machinery, but with the service team covering everything.

The result is improved efficiency through the more effective use of engineers. This demonstrates a differentiation strategy in terms of the improved service received by the customer.

8.2.10   Peat Marwick McLintock: Management Consultants (D)

In order to reinforce its corporate strategy as a supplier of high quality consultancy services, PMM:MC introduced a substantial local area network in six sites in the city of London. This system was based on a series of minicomputers connected though EtherNet to in excess of 400 workstations. The system is also accessible remotely through laptop personal computers supplied to members of staff.

PMM:MC considers it has two strategic applications on the system. The first strategic application is its ability to produce high quality proposals and reports in a very much shorter period than it was able to previously. The preparation time of a proposal has been reduced from between seven and ten days to two days. The second strategic application involves its consultant database. With more than 600 consultants in its London offices, it is often difficult to determine who is best for a particular job. By using this staff curriculum vitae database, it can now quickly locate the consultants with the most appropriate qualifications for a particular task. It can also use details of previous jobs in the proposal to the client in order to establish its expertise in the field.

8.2.11   McKesson (C) (D)

McKesson is the largest drug distributor in US. Following the pattern established by American Hospital Supplies, it has supplied its customers with terminals for ordering, receiving and preparing invoices. In addition to simply selling McKesson products it also uses its strategic DC&N to sell associated products and other services.

McKesson has used its strategic DC&N to provide information to retailers and suppliers to manage inventory and to assist them in marketing and sales. It also supplies assistance with shelf management, pricing and labelling. Seminars are provided for retailers and suppliers. It has also engaged in joint software development projects. However the software side did not take off as well as anticipated and McKesson has subsequently withdrawn.

The result is that customers are tending to place larger orders and McKesson has streamlined its order processing.

8.2.12   CompuCard (D) (C)

CompuCard is an example of a company created as a result of IT. It provides a videotext home shopping service whereby buyers use personal computers to browse electronic catalogues to compare prices and specifications. The system allows the company to keep prices 25-30% lower than the recommended retail price.

The result is that the revenues of CompuCard have quintupled in two years to US$ 9.5 million.

Membership in the US is 15,000 and it is estimated that by the mid 1990s 75% of US householders will use such a system and that CompuCard's income will be hundreds of billions of dollars. The concept of electronic shopping is sometimes referred to as Information Wholesaling. CompuCard has recently successfully established its service in the United Kingdom.

The result is a company which, through the strategic use of DC&N, competes with traditional mail ordering companies, and in addition can maintain low running costs and thus offer products at a lower price, ie implementing a cost leadership strategy.

8.2.13   Shelernet (D)

Shelernet is an electronic information exchange, developed by the First Boston Corporation to allow real estate brokers to find, quickly, what mortgage packages are available at a particular time, and whether a buyer will qualify for financing. Both parties can make preliminary commitments within 30 minutes.

The result is an improved position for both broker and buyer when looking for mortgages.

8.2.14   American Airlines (D) (P)

American Airlines used computer and communications technology to build an entirely new business. It developed a reservation system (Sabre) which lists the flight schedules of every major airline in the world.

Of the 24,000 automated travel agents in the US 48% use the system. The American Airlines reservation system displayed AA flights on any particular sector on the terminal before any other airline's flights. This took advantage of the reservation clerks' natural tendency to choose the first flight offered. This in turn resulted in greater load factors for AA. In addition, for reservations made on other carriers AA charged US$ 1.75 per reservation made through its system. Sabre earned US$ 338 million in 1985 of which US$ 170 million was profit. An anti-trust case was made against AA by other airlines for unfair competition.

The result is an airline entering the data processing business with a new product and also, by the ability to make easy reservations, improving its own productivity. American Airlines, which was market leader with this type of system and having gained a leading edge, now competes with United Airlines and several others.

8.2.15   Intermodal Transportation Services (D)

Intermodal Transportation Services used IT to change its system for quoting prices. It uses microcomputers to create a strategic DC&N which links the various offices to a central point which calculates all prices.

The system gives the company the capacity to be able to introduce new pricing policies, or to offer discounts to national accounts, which actually place their orders from all round the country. These were previously handled locally by each office manually calculating prices – thus making national discounts near impossible.

The result is more flexibility to quickly respond to trends.

8.2.16   Western Union (P)

Western Union has developed Easy-Link, a sophisticated high-speed data communications network which allows personal computers, word processors and other electronic devices to send messages to each other and to telexes around the world.

8.2.17   Sears (P)

Sears took advantage of its experience in processing credit cards to sell the service to others. For example its credit authorisation and transaction processing system has been adopted by Phillips Petroleum and a retail remittance processing service is used by Mellon Bank.

The result is a new product line allowing the company to compete in a new market and to enter that market as an established user of IT.

8.2.18   A O Smith (P)

A O Smith developed a data communication expertise to meet its own requirements as a manufacturer of automated parts and then sold this expertise to a bank consortium who were looking for a contractor to run a network of automated teller machines.

8.2.19   Citicorp (D)

Citicorp set up a high level technology committee to explore possible strategic applications for IT. In addition it publishes a newsletter on technology to keep officers abreast of new opportunities. The current Chairman,

John Reed, has been the architect of much of the firm's technological innovation over the last ten years, which guarantees its commitment.

The result is that Citicorp has become a leading edge user of IT which has decentralised the authority to acquire new equipment. This leading edge strategy is coupled with a close to free market attitude to suppliers. This has meant a high rate of expenditure which has kept Citicorp ahead in the IT opportunity stakes.

Citicorp uses its strategic DC&N to process over 15 million card holders for Visa, Mastercard, Diners and Carte Blanche. It sells marketing information over its strategic DC&N to assist subscribers with merchandising, promotions and advertising, etc.

8.2.20 Levi Strauss Europe (C)

In the garment industry there are only two major buying seasons per year. It is critically important for superior performers to know as early as possible what the firm's fabric purchasing requirements will be.

In order to expedite the receipt of orders Levi Strauss equipped its salesmen with hand-held, battery powered, data collection terminals. These devices were used to enter volumes and details of products determined by the sales people on the premises of the client. The hand-held terminal had a simple printing device which produced a paper copy for the client as confirmation of the order placed. The sales people then transmitted the orders received overnight to Levi Strauss's central computers via a dial-up line and acoustic modems. This provided a rapid update of the materials required by the firm during its next manufacturing phase.

Levi Strauss achieved approximately a ten day lead on its competitors through the use of this system thus allowing Levi to take a firmer position in the market. This meant having a greater choice and flexibility as to the fabrics it would have at its disposal for the forthcoming season.

8.2.21 Federal Express (D)

In the early 1980s Federal Express revenue exceeded $1 billion by carrying 43 million packages for 550,000 customers. It used 75 aircraft and 5000 delivery vehicles. To maintain its position in the market in the face of continuing competition, Federal Express used a strategic DC&N as follows:

- Requests were received by local centres and communicated by them to a computer and video display in the vehicle nearest to the client.
- Drivers communicated directly through their on-board computers with the local centres when a pick-up took place.

- Shipping documents and airway bills were supplied with bar codes which were used for scanning at various stages of the delivery process to provide online information as to the exact status of any consignment.

This use of strategic DC&N built up the public's confidence in Federal Express and gave it a commanding share of the market.

The effect of this strategic DC&N was to actually change the structure of the air courier industry. A number of firms dropped out of the industry or were forced into niche markets, and Federal Express' major competitors including DHL and UPS, were obliged to embark on major investments in strategic DC&N in order to maintain market share.

8.2.22   Finnpap-Finnboard (D)

Finnpap-Finnboard is the industry representative of the Finnish National Paper and Board manufacturers. Its main corporate objective was to sell Finnish P&B products. In the early 1980s it discovered that certain Finnish P&B manufacturers were dealing direct with buyers in Europe and this suggested that the existence of Finnpap-Finnboard had a limited time horizon.

Finnpap-Finnboard responded by establishing a strategic DC&N in the form of a VAN based in Helsinki, through which its members' inventories and catalogues could be accessed. Finnpap-Finnboard sales people could then place orders directly with the manufacturers both for goods in stock and also for special product orders. This new system had the effect of discouraging most of the Finnish manufacturers trading independently.

8.2.23   General Electric (D)

Following a survey in 1980 General Electric realised that it was not adequately responsive to user enquiries – not enough product information was available to the consumer, both before and after a purchase.

It responded by installing a toll-free calling telephone system and established the computerised G E Answer Centre. The Centre now covers the full product range and handles an average of 1.5 million calls per year. The database used by the Centre can retrieve 500,000 pieces of information, which has often been entered onto the central computer by skilled appliance service engineers, and represents about 8,500 products. Ninety-four percent of customers are reported to be satisfied with the service.

The result is that G E has restructured the way it deals with its end-point customers, which has significantly increased their satisfaction with G E.

8.2.24 General Tire (C)

General Tire introduced a telemarketing centre for service support. The service support centre was based on a mainframe computer on which full details of clients were maintained on a database. The aim of the centre was to free the salesforce in the field from dealing with customer queries and to enable them to do more selling. The service was successful and later took over the selling and account management function for some of the marginally profitable accounts, ie those that could not be profitably serviced by a sales team. In the first month the telemarketing service had sold more to those accounts than the salesforce had done in the whole of the previous year.

The result is a cost leadership strategy by reducing salesman costs in the field. The improved sales of the normally less profitable accounts are now able to contribute to the total corporate profit.

8.2.25 Sulzer Brothers (D)

With the aid of computers Sulzer Brothers has improved the design of diesel engines in a way that previous techniques could not. It has been able to increase the number of cylinder bore sizes from five to eight in low speed marine engines, allowing ship owners to more precisely choose the engine for their needs and thus reduce their fuel bills.

The result is the company's improved ability to compete in the marketplace with a wider range of products to suit a wider range of client requirements.

8.2.26 Schlumberger (D)

Schlumberger has developed an electronic device to measure the angle of a drill bit, the temperature of rock and other variables while drilling oil wells.

The result is reduced drilling time and the ability to eliminate some steps in the normal process, therefore making the Schlumberger product more attractive to the market than competing products.

8.2.27 Canon (C)

Canon built a low-cost copier assembly process based around an automated parts selection and materials handling system. Assembly workers use bins which contain all the parts required to make a particular model. This is part of the Kanban inventory and production management system and has the effect of drastically reducing inventory carrying and material handling costs. The success of the process is largely due to the software controlling the parts inventory and selection.

The result is substantially reduced production costs leading to the ability to sell lower priced copiers and thus compete in the marketplace through a cost leadership strategy.

8.2.28   Caesar's Palace (C)

The casino Caesar's Palace installed a system to analyse the data collected on large spending customers by the more accurate identification of their spending patterns.

The result was to save money by being able to lower the complementary budget by more than 20%.

8.2.29   Dow Jones (C)

As publishers of the *Wall Street Journal* Dow Jones developed a page transmission technology linking its 17 US printing plants to produce 'a truly national newspaper'.

This has led to the *Asian Wall Street Journal* and the *Wall Street Journal, European Edition* being started, with printing taking place all over the world, using shared editorial which is electronically transmitted.

The result has been the ability to produce newspapers at greatly reduced costs and has allowed Dow Jones into an international market that it previously could not afford to enter.

8.2.30   Intermodal Transportation Services (D)

Intermodal Transportation Services used IT to change its system for quoting prices. It uses microcomputers to link the various offices to a central point which calculates all prices.

The system gives the company the capacity to be able to introduce new pricing policies, or to offer discounts to national accounts, who actually place their orders from all round the country. These were previously handled locally by each office manually calculating prices, thus making national discounts near impossible.

The result is increased flexibility to quickly respond to trends.

8.2.31   Eastman Kodak (P)

Kodak recently offered a new service of long distance telephone and data transmission services through the use of its internal telecommunications system.

In a different area, Kodak installed the TechNet System, a quality-control computer installed in photo-finishing laboratories to monitor equipment utilisation.

The result is that the company has been able to utilise spare capacity and at the same time increase its revenue through the utilisation of its telecommunications system. Through Technet it has been able to maximise the efficiency with which equipment is used in photo-finishing laboratories and thus help improve productivity in this area.

8.2.32 Imperial Oil (C)

As an affiliate of EXXON, Imperial Oil has made dramatic internal staff changes by:

- putting a marketing man in charge of data processing;
- putting a system manager on management committees of the business units;
- measuring how much competitors spend on processing.

The result has been a much better educated staff, leading to better decisions as to how to employ IT to effect cost reductions.

8.2.33 General Foods (C)

In 1980 General Foods began to involve IT in the corporate strategic planning process. It made all the managers in the ISD consultants, and told them to go to each department in the company and teach as many people as possible how to utilise end user computing.

The result is that IT soon became an integral part of most people's work and subsequently of the planning process. Furthermore, there was an improvement in staff productivity which led to cost reductions.

8.2.34 Hunt Wesson (C)

Hunt Wesson developed a computer model to help study the expansion of distribution centres. It was able to evaluate many more variables, scenarios and alternative strategies than had been possible before.

The result is the more effective expansion of, and improved decisions on the most appropriate location for, distribution centres leading to various forms of cost reduction.

8.2.35 Datsun Nissan (D)

Datsun Nissan uses a business modelling system to demonstrate the performance of its vehicles, both in terms of operating costs as well as maintenance and replacement schedules. The model has been supplied to dealers who use it as a selling aid to fleet owners. Fleet owners are invited to enter details about their own fleet into the system which will then calculate the various costs of operation per vehicle, and per driver within their firm.

The result is that Datsun Nissan dealers have become transportation consultants to their clients who run large fleets and are able to demonstrate to them the savings to be made by purchasing their vehicles.

8.2.36 Pearscor S A (D)

As a large distributor of newspapers, periodicals and magazines, Pearscor was faced with the difficulties of newsagents over-ordering in all three categories. It established a large computerised database to itemise sales for each newsagent over a five year period. It then used the database in conjunction with a forecasting model to be able to predict the demand required by each newsagent.

The result is much more effective use of Pearscor products and a much more satisfactory relationship with the network of newsagents.

8.2.37 Shell Aerofuels (D)

Shell Aerofuels supplies international airline carriers with fuel on a world-wide basis. Air carriers previously had considerable difficulty in settling their accounts due to their having to pay for fuel obtained from different locations in different currencies. To assist with this problem Shell supplied its clients with a list of all purchases on a floppy disk in IBM-PC compatible format.

The result is the ability of air carriers to much more easily analyse and reconcile their accounts with Shell. This in turn enables Shell to be paid with less delay.

8.2.38 Benetton (C)

Benetton uses its strategic DC&N to connect its chain of retail outlets with its own manufacturing and contracted manufacturing firms.

It does this through a data collection system based on electronic point of sale (EPOS) which rapidly updates centralised sales and inventory statistics. The rapid availability of these figures allows the merchandising managers of Benetton to react very rapidly to any changes in the market, thus allowing them to maintain adequate stocks of garments in retail outlets while only holding limited central inventories.

8.2.39 Japan Airlines (JAL) (D)(P)

With a multi-million dollar worldwide network in place Japan Airlines (JAL) found that its network was under-utilised.

This resulted in a search for additional uses which in turn resulted in JAL offering a wide range of other purchasing services over the network. This included the sales of cinema tickets, theatre and concert tickets as well as tickets for sporting events such as Wimbledon.

8.2.40 Marks and Spencer (C)

Marks and Spencer has established trading rules whereby all its regular suppliers are required to subscribe to the TraderNet Electronic Data Interchange network within the UK.

This EDI connection not only allows for easier and more efficient paper handling, but also provides Marks and Spencer with access to the current stock and production schedules of its suppliers. This enables Marks and Spencer to call off merchandise as and when required to respond to market dynamics. This effectively converts its suppliers to buffer stock holders.

8.2.41 IBM (C)

IBM has recently introduced an EDI system into its UK and European operations. The objective of this system is to improve its purchasing procedures for the raw materials and component parts required by its manufacturing facility at Greenock in Scotland.

The impetus behind this initiative is that IBM perceives EDI as a CSF to the establishment of a Just-In-Time (JIT) manufacturing arrangement at Greenock. The aim of the JIT is to reduce the manufacturing cycle of PS/2s to under 24 hours. To achieve this IBM believes that it must know to within minutes when various raw materials and component parts will arrive at the factory gates. By connecting its suppliers to an EDI system IBM can monitor its inward bound material requirements.

8.3 ANALYSIS OF INFORMATION SYSTEM TYPE

There are now thousands of examples of firms who have successfully implemented SIS. These include firms from every industry as well as both large and small businesses. From the extensive literature it appears that the systems used by these firms to gain an advantage break down into a number of fundamental classifications. The following four categories shows the type of business advantage offered by SIS.

- *Client Direct Connection for Expediting.* The first group are those who have supplied their clients with hardware and software to enable them to expedite their ordering and inventory control processes. This has had the effect of introducing a switching cost for the client if he were to move to another supplier. In addition, this technique has generally reduced costs for the supplying firm as well as the purchaser. A variation of this approach is the equipping of sales staff with hand-held data capture equipment which provides the capacity to transport data over public telephone lines to centralised computers.

– *Internal Databases used to Improve Client Service.* The second group consists of those who have taken traditional data processing systems, added a SIS dimension, and thus re-oriented them so that they become useful to sales or service personnel in their interface with their clients. The effect of this has been that the firm has achieved superior performance in marketing and client service. This has been especially successful when applied for the purposes of prospecting for new business.

– *Marketing Network Capacity.* A third group have taken their information system infrastructure and used it to create a completely new service. In so doing, they have established a new business for relatively little cost and relatively little risk. This ranges from selling time on their systems, to making them available as a VAN or VADS, to undertaking transaction processing of third parties.

– *Developing Entirely New Businesses.* A fourth group consist of completely new businesses which could not have existed before the current state of IT. Many of these businesses are in the area which has become known as information wholesaling. This includes data via services, subscription databases and home purchasing.

Finally, there are numerous other examples which do not conveniently fit into any of the above groups, but which have used a creative and innovative approach to exploit the SIS opportunities available to them. Sometimes the approach taken by these firms is criticised for being opportunistic, and therefore not part of the corporate strategic planning process. However, all marketing-oriented firms must be, by their very nature, close to their clients, and be prepared to respond immediately to satisfy perceived gaps in the market, and this by definition is opportunistic.

Recent research indicates that SIS of the above types have been implemented by firms in the following proportions:

Client Direct Connection	45%
Internal Databases	42%
Marketing Network Capacity	12%
Developing New Businesses	1%

These percentages reflect the difficulty in achieving a strategic advantage through these different types of DC&N applications.

8.4 SUMMARY

It is clear that there are many different opportunities or different ways to gain a competitive advantage using SIS. The exact extent to which these opportunities have been exploited is not fully known. The Butler Cox Foundation claims that it is extensive and Wiseman claims that any firm using his SOG technique will find their own SIS opportunity. From the cases histories discussed in this chapter it is clear that a lot of different approaches have been used. In most of the cases, firms have used an existing hardware or software system as the basis for their SIS and that this principle of platform development appears to be crucial for any organisation wishing to gain a competitive advantage.

Readers interested in more detail as to how firms formulate and implement strategic information systems are referred to the NCC book *Strategic Information Systems, Development, Formulation, Case Studies* by Dan Remenyi.

9   Strategic Data Communications and Networks

9.1   INTRODUCTION

In considering the case histories of competitive advantage in Chapter 8, a very large percentage of these firms achieved their SIS through the use of data communications and networks. It is therefore important to address this subject separately as part of any comprehensive SISP.

Data communications is the process of transmitting information from one computing device and receiving it at another. A network is a coordinated series of computing devices, able to pass information from one to another as required for the management of the firm's information resources, using data communications software.

The concept of Strategic Data Communications and Network (DC&N) is an example of SIS or Information Weapon Theory. It is essential that strategic DC&N be included in a SISP study. DC&N may be strategic by allowing the firm to make a dramatic change to its approach to the market through applications such as IOS or EDI, or by providing the means for many improvements to applications such as invoicing, inventory control, debtors, etc. DC&N are also strategic because they require a large investment, they have high operational costs and are intrinsically high risk.

In the development of a SISP, DC&N should be addressed separately during both the system audit and brainstorming sessions. DC&N should also appear as a separate section in the action plan. There should be a separate budget and a separate staff requirement for DC&N in the SISP.

In a general sense, networks may be defined as the ability to connect together points of importance. Networks have been a business issue for centuries, from the network of canals and railways to telegraph and telephone systems. Today it is already clear that data communications networks play a vital role in the struggle for profits and are a technology which businesses must learn to exploit.

Networks have become important because computing and communications technology have now converged, and many businesses are using the opportunity which this convergence of technologies offers to produce a new form of network to gain a competitive advantage. Such networks are sometimes referred to as Strategic DC&Ns.

Although data communications networks have been used to some extent in business for 20 years, until recently they have been seen not as an opportunity, but rather as a necessary evil, required because of the geographical remoteness of business locations. Figure 9.1 is typical of the sort of traditional networking used by companies needing to communicate across remote locations. Such a network might extend throughout London or Manchester, or even the UK or the EEC. A network such as the one described here would not necessarily provide the firm with a competitive advantage but might represent a platform from which such a system could be developed.

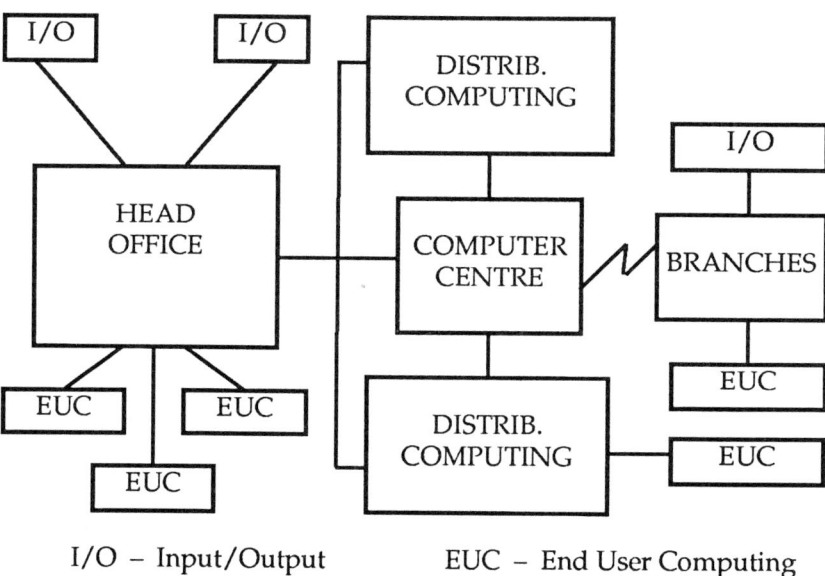

I/O – Input/Output   EUC – End User Computing

**Figure 9.1   A typical internal information network
with platform potential**

9.2   WIDE AREA NETWORKS

As networks grow both in geographical size and in complexity of applications, so managers must learn to exploit their strategic potential as well as use them with maximum efficiency. By spending more money on networks and ensuring they are efficiently managed, substantial savings can be made elsewhere in the business, by concentrating data and thereby eliminating duplicate databases for example.

Many large companies have reached the stage of having their own private information networks to better control the movement of information and data around the organisation. These networks are often spaced widely throughout the country, or even the world. These extensive networks are referred to as Wide Area Networks (WANs). Initially such networks are used only for administration, and taking the next step to use the network to improve communication with suppliers and clients as shown in Figure 9.2 has so far only been taken by a few. This is referred to as using information networks as a strategic or competitive weapon. Electronic links can be forged with customers and suppliers, exploiting the company's information more effectively, introducing innovative new services and thereby getting ahead of the competition. In this respect ETO and EDI are some of the most important examples of an IOS. In Figure 9.2 the original administrative WAN has had a gateway added which allows both customers and suppliers to have access to the firm's information systems.

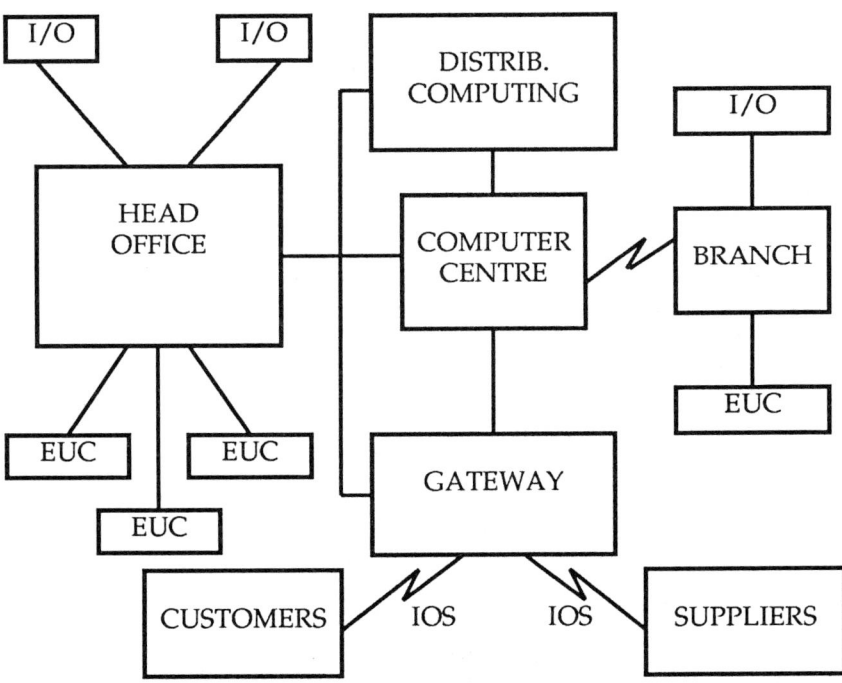

Figure 9.2   **An enhanced information network based on an existing platform**

To move into the area of competitive advantage from networks the first step is to find a strategic opening for the use of this technology. This is sometimes referred to as a vision. Clearly this vision must be congruent with the firm's objectives, strategies and CSF. The approach described by Wiseman in Chapter 4 which used a strategic options generator could be employed. The next step is to create a pilot scheme. This will show if the idea is viable. It will be an opportunity to learn how the real system should be developed by highlighting technical inadequacies. It will build confidence in the staff because they will be able to see what can be achieved by implementing such a system. Because the establishment of a strategic network is very expensive, without such a pilot scheme vast amounts of money may be invested in developing an information network which for one reason or another does not fit in with the organisation. This could at best dampen staff morale, and at worst result in competitive disadvantage.

There are many benefits to be gained from networks. They may be used more readily to make a product available in the marketplace, they may be used to lock customers into the supplier and/or they may create a halo effect. The halo effect means that they engender loyalty and comfort in the firm's clients who see the network as an additional service. This is one of the roots of competitive advantage.

9.2.1   Some Advantages of Strategic DC&N

The advantages of information networks are not limited to any one industry. However, fast moving businesses such as retailing, banking, transport, finance, and manufacturing can probably make most use of a network.

In the case of retailing the following can lead to competitive advantage:

- faster invoicing and ordering;
- minimum stock levels;
- improved cost control;
- more effective marketing and pricing;
- faster response to customer demand.

Computers can typically be placed in branches networked to head office so that electronic ordering ensures the shelves are always full, but stock levels are controlled. More information can be supplied to the customer in the form of detailed sales slips and the sales information can be collected and used for decision making throughout the firm.

TraderNet, which is a value added network (VAN), is used widely throughout the retail industry in the UK. It is an electronic clearing house which allows companies to exchange orders and invoices by way of a computer link as opposed to through the post. Companies using the system claim considerable competitive advantage by being able to respond more quickly to customer requirements, which is a vital factor in the highly competitive high street retailing business.

In the area of banking and finance, information networking can provide the following areas of competitive advantage:

- smart cards and electronic funds transfer;
- more marketing and planning data;
- closer links with agents and customers.

It is clear that one of the keys to the success of networks as devices of competitive advantage is their ability to give people the right information in the right place at the right time.

An area that the banking industry has been researching for some time is that of home banking. The potential success of this is still to be proved in the UK. It has been tried on an experimental basis in several parts of the world, but has not attracted as much attention as was hoped. However remote corporate banking is continuing to grow. In France, the Minitel viewdata systems are common in the home and the office and this has contributed to the relative success of home banking in France.

In the manufacturing industry the following areas of competitive advantage may be achieved through information networking:

- stronger links with customers, distributors and suppliers;
- reduced spare parts stock;
- increased production flexibility.

Electronic links with customers and suppliers are crucial to remain competitive in the manufacturing industry, and in this respect integration is the key goal. By integrating suppliers' applications with the manufacturing company's means that quantities of components held can be reduced, flexibility can be increased and as a result prices of the end product can be held down.

9.2.2   DC&N and the Value Chain

The Porter value chain expresses the relationships which strategic networks frequently exploit. In Figure 9.3 it may be seen that both the firm's and its clients' business value chains may be directly connected through an IOS network. In most cases this involves linking a firm's inbound logistics with its suppliers' outbound logistics. However this is not exclusively the case as there are a large variety of different types of connections, as shown in Figure 9.3. In addition the firm may also exploit DC&N by directly connecting with its suppliers using the same value chain concepts as described above.

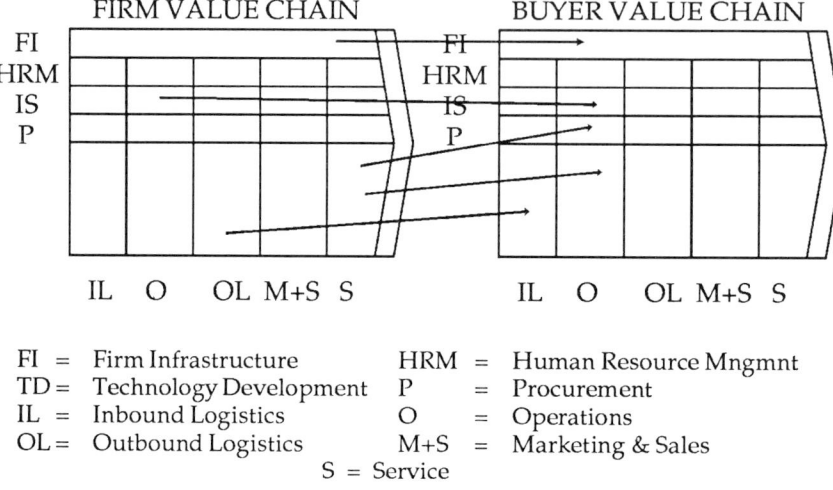

FIRM VALUE CHAIN   BUYER VALUE CHAIN

IL O   OL M+S S   IL O   OL M+S S

FI	=	Firm Infrastructure	HRM	=	Human Resource Mngmnt
TD	=	Technology Development	P	=	Procurement
IL	=	Inbound Logistics	O	=	Operations
OL	=	Outbound Logistics	M+S	=	Marketing & Sales
			S	=	Service

Figure 9.3   An IOS network connecting two value chains

9.2.3   Management Issues for Strategic DC&N

Whatever the industry sector, the main obstacle facing the successful implementation of information networks is management. Most senior managers who have to formulate and perhaps contribute to the implementation of business strategies know little about DC&N, nor in many cases do they want to acquire knowledge about them. As a result they do not know about the potential that such systems have for their organisations. IS departments are in many cases aware of the technical advantages of networking, but as they probably do not know the aims of the company it may be difficult for them to see the commercial potential.

For networking to succeed a champion at board level is frequently required. This should be someone who understands both the business and the technology. It is becoming increasingly clear that people who can see the business value rather than the technical value of a scheme are better able to push through an innovative plan. Making the decision to expand networks beyond internal usage is a difficult one which has many implications. For example, data that was previously held to be confidential may be released to large numbers of users through customers and/or suppliers.

Solving the technical problems associated with forming an information network is not a trivial matter. It would be an extremely costly and time consuming process to start from scratch. The best position is to have a platform from which to develop. This will be an already established internal system which can be extended to include clients and/or suppliers. It is common for firms who decide to expand their networks to purchase the expertise from outside to perform the development. An essential part of the implementation is education and training. Education is required so that users can see the advantages to be derived from the network and training so that they will actually make use of the facility.

Vital to the success of any development is the ability to manage the network. In the past network managers were concerned only that the physical components were working efficiently. In order to use networks strategically managers must be able to focus on the business applications for which they are being used.

There are important security issues with networks. Networks are very vulnerable to fraud. Hackers can access networks and help themselves to funds or perhaps even products. The level of security at which the firm is accustomed to working will usually have to be improved.

Another important issue is that of compatibility of equipment used on the network. The firm's and its clients' or suppliers' hardware may be incompatible. Providers of networks are having to supply a support service to ensure maximum effectiveness regardless of the mix of hardware being used.

Companies must establish corporate network strategies in order to ensure that new initiatives are driven by the real business goals of the organisation. This must be done through the firm's SISP activity. The SISP must bring together both the business and technical issues. To this end personnel such as accountants and sales people should be incorporated into the planning and design team for the new network in order that they can both contribute ideas and help prevent IS staff implementing great ideas that have nothing to do with the goals of the business. It is therefore most important that DC&N be explicitly addressed in the SISP, and any SISP which does not address these issues is incomplete.

With regard to the future of wide area networks, companies of all kinds will be able to spread into new businesses due to the increased ability to communicate information. However, large companies will set the pace as they are the only ones who have the resources for such developments. This will inevitably lead to a decrease in competitiveness in some industries where wide area networking is common, as smaller firms may no longer be able to afford to compete on the same level. It is still uncertain as to the overall impact information networks will have. However, it is sure that they will bring change and with it new opportunities. Therefore wide area networking will remain a strategic issue for some time to come.

9.3   LOCAL AREA NETWORKS

In addition to WANs many firms are using local area networks (LANs) for strategic purposes. LANs can provide many of the competitive advantages of WANs but on a smaller scale. LANs are becoming extremely popular. It is estimated that 95% of all businesses will be using LANs within the next five years. It is therefore essential that the issue of LANs should also be separately addressed in a SISP.

The following pages examine some of the variety of computer networks that are currently in use, including topologies, components, standards and the hardware/software requirements. The aim of this section is to introduce the types of issues which will have to be addressed in developing the LAN section of a SISP.

A personal computer LAN consists of a number of standard PCs or workstations which can be operated as standalone systems independently as well as nodes on the LAN. Each computer can have a variety of different peripherals including disk drives, monitors, printers etc. The LAN is formed by linking the computers with a high speed data communications link. The sophistication of the PCs on the LAN can vary, but if establishing a PC LAN today a minimum of 80386 processors is recommended and 80486 machines will give substantially improved performance.

9.3.1   Benefits of a LAN

Depending on the type of organisation concerned, a LAN may produce a wide variety of benefits ranging from improved efficiency and effectiveness to direct competitive advantage. From a functional point of view the benefits of using a LAN may be divided into three specific areas:

- sharing information;
- sharing peripherals;
- electronic mail.

Through the efficient application of a LAN environment, not only can the collective productivity of PC users be increased, but the operating costs can be substantially reduced:

9.3.1.1   Sharing Information

Information can be exchanged far more easily through a LAN. Reports can be copied from one user's directory directly into another user's, without the need to necessarily print out a hard copy, or to put the information onto a floppy disk. Because of the faster and more direct access to information that a LAN offers, it is likely that the quality and number of business decisions will improve.

9.3.1.2 *Sharing Peripherals*

Although each PC on the network can have its own full complement of peripherals, costs can be considerably reduced through the ability to share large disk drives and high quality printers.

9.3.1.3 *Electronic Mail*

Messages can be sent from one user to any other user or number of users on the network. The recipient of the message need not be at his/her PC as it will be stored in an electronic mailbox in the file server for later reading. This speeds up interpersonal communication by decreasing paperwork and reducing time and money wasted waiting for replies to written memos or telephone messages.

9.3.2 Local Area Network Components

9.3.2.1 *Network Servers*

In order for information to be interchanged between the PCs on a LAN it is necessary for one PC to be designated as a server. This server PC has the ability to share its peripherals with other computers. There are different types of server including file servers and printer servers.

A file server provides disk space that is accessible to other PCs on the network. A print server has a printer or other hard copy device that can be used by other users on the LAN. A dedicated server is purely a central processing unit (CPU), often without a keyboard, monitor, etc, which simply services the requests of other computers on the network.

9.3.2.2 *File Servers*

File servers control user access to files, ensuring that only one user at a time is able to write to a file – or specified part of a file. In addition the file server will maintain file access control through the use of passwords. The file server will usually be a faster, more powerful PC than others on the LAN and will have a high capacity hard disk.

9.3.2.3 *Print Servers*

In the same way that PCs on a LAN can share data through the use of a file server, they can also share a printer through the use of a print server. This will typically enable each user to have an inexpensive dot matrix printer attached to his/her machine and for one PC in the LAN to have a high quality laser printer which will be designated the print server machine. This does not necessarily have to be the same PC as the file server.

9.3.2.4 *Terminal Servers*

A terminal server is a special device that reduces the number of network cards that must be purchased. Two or more PCs may be connected to the terminal server, which in turn is connected to the network in the same way as a normal device. Thus the PCs have the benefits of being able to use the network as if they were connected directly, but do not require expensive individual network cards.

Figure 9.4 shows a typical LAN with a file server, a printer server and a terminal server.

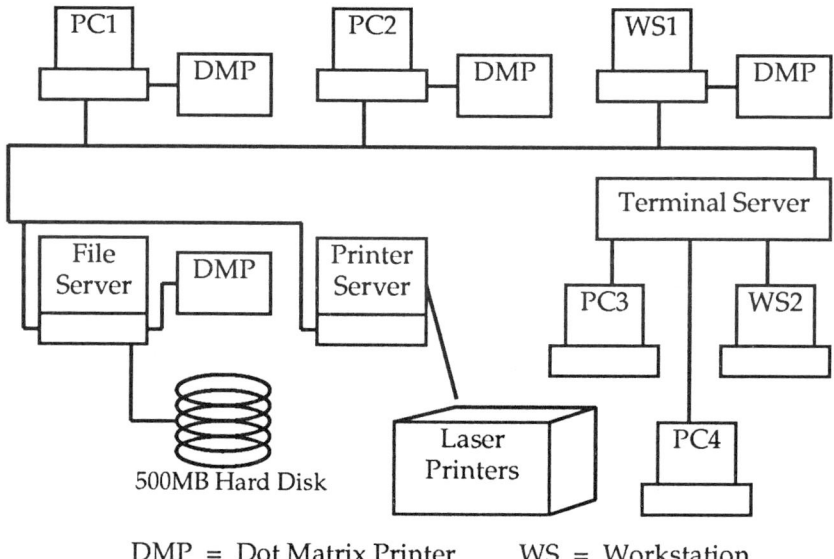

DMP = Dot Matrix Printer   WS = Workstation

Figure 9.1   A typical LAN configuration

9.4   TYPES OF LAN

The way in which the PCs on a LAN are connected together affects the efficiency of the system. There are four main configurations or topologies, referred to as:

- Star;
- Ring;
- Bus;
- Tree.

In addition to these basic topologies, there are various combination or hybrid topologies including:

- triangulated stars;
- complete connections;
- irregular patterns.

9.4.1 Star Network

Figure 9.5 shows a typical star network. This LAN will always have a central controller which will be a file server and a print server. Any information that is to be passed from one computer in the LAN to another must be routed through the central machine. This LAN topology is based on the way the original mainframe and mini computer networks were configured. It is still popular for large network systems. The main disadvantage with this type of network is that if the central computer fails then the entire network ceases to function. It is therefore said that the star network has a single point of failure (SPF).

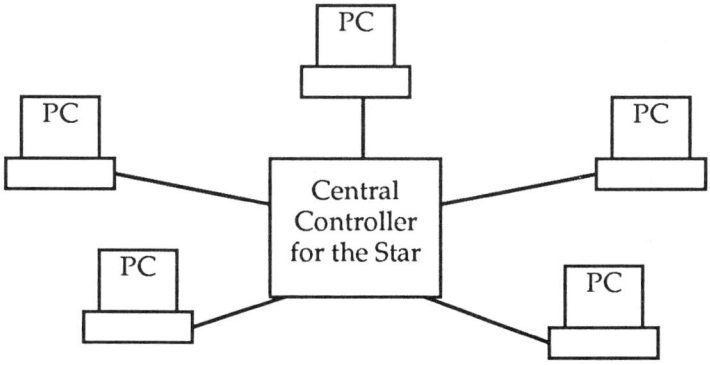

Figure 9.2   The star network topology

9.4.2   Ring Network

The PCs in a ring network are wired together in a circle and data may be passed in either direction around the circle. Each PC is recognised in series and information sent from one machine to another is passed through the intermediary computers along the circle. For example, in Figure 9.6, if the user of PC1 wished to send a file to PC3 the data would be dispatched around the ring, first to PC2 which would recognise that the data was not for it, and would retransmit the data to PC3.

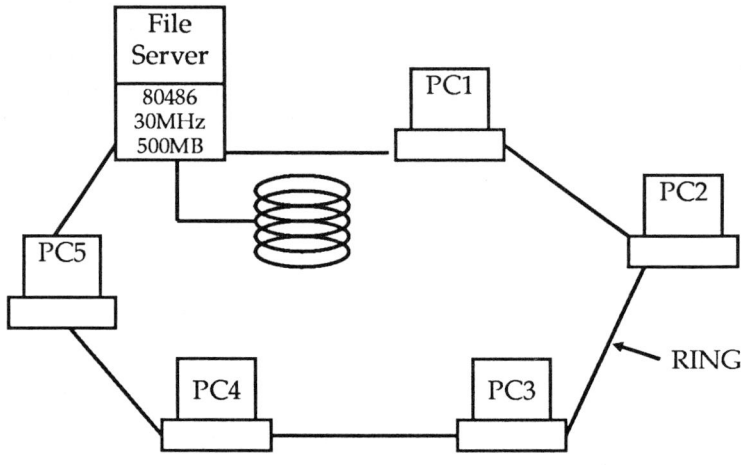

Figure 9.3   The ring network topology

With this methodology, failure of one PC in the ring can cause the whole ring to malfunction. However, with certain proprietary ring networks, this would not necessarily mean the complete failure of the system as data may be redirected around the ring in the other direction, thus avoiding the failed machine. Some systems automatically bypass failed machines, causing data to be transferred straight along the wire. This allows data communications to continue normally. This technology is generally referred to as a token ring, because the transfer of data around the ring is accomplished with an electronic token or signal. The token technique is used to ensure that messages on the ring do not collide. The token ring topology is therefore sometimes referred to as a collision avoidance system.

9.4.2.1   Token Ring

The term Token Ring is both a generic term for a type of ring network and the name of an IBM network. It is one of the most popular LANs and is particularly useful to companies wishing to connect a large number of PCs together, but also requiring access to mainframe and/or minicomputers.

A Token Ring LAN connected with twisted pair wiring gives a powerful, well-controlled but flexible system. The number of users that can be attached to one ring is a variable figure, depending on how much traffic there is likely to be for what proportion of the time. However, it is generally regarded that having more than about 30 users on any one LAN is unadvisable due to the administration and maintenance that is required to keep the system running. With a Token Ring LAN it is easy to join two or more rings together which in effect removes the barrier as to the number of users that can be installed. In addition to hard wiring, the company will need to use modems to connect users in remote locations. With so many users a number of interconnected rings will be required and it would be possible to isolate one or more rings serving certain parts of the company such as payroll or accounts.

The way in which this type of LAN operates is to constantly pass a token around the ring. When a user wishes to receive or send information they call for the token so that when it is next passing their system they can take control and transmit or receive data. Only one message at a time is passed around the LAN and thus the overall data control is good and the system rarely fails.

This type of network is therefore suitable under the following conditions:

- A large organisation with more than 60 to 70 users;
- PCs located in different buildings or in excess of 1000 feet apart;
- The need to share information between PCs, terminals and mainframes;
- Frequent changes in PCs, network configurations or network resources;
- Unplanned growth.

9.4.3   Bus Network

A bus network configuration depends on a common data roadway referred to as a bus, onto which all the PCs in the LAN are attached. The PCs on the LAN listen to all the messages that are passed along the bus, but each one will only access messages addressed to it. If one PC on the LAN fails the others will not be affected. DEC has adopted the bus as its main LAN offering. Figure 9.7 illustrates a typical bus configuration.

Bus networks use a transmission scheme known as *Carrier Sense Multiple Access with Collision Detection*, (CSMA-CD). Under this technique, the system constantly monitors all transmissions that are taking place over the network. If a collision between two transmissions is detected, ie two different nodes are transmitting at the same time, then all transmitting stations cease transmitting, and wait for a random length of time before transmitting again.

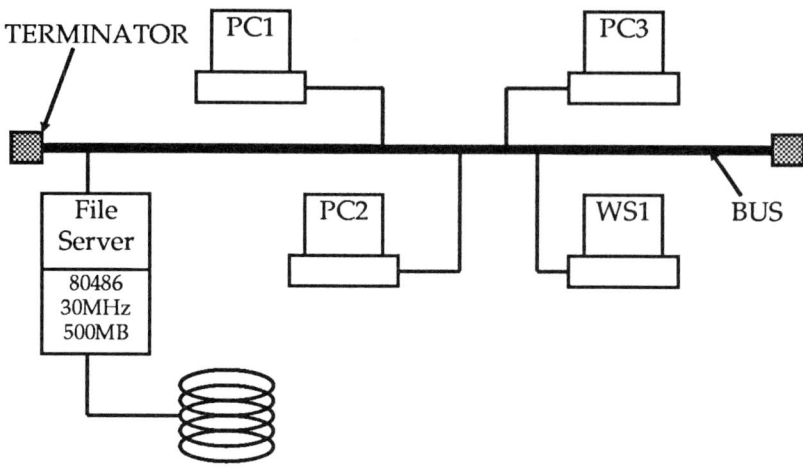

Figure 9.4   The bus network topology

9.4.3.1   EtherNet

EtherNet LANs are the main form of bus systems and are the primary competitors to the Token Ring. They are currently a popular choice for many users.

The main difference between the EtherNet and Token Ring LANs is that an EtherNet network passes information directly from one PC to another via the bus. This means that the transmission and retrieval time can be much faster than with the Token Ring. However, if information is being transmitted and received by the same PCs at the same time a collision can occur which causes the data to be returned to the originating machine and for it to then be retransmitted. When a collision occurs the system will generate a random number to represent the length of time it will wait until the message is retransmitted. The result is that with a large network carrying a lot of traffic the wait time can be considerable and the LAN can be prone to suffering unacceptable periods of delay. Another advantage of EtherNet is its ability to relatively easily link hardware from a number of different manufacturers. Mainframes and minicomputers can also be included in the LAN and these devices can act as file servers if required.

9.4.4   Comparisons of These LANs

Figure 9.8 shows how the Token Ring and EtherNet networks compare to each other in terms of standards, performance and cost. It should be remembered that only a correctly implemented and well managed network will produce the maximum benefits and performance figures.

	Token Ring	EtherNet
Standard	IEEE 802.5	IEEE 802.3
Main proponent	IBM	DEC
Systems connectivity	Mainframes Minis PCs	Minis Supermicros PCs
Cabling system	Structured	Flexible
Bandwidth	4 Mbits/s or 16 Mbits/s	10 Mbits/s
Performance	Medium/High	High
Cost	Medium/High	Low/Medium
Maturity	Medium	High
Primary advantage	Systems Connectivity	Price/ Performance

Figure 9.5   Comparison of Token Ring and EtherNet

9.4.5   Tree Network

A tree network is another network topology which as can be seen in Figure 9.9, has some of the characteristics of a bus, but also has a higher degree of flexibility.

A tree network uses a series of hubs which may be active or passive. A hub is essentially a junction box which allows different branches of the network to be interconnected. An active hub boosts the signal for covering a greater distance than a bus system. ARCNET is the most popular type of tree LAN.

9.4.6   Connecting Networks

Connections can be made between different networks through the use of a variety of devices. There are three ways of connecting LANs to either other LANs or WANS. These connections are made by using devices called repeaters, bridges and routers.

Figures 9.10 through 9.12 show how these devices can be used to connect different configurations and topologies.

The repeater is the simplest form of connecting device and would be used to connect quite similar networks, as shown in Figure 9.10.

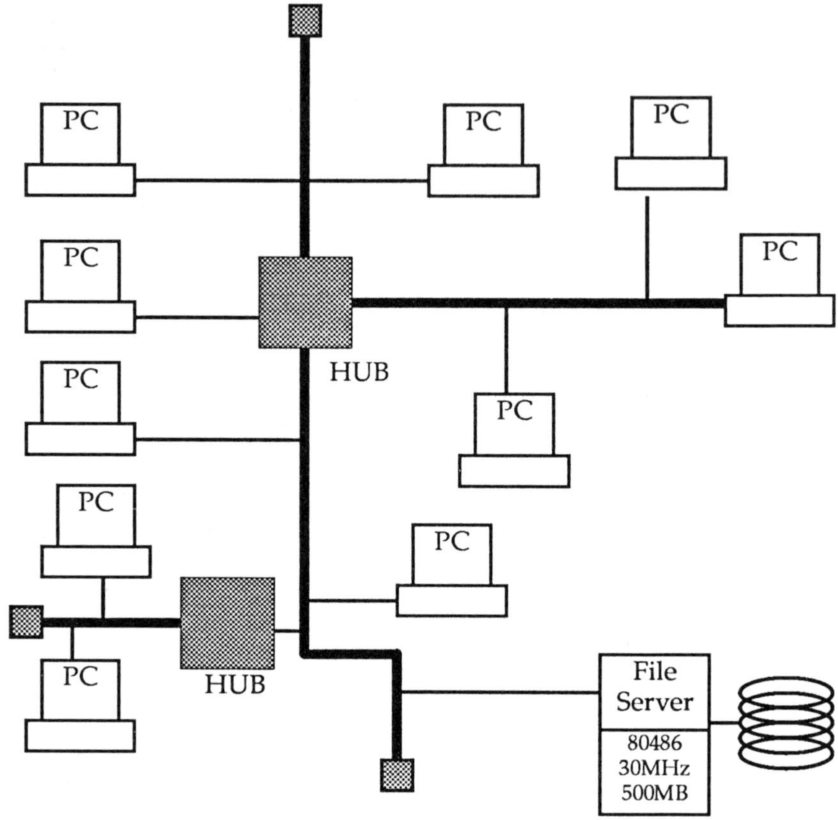

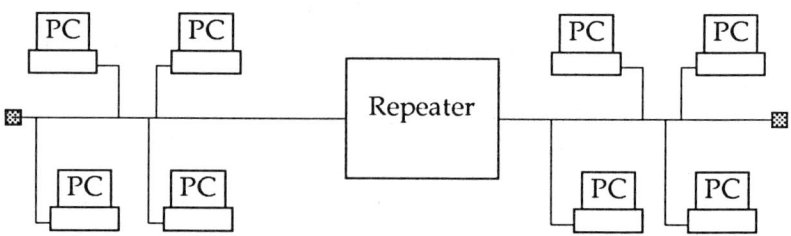

Figure 9.6　The tree network topology

Figure 9.7　Using a repeater to link a bus to a bus

A bridge is a more sophisticated network connector, and is used to connect different types of LANs, as shown in Figure 9.11.

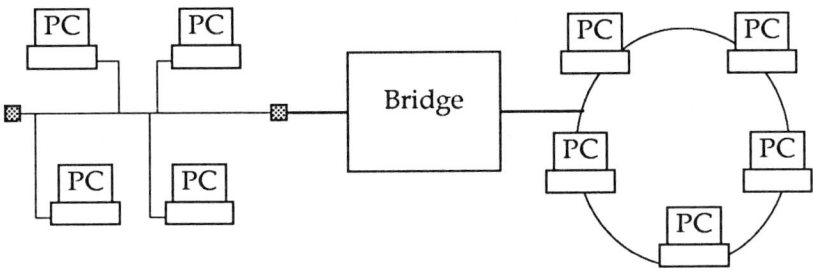

Figure 9.8   Using a bridge to link a bus to a ring

A router may be used to connect LANs to other data communication devices, as shown in Figure 9.12.

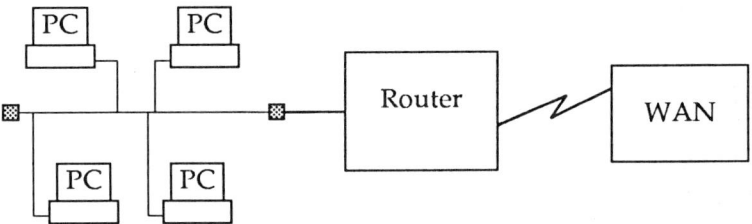

Figure 9.9   Using a router to link a bus to a WAN

9.4.7   Network Management

Network control or management may be defined as the structured approach taken to ensure the system's integrity is maintained and that the network continues to operate at an acceptable level. Network management includes not only the on-going issues of fault detection and correction, but also the more general topics of network design and implementation.

Network management has become strategic as more and more firms are using networks for strategic purposes. Whilst these systems are operating correctly, they offer opportunities to provide substantial benefits to the organisation, but should the systems fail, the firm will suffer correspondingly greater losses. Thus it is essential to plan and control network operations in order to minimise this risk and thus maximise the strategic benefit.

It is particularly important to consider the issue of network management when selecting a network topology. Certain topologies and inter-network connections allow a greater degree of control than others. Additionally, it is easier to monitor the work that is being carried out on different workstations and devices if an appropriate network topology is selected.

Figures 9.13 through 9.15 show how three different network topologies affect the level of network management, from the web topology in Figure 9.13 which offers no overall systems management, to the connected rings in Figure 9.15 which allow maximum control and monitoring to be performed. It should be decided during the SISP which level of network management and control the firm considers most appropriate to its circumstances.

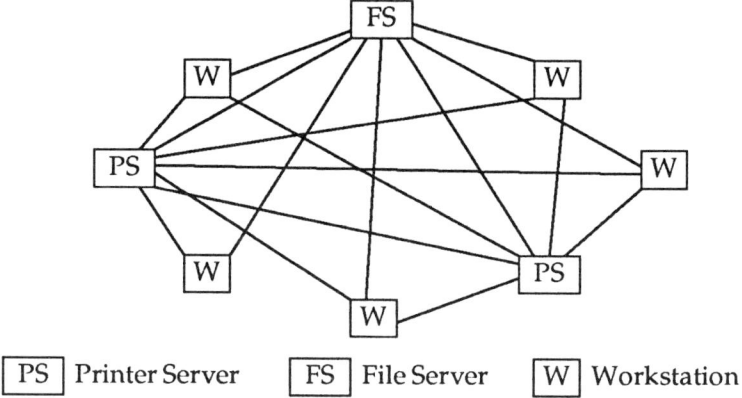

Figure 9.10   A web topology with no network management

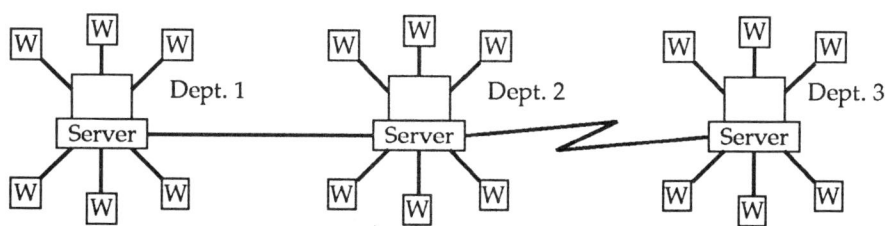

Figure 9.11   Server-level management

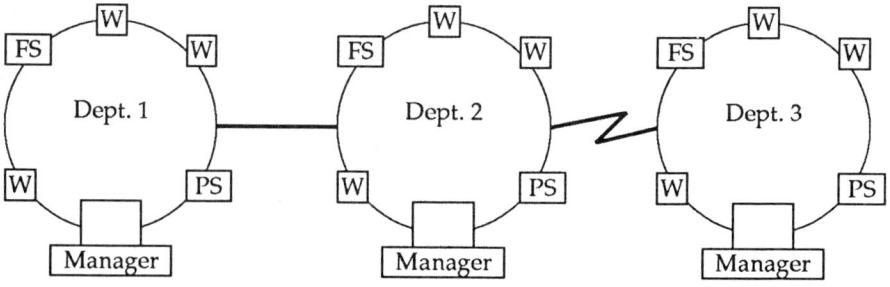

Figure 9.12   Domain management

9.5   INSTALLING AND USING A LAN

Having decided to implement a LAN, and selected the appropriate topology and supplier, it is then necessary to prepare the site location and users in advance.

9.5.1   Wiring

One of the key issues that affect the successful installation of any LAN is the way in which it is wired. There are generally three options available:

- coaxial cable;

- twisted pair;

- fibre optics.

Coaxial cable is the type of wire used for television aerials. It is circular with a central core of copper. This is a solid wire which is able to pass a single signal. The copper wire is surrounded first in a plastic insulator and then covered in braided wire which passes the earth signal and works as a screen. A PVC covering provides the outer sheath. Coaxial cable is particularly good for sending high frequency signals over long distances. It is, however relatively expensive.

Twisted pair is, as its name suggests, two or more wires twisted together and held in a PVC sheath. The number of wires in the cable can vary, but one will normally carry the earth signal and each of the others can carry a single signal. As this cable is generally not protected with the braiding found on coaxial cable it is subject to electronic interference or 'noise' which can effect the transmission of data. It is however a cheap option, and is widely used in the LAN environment, particularly where distances between PCs are relatively short.

The fastest, but most expensive wiring option is fibre optics. A fibre optic cable is capable of sending a large number of signals down a single glass fibre light guide by utilising a large number of different frequencies. Because the data is sent in the form of light as opposed to electricity there can be no electronic noise from external devices, and thus this is a very fast and reliable form of wiring. Primarily due to its cost it is not yet widely used in the LAN environment.

The supplier of a LAN will normally advise on the type of wiring that should be used and it is advisable to install the wires around the building prior to the PCs being installed or joined to the LAN. The wiring decision is a most important one as it can directly affect the performance and reliability of the system and thus affects its strategic impact. Also if wiring has to be retro-filled into a building it may be a more costly exercise.

9.5.2   Using a LAN

Until recently LANs were only perceived as being suitable for the processing requirements of a department or function. They were often initiated by end users with little or no help from the ISD. For this reason many LANs were very limited in size, functionality and facilities. In recent years this attitude has begun to change and a new term, *Enterprise LANs* has emerged. An Enterprise LAN has a much wider scope with one of its primary objectives being to serve the needs of the whole enterprise. This trend means that LANs will be used far more extensively throughout the entire organisation. This will result in more applications being available on LANs with higher levels of traffic and the need for more professional LAN management and control. In these circumstances the need for the ISD's involvement becomes critical.

9.6   NETWORK STANDARDS

The final issue which SIS planners should be aware of is that of international standards.

Although there are many standard setting organisations working in this field, there are two main standards for network communication referred to as IEEE and ISO/OSI.

IEEE is an acronym for the Institute of Electrical and Electronic Engineers. This is a US computer and data communications standards setting body which has established a whole range of standards in this industry. The IEEE has formed a special committee called IEEE802 to define guidelines and standards for LAN communications. Because of the definitions laid down by the 802 committee a manufacturer can develop hardware and software that will be able to communicate with another manufacturer's products. Networks that have conformed to the IEEE standard include IBM's token ring which is referred to as IEEE802.5 and EtherNet which is IEEE802.3.

ISO/OSI is an acronym for International Standards Organisation/Open Systems Interconnection. ISO is an international standards setting group based in Geneva. OSI is a set of communication standards which ISO has established and which is beginning to be widely accepted. The OSI standard is based on a seven layer model for data communications in which each layer defines a different function in the model. Figure 9.16 shows the definition of the seven layer model.

Layer 1 defines the hardware and electrical specifications that must be met. Layer 2 specifies how the data is to be transferred from point to point. Layer 3 defines the internetwork routing specifications. Layer 4 specifies how the data is to be transmitted, in a reliable form, from one point to another. Layer 5 specifies how the dialogue between nodes will be handled. Layer 6 specifies

Users Programs and Devices

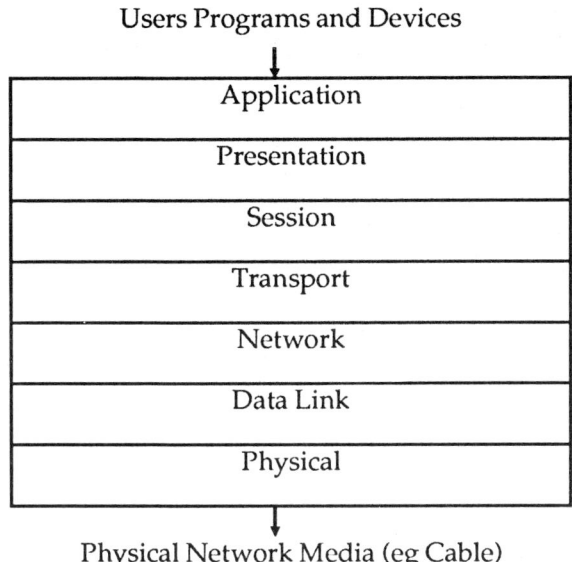

Physical Network Media (eg Cable)

Figure 9.13   The seven layer model definition

how the data will be represented, and how it is to be formatted. Layer 7 specifies any special purpose services that may be required.

In addition to the network standards set by the IEEE and ISO, many manufacturers have defined their own standards. Two of the most common of these independent models are the IBM and the TCP/IP architectures.

Although IBM is still the most powerful de facto standard setting body, the work done by the ISO is being more and more recognised. This is because of pressure exerted on all suppliers by bodies such as the US Department of Defense, the EEC and a number of other government bodies. It is now clear that there is a major movement towards OSI standards and any IS planner must bear this in mind.

9.7   SUMMARY

This chapter has given a general introductory overview of some of the issues related to data communications and networks. This is included in this work because it is believed that management decision makers should have some knowledge of the scope of data communications and networks as well as an acquaintance with some of the issues involved.

Strategic DC&N are a vital issue in many organisations and should be explicitly addressed when producing any SISP. There are numerous applications of DC&N in most firms, ranging from WANs to LANs. Therefore, strategic DC&N are important both from a WAN and a LAN point of view. It is therefore essential that strategic DC&N be clearly understood by management and that the players in the development of a SISP address these issues directly. As most SIS are network based, strategic DC&N is an issue that cannot be avoided. In addition the demand for networks, both LANs and WANs, is likely to grow exponentially for the rest of the decade.

10 Office Automation

10.1 INTRODUCTION

In a similar way to data communications and networks, Office Automation (OA) is an important subject to separately address as a part of any comprehensive SISP. After a somewhat false start in the 80s, OA is beginning to play a more important, and frequently strategic, role in many enterprises.

The strategic importance of OA rests in the fact that it can dramatically improve office staff or white collar access to information. As OA can make a significant contribution to improving the performance of many organisations it is most important that the issues of OA be specifically addressed in any SISP and that funds be allocated to its development during this planning process.

Although in certain situations OA has a very high potential to improve productivity the real benefits to be derived from OA result from the improvement in information availability which may be used by the firm to help improve the decision making process and thereby increase the organisation's effectiveness. This is important because a major industry driver of the 90s is optimum quality, which implies getting it right the first time. To achieve this optimum quality concept the enterprise must be able to ensure that it can offer its clients a reliable and rapid response to their requests, and OA can certainly play a central role in achieving this objective.

The strategic dimension of the increased effectiveness aspect of OA may also manifest itself as a differentiated organisation, depending on the firm and the industry in which it functions. Of course there are firms which may derive only marginal improvements from OA and in these situations OA will not have much, if any, strategic value. The extent to which OA may be strategic to the firm is a function of the role and intensity of information both within the industry in which the firm functions and the firm itself. Industries which are information-intensive such as banking and insurance will find the benefits available through OA critical to their success. Similarly, professional firms such as accountants, architects, engineers, lawyers, and management consultants are finding OA invaluable. For many of these professional firms OA represents an opportunity to gain a competitive advantage by substantially increasing the level of service which may be offered to clients. Furthermore, OA systems have been very effectively implemented in the management services departments of many firms.

In general, as many firms attempt to increase their competitive advantage to some extent by the use of OA, firms should perceive OA at the very least as a defensive strategic move.

10.2   DEFINITION OF OA

OA may be defined as the use of computer technology to serve business goals by raising the effectiveness and the productivity of office staff, particularly those who are not specialists in IT. OA represents a critical development in IT because it brings computing power to the assistance of white collar workers and management professionals in a way in which the more traditional accountancy based data processing applications completely failed to achieve. For many users OA is either the first step into personal productivity tools or an extension of the standalone productivity tools available on PCs to encompass departmental or group issues. A very important feature of OA, which is not addressed by systems analysis alone, is that it recognises that much of the work undertaken in an office relies on interaction between a number of people. Thus OA technology emphasises the need for a high degree of connectivity between individuals in the office, and thus the various parts of the system. It is this focus on connectivity that makes OA such a beneficial aid, especially to the knowledge worker.

Although OA is vitally concerned with productivity improvement it is not essentially a cost reducing endeavour. As a by-product OA may possibly reduce administration costs, but this is not always the case, and in any event it is not likely that any such cost reduction could in itself lead to the firm becoming a cost leader.

OA may enhance office productivity by improving the quantity and/or quality of output from office workers or reducing the direct or indirect cost of office workers. These include all levels of staff from clerical and secretarial through professionals to top management. OA, unlike personal computers and other forms of end user computing, does not generally provide computing power to blue collar workers or other technical staff outside the office.

Office productivity may be enhanced by:

–   improving the speed and ease of completing tasks especially by the automation of clerical and secretarial activities;

–   increasing group effectiveness by facilitating information exchange thus ensuring everyone is kept as fully informed as possible – information support ensures greater ease of attaining objectives;

- reducing costs of labour, consumables and office space; labour cost reduction is often most easily achieved among more junior staff whose work may be fully automated as opposed to having only part of the work automated.

In addition OA can support better management by providing an EIS system comprising the following:

10.2.1   Personal productivity tools

OA systems typically provide spreadsheet systems, databases, electronic mail, etc, which give management the opportunity of performing extensive analysis and communicating their findings rapidly through the organisation.

10.2.2   Interfaces to corporate data

A key reason why OA is superior to standalone personal computers is that through the system's connectivity, the latest transactional data may be accessed by management for immediate analysis. This type of interface which may be linked to DSS and EIS requires the use of sophisticated 4GLs.

10.2.3   Interfaces with external data including Viewdata

Decision makers need access to a wide range of data including much data which will not be on the firm's own computers. OA must therefore provide the capability of accessing other commercial online databases.

Management applications are often dogged by implementation delays, cumbersome access procedures and lack of comprehensive data. This has resulted in top management turning against OA claiming that their work is not assisted by it.

10.3   DEPARTMENTAL AND CORPORATE NATURE OF OA

OA systems are departmental in nature, providing facilities to groups. These group facilities are broadly similar to those provided to individuals through the use of PCs. Although this situation is changing rapidly, at present many PCs are still mostly used in a standalone mode and thus are mostly of benefit for personal productivity. OA goes beyond what is available through PCs by extending personal productivity to departmental productivity and further providing a bridge between personal and/or departmental computing and corporate computing. Thus a link to the corporate mainframe is a critical part of the OA hardware system.

In fact more and more firms are extending their departmental OA systems to embrace the whole organisation, and in some cases this involves linking PCs to minicomputers and then to mainframes through LANs and WANs.

Another aspect of the link to the mainframe is that the OA system may generate such large volumes of data that it cannot store it in an effective way on its own mass-storage devices. In such cases the storage capacity and processing power of a mainframe or super mini is required. At present systems sold for OA do not have the intense processing power of a mainframe.

OA has been primarily driven by minicomputer hardware manufacturers. Most of the original OA systems were supplied on proprietary hardware using proprietary software. In many cases these OA vendors over-sold and under-delivered. Today the market has changed. There is a wide range of vendors with an extensive variety of hardware and software OA products. This range extends from IBM who supply PROFS as a mainframe OA system to many vendors of LANs with applications software. Major minicomputer vendors are DEC with their All-In-One system, Wang with Wang Office, ICL with Office Power, Data General with CEO, and Unisys with Office Ensemble.

10.4   OA APPLICATIONS

OA applications are typically not transaction-based. They are often text and number related activities which support the efforts of the knowledge worker. These applications relate to fact gathering, fact organising and information presentation. These activities are crucial to managers, professionals and their personal assistants or secretaries.

OA applications may be divided into five main groups.

Text processing

This includes, but is not limited to, word processing, as it also includes electronic document distribution (E-mail) and filing. It also includes interfacing with online source material from internal and external databases as well as newswire services. In an OA context text processing is aimed as much at non-clerical and non-secretarial staff as at the traditional users of word processing. Spelling checkers, thesaurus, and mailing systems are also important here.

E-mail's importance is rapidly growing especially as it is seen by many as an absolutely essential prerequisite before a firm can move to EDI and other IOS.

Another major issue which is considered under the heading of text processing is desk top publishing (DTP). Many OA systems now incorporate some degree of DTP.

Record storage and retrieval

This application area includes a wide range of software products which will store data, provide an updating facility and allow quick and easy retrieval.

Typical uses for these systems are project records, resource records and client and personnel details. As the central feature of OA is the system's ability to allow resource sharing, emphasis is placed on the multi-user nature of these systems. This means that such systems should have adequate file and record locking procedures. The data input procedures should be easy to use and preferably based on data forms which should address multiple systems. It is important for this software to provide an easy interface to other programs especially word processors and spreadsheets. A report generator should be available for quick and easy reporting. These systems should have capacity for a large number of records and each record should be capable of holding a large volume of data with the ability to hold a large amount of text.

Figure work

Spreadsheets have become the usual vehicle for providing individuals with personal productivity tools for numeric analysis. The primary application areas for spreadsheets are budgeting, estimating, costing, capital investment appraisal and forecasting. The better spreadsheets have integrated graphics, data management, word processing and telecommunications. Data from the spreadsheet should be easily transferable to a word processor and database system.

Communications

As connectivity is a corner stone of the concept of OA it is essential that all hardware and software components of the system can quickly and easily communicate with each other. It is equally imperative that the OA system is interfaced to the corporate mini and mainframe computer systems as well as public subscription databases.

Other business productivity tools

These include a series of business utilities such as diaries, memos, calendars, directories, calculators as well as graphics packages.

By definition OA applications must be multi-user and multi-tasking. This facility will be provided by either proprietary software developments or increasingly through Unix or Xenix based systems.

It is important not to select OA applications on the basis of the suitability of the equipment only, but rather for the relevance of the system to the organisation.

Figure 10.1 shows a typical set of OA tools which have been configured in order to provide a London based enterprise with a strategic or competitive advantage. The competitive advantage will be derived from the enterprise's ability to use these systems to enhance the level of service which it offers its clients. The service level will improve as OA will allow the firm to provide

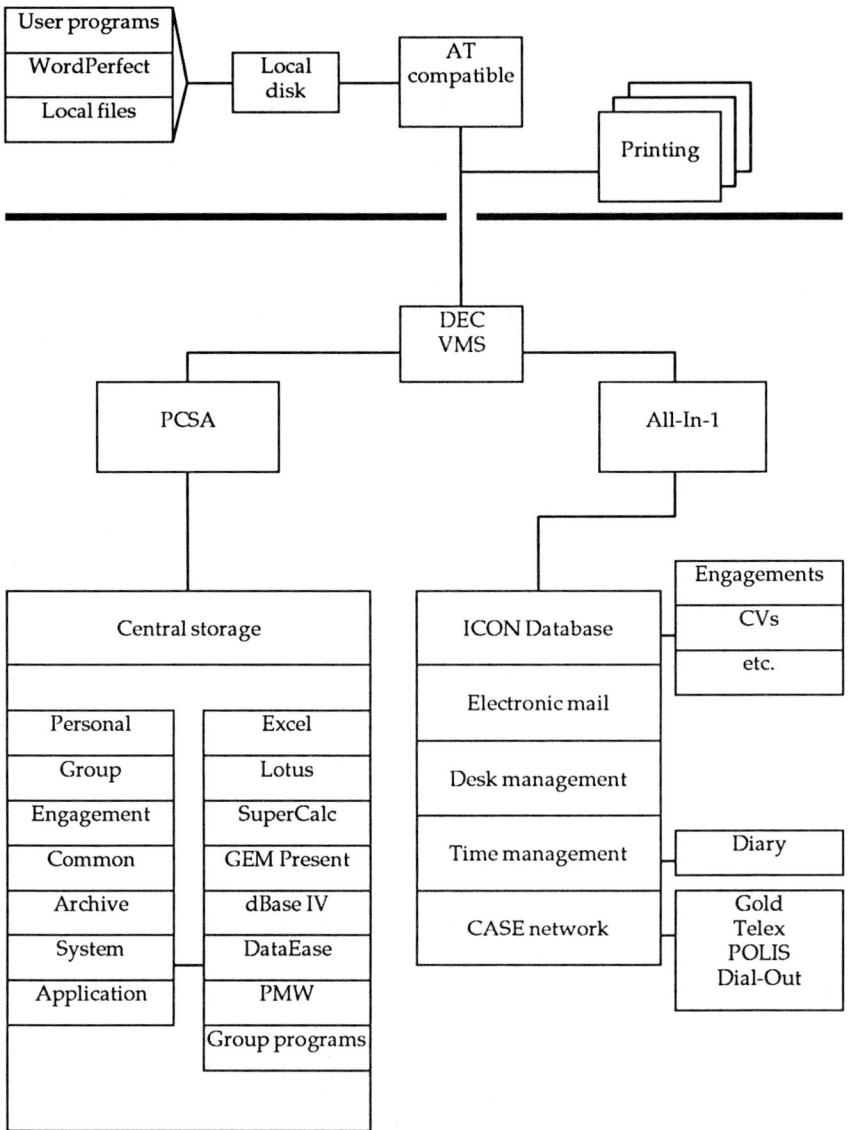

Figure 10.1　A typical set of OA tools

more comprehensive information to its clients as well as dramatically decreasing the time required to respond to requests. In this way the firm will continue to differentiate itself relative to its competitors.

Figure 10.2 indicates how various elements of the OA system communicate in order to provide the necessary degree of connectivity. Within each of the nodes in the system there are EtherNet-based LANs. Each of these LAN systems function independently and are connected to the central system at head office by means of a WAN. Each node has its own minicomputer with a substantial network, as well as a sizable disk storage capacity. In order to ensure that each node within Greater London will be able to communicate with each other node without having to rely on the head office system, the WAN is triangulated. This means that there are several different routes by which a system may access other systems.

10.5   OA STRATEGY

An OA strategy gives a general sense of where an organisation's OA activities should be heading. It should specify how the firm is to get started and provide general guidelines as to how to proceed. It must state objectives so that the firm's performance with OA may be monitored and assessed. It should have a three to five year timescale and therefore match the planning period of a SISP. As this technology is still in a state of reasonably rapid change the strategy should be reasonably broad and flexible.

An OA strategy may be positive, negative or neutral. A positive strategy seeks out opportunities to enhance the firm's performance through OA. A negative strategy sees OA as a cost which must be kept as low as possible. A positive strategy risks considerable expense and the possibility of no material benefit whereas a negative strategy risks lost opportunities and the possibility of competitors becoming more effective through their application of OA. A neutral or indifferent strategy is probably the least effective as it risks both the disadvantages of the positive and the disadvantages of the negative strategies.

OA strategies are sometimes only pursued when end user computing has grown out of control and must be rationalised to prevent further waste. When this occurs some firms turn to OA as the main vehicle for providing computing power to their management, professional and office staff.

The OA strategy pursued by many firms ties in closely with their generic IS strategy. If the firm is following a centrally planned or leading edge information systems strategy it will have a positive attitude to OA. If the firm is following a scarce resource or necessary evil policy then OA will be treated negatively. Neutral attitudes to OA may result from free market and monopoly strategies.

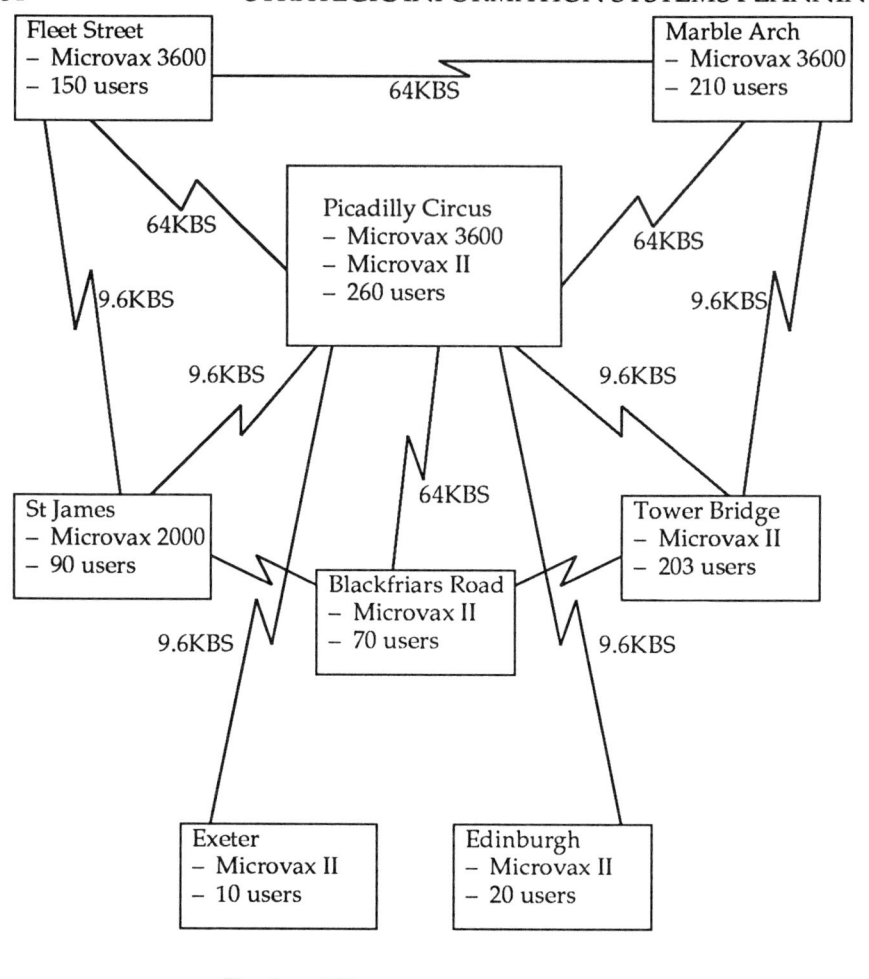

Total: 830 users
          520 workstations
          120 printers

Figure 10.2   Interconnections in an OA system

10.6   SUMMARY

OA should be an integral part of almost every firm's IS strategy. At best it can produce very considerable competitive advantage, and at worst it must be seen as a defensive strategy.

Whatever the firm's IS strategy the OA strategy must be explicitly incorporated into the SISP. This is done by requesting different departments to submit their OA plans during the corporate strategic planning exercise. These individual plans must then be aggregated and finally consolidated into the overall SISP. OA issues are closely related to strategic data communications and networks considerations, and must be reviewed at the same time as the firm establishes its policies on LANs and other end user computing issues. In recent years these have constituted a larger part of the SISP.

11   When is a SISP Required ?

11.1   QUESTIONNAIRE TO DETERMINE THE NEED FOR A SISP

As mentioned in Chapter 1, not every firm will have to, or want to, perform a SISP. Some firms are too small for a SISP. Some firms cannot afford the funds required. Some firms are too immature in their IS experience to be able to profit from a SISP. Some firms and the industries in which they function are sufficiently stable that a SISP is, perhaps, not seen to be necessary. Furthermore, the culture in some firms would either make a SISP impossible, or render its results of little or no value.

Therefore an important question which senior management must face is "Would a SISP be beneficial to this firm, and if so when should it be undertaken ?". The subsidiary question which should also always be asked is "If a SISP is required, what should be its scope?"

11.2   ASSESSING WHETHER A SISP WILL BE BENEFICIAL

The following is a series of lists of circumstances under which a firm will usually need to perform a SISP. It is not intended that all these circumstances be perceived as having equal importance, nor is it suggested that the lists are exhaustive. These lists may be used to develop a questionnaire which may be used by the reader to discuss the likelihood of the firm requiring to conduct a SISP.

11.2.1   Corporate-Wide Issues

Corporate-wide issues are those which have an impact on most aspects of the organisation and which can radically affect the way the firm conducts its business. A checklist of such issues will include:

–   Has the fundamental structure of the firm been recently changed or are there plans to change it?

–   Have any major acquisitions or divestitures been made recently or are there any intended in the near future?

–   Has unusually fast growth been experienced in recent times or is it expected soon?

- Has the firm experienced difficulty in obtaining the information needed for effective decision making?
- Is prompt, accurate operating information available from decentralised locations, or are there unacceptably long delays?
- Is the firm having excessive difficulty obtaining suitably qualified staff, and retaining their services?

11.2.2   Industry Drivers

Industry drivers refer to conditions in the environment in which the firm functions which impact all organisations in the industry. Each firm faces many industry drivers. A checklist of these will include:

- Has the industry been, or is it about to be, deregulated?
- Have there been any major changes in the balance of business power which may have affected the industry's image?
- Are there any major socioeconomic shifts which will affect demand and/or supply?
- Have competitors been able to outmanoeuvre the firm because of better or more timely information on markets, specific customer needs, or other key factors?
- Has any competitor used IT creatively to reduce costs, improve productivity, enhance product or service value, speed delivery or create new products or services?
- Has there been any major breakthrough in the IT hardware or software industry which could affect how the firm functions?
- Is the quality of the firm's information systems perceived to be below average for the industry?

11.2.3   Information Quality

Information quality refers to the standard of reporting facilities supplied by the ISD. Information quality is a measure of how efficiently and effectively the ISD personnel are applying the technology at their disposal. The questions they will be looking at include:

- Could the firm lose credibility in the financial community because of inaccurate or delayed financial reporting/forecasts?
- Is there, or is it suspected that there might be, a problem regarding security of financial, personnel or marketing information?
- Have the accounts been qualified by the auditors?

- Have there been any inventory surprises – obsolete stock, major stock outs, late delivery from suppliers – due to inaccurate, late, or inadequate information?
- Do information users regularly express dissatisfaction with what they get, when they get it or how they get it?
- Is there frustration because redundant data sources are producing inconsistent or conflicting reports and information?

11.2.4 Information Management

Information management refers to a group of issues relating both to how information is presented to appropriate end users as well as how the ISD is managed. The following situations should be assessed:

- Is the firm failing to get a steady flow of creative ideas concerning the effective use of IT?
- Do critical systems fail to meet the information needs and expectations of information users?
- Is it believed that senior management is out of touch with the information systems operations?
- Do systems fail to reflect the business priorities which have been established for the organisation?
- Is there an increasing maintenance backlog?
- Do the information systems fail to contribute positively towards the achievement of corporate goals?
- Is the cost of the ISD escalating exponentially?
- Are there problems in staffing the ISD?

11.3 WHAT SHOULD THE SCOPE OF A SISP BE?

The broader the scope of a SISP, the greater the chance of effecting real strategic improvements. However, these possible gains must be offset against cost, time and the firm's internal politics. It is often better to undertake a SISP with quite a narrow scope in order to establish that this is part of the way the firm conducts its planning. Once the SISP process has been established the scope of the project may be extended to address additional functions, geographic areas, products lines etc. Alternatively the SISP could be repeated each year in order to look at different areas of interest. In short the scope of a SISP is determined by a whole range of factors which are quite specific to each individual firm.

11.4 SUMMARY

A SISP is an expensive, time consuming activity. It is not relevant to every enterprise, and to those to which it is appropriate, it will only be necessary under certain circumstances. This chapter lists some of these circumstances. Not all of the points listed here are of equal importance. Also, the importance of these points will substantially vary from industry to industry, as well as from firm to firm within any given industry.

12 Steps Required to Develop a SISP

12.1 INTRODUCTION

The SISP is a document produced annually which will indicate what the firm intends to achieve with its IS department in the next 12 to 18 months as well as the next three to five years. Thus the SISP has both short and longer term implications for the firm.

In a previous chapter the design of a systems architecture for IS was discussed, in which it was stated that the firm must stake out a goalpost up to about ten years ahead towards which it can aim. As already mentioned, these targets are not the same as the SISP itself as they are really definitions of the IS environment in which the firm intends to be working in the future. The architectural plan also addresses standards and policies to which the firm intends to comply during the longer term planning period.

The format and detail of the SISP is directly dependent on a number of variables including the reasons for initiating the SISP and the constraints placed on the study. It is also affected by who conducts the study and the amount of funds allocated to the work as well as the time period allowed.

12.2 REASONS FOR A SISP

A SISP may be initiated for one of several quite distinct reasons, some examples of which follow:

- The old mainframe must be replaced.
- There has been a mass proliferation of PCs which have got out of control.
- The IS budget is clearly no longer being complied with and is thus out of control.
- The systems no longer supply relevant information.
- There has been a merger or acquisition.
- A new IS director is appointed.

This list is by no means exhaustive and other suggestions as to when to perform a SISP are supplied in Chapter 11. If the SISP were initiated because of a limitation in the mainframe then it will probably be less probing than if it were initiated because the systems are perceived to no longer supply relevant information.

12.3   CONSTRAINTS UPON A SISP

There may be a number of constraints placed on the scope of the SISP:

- *Business Scope of the Plan:* A SISP may be performed for the whole enterprise or for one business area or a group of business areas.

- *Geographical Scope of the Plan:* A SISP may be performed for head office only or perhaps for the IS requirements in Europe ignoring the enterprise's IS in Asia, etc.

- *Hardware:* The SISP may be drawn up subject to the constraint that the mainframe will not be changed for five years.

- *Software:* The SISP may be drawn up subject to the constraint that certain software products will not be changed for a given number of years.

A SISP which only concerns itself with computing in head office will obviously be less substantial than a SISP conducted for the whole of the company.

The time required to develop a SISP will of course vary enormously from one firm to another. In most circumstances a thoroughly developed plan will require a minimum of three to six months and possibly longer, to prepare. To develop a SISP a team should be established which incorporates a member of top management as well as a senior IS executive. Some formal project management procedures should be used to plan and control the work of the team. Frequently SISPs are developed with the help of consultants who will act as catalysts in the team. However it is essential that at least one senior executive from the organisation itself participates in the development of the plan and endorses the proposals put forward in it. It is not appropriate for consultants alone to prepare a firm's SISP as it will then belong to outsiders and not to executives within the organisation. Also if consultants alone prepare the plan a methodology may be used which no-one in the organisation understands. However, SISPs prepared with the help of consultants are sometimes longer and more thorough than others.

12.4   BACKGROUND WORK BEFORE THE SISP BEGINS

A SISP is concerned with defining the hardware, software, communications and people required to support the IS function. It is also concerned with the organisational procedures within which the ISD will operate. The SISP is a direct derivative of the corporate strategic plan which defines how the enterprise will attain its business objectives. Thus before the SISP may be prepared the corporate strategic plan must be developed and a list of critical success factors (CSFs) established, as the IS planners will need to draw on them to ensure that they are on course. In fact throughout the development of the SISP continual reference will be made to the CSFs.

These CSFs are the things which must occur if the corporate strategic plan is to be realised. In the process of developing the SISP they will be matched against specific application systems to see the extent to which they assist the realisation of the plan.

If a corporate strategic plan does not exist or if CSFs have not been identified then the SISP team leader must attempt to obtain this information from top management. However, this is not an easy process as the production of a Strategic Plan is a major exercise in its own right. The first issues which a strategic planning process address include:

- the environment;
- the product-market mix;
- the firm's strengths and weaknesses;
- the competition;
- the legal infrastructure;
- established and new technology;
- human resources;
- required investment levels;
- financial markets;
- other stakeholders.

Each of these areas are analysed in order to determine the firm's strengths and weaknesses. Having completed such analysis the planners are in a position to establish realistic goals and objectives for the firm.

Figure 12.1 shows the structure of the planning activities required to establish the firm's goals and objectives.

Having established the firm's goals and objectives, the next step is to establish a corporate strategy which in simple terms represents the way the firm intends to achieve these goals and objectives.

In Figure 12.2 the steps required in the first phase of establishing the corporate strategy are shown.

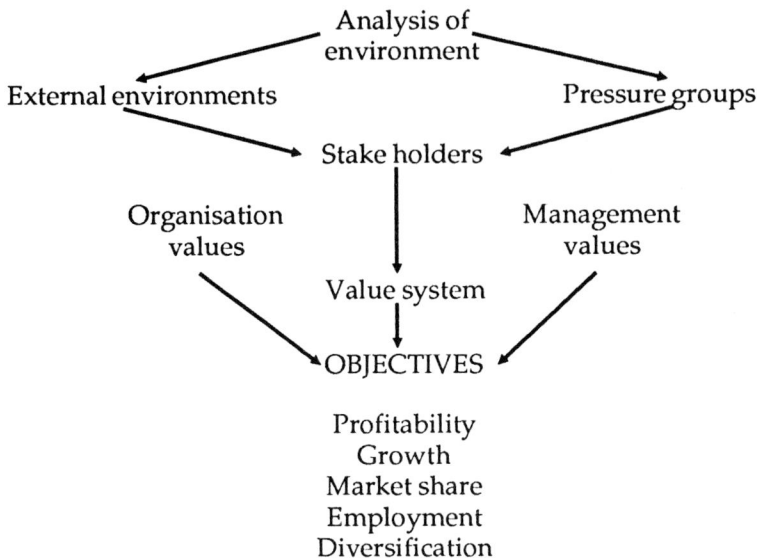

Figure 12.1   Establishing goals and objectives

At this stage the CSFs may be derived. These CSFs should be established for the firm as a whole as well as for each function within the firm. For every CSF there should be a Key Performance Indicator (KPI) which may be used to establish whether the firm has been successful with the CSF. The definition of the KPI determines the data required, and this is formalised in the culture data set. In many firms, the objectives setting, the corporate strategy formulation and the CSF identification will have already been completed before the SISP begins.

In a similar way the organisation should have already considered the issue of its IT architecture and this will be another important input to the SISP. These activities refer to the top down aspects of the planning process.

12.5   DETAILED STEPS REQUIRED TO PRODUCE A SISP

As will have been seen in Chapter 1, there are many approaches to a SISP. The author proposes a 20 step approach which he has found produces satisfactory results wherever it is possible to follow this route. The 20 steps are shown in Figure 12.3

Figures 12.4, 12.5 and 12.6 show the logical order in which these steps are performed, and indicate which can be performed concurrently. The 20 step programme has been divided into three major phases, each of which is addressed separately.

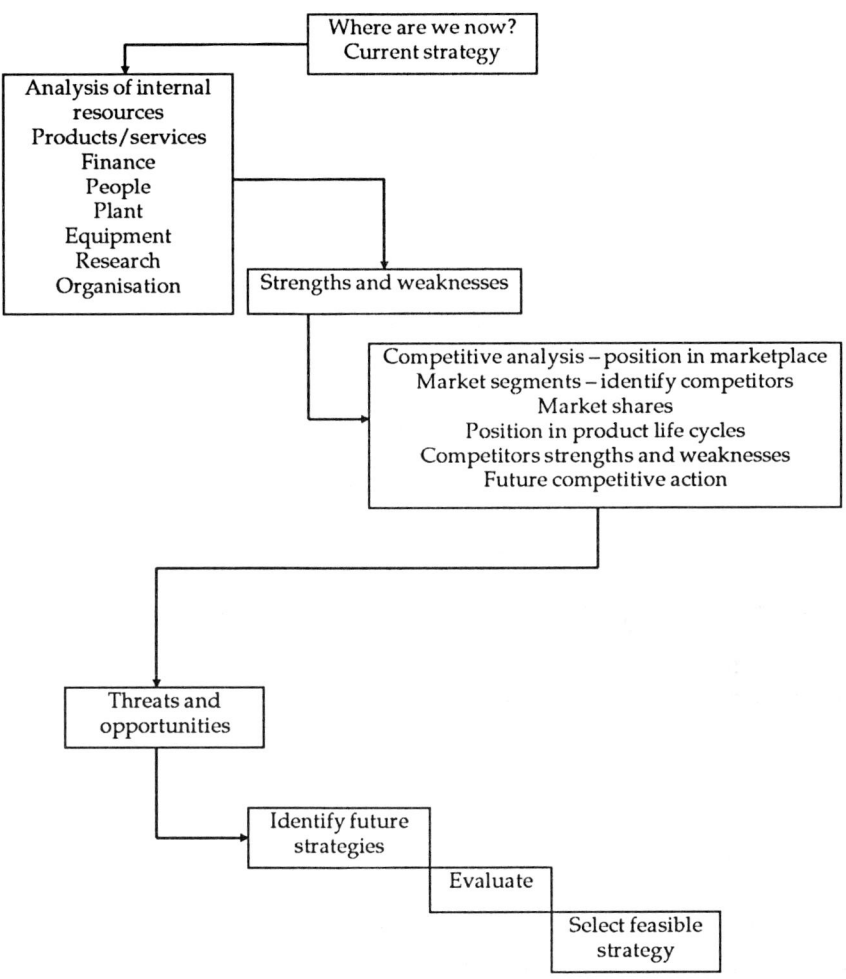

Figure 12.2   Establishing the corporate strategy

Twenty Steps to a SISP

1. Obtain authorisation.

2. Establish a team and arrange accommodation, tools etc.

3. Allocate responsibilities and create a timetable.

4. Determine the corporate goals, objectives, mission etc.

5. Establish the firm's corporate strategy, explicitly or implicitly.

6. Define the Critical Success Factors.

7. Establish the Key Performance Indicators.

8. Define the critical data set.

9. Incorporate the firm's Information Technology Architecture.

10. Conduct a systems audit.

11. Rank current systems condition and prioritise current systems proposals.

12. Brainstorm for new systems and create an IT opportunities list.

13. Perform cost benefit and risk analysis.

14. Conduct filtering workshops.

15. Produce an action plan.

16. Communicate the action plan to all appropriate staff.

17. Identify and appoint project champions.

18. Arrange for top management to publicly commit to the SISP.

19. Create feedback mechanisms.

20. Update the SISP.

Figure 12.3   The 20 steps in creating a SISP

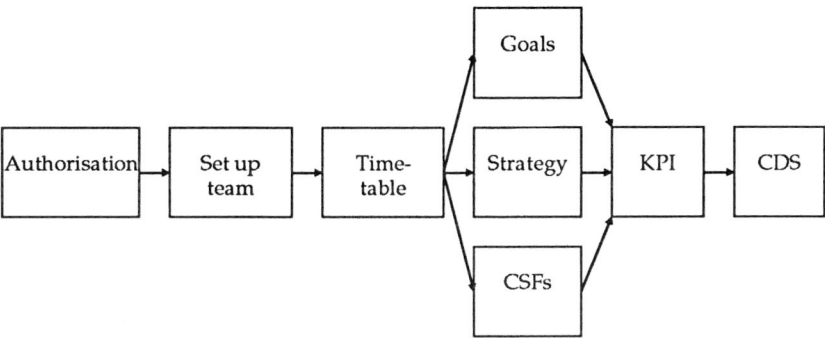

Figure 12.4   The first phase of the SISP

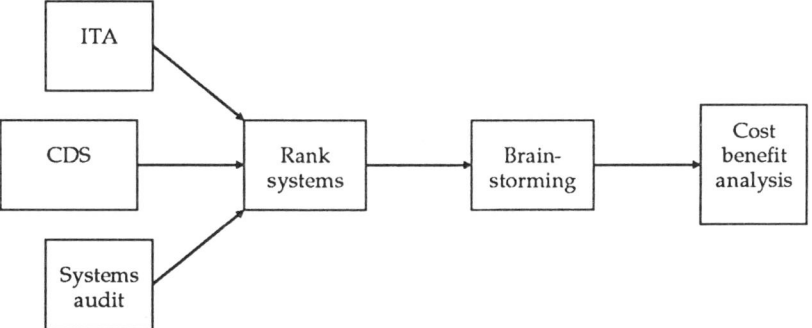

Figure 12.5   The second phase of the SISP

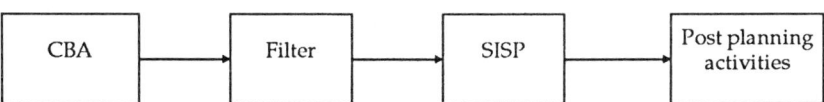

Figure 12.6   The third phase of the SISP

12.5.1   Step 1 – Obtain authorisation

Before any progress can be made the concept of a SISP must be presented to senior management. In some incidents this is done by the information systems director while in other cases the motivation may come from other directors. Consultants are sometimes used to motivate the SISP and perhaps write a proposal for the board of directors. Once the senior team has accepted the proposal, authorisation should include:

- A budget
- A team leader

It is most important that sufficient funds are made available and it should be remembered that a SISP is an expensive exercise. If the project runs out of funds before it is completed the entire SISP is put at risk. With regards the team leader a senior executive is required. The more senior the executive the better as this will give the SISP team the status which it will require in order to bring the project to a satisfactory conclusion.

12.5.2   Step 2 – Establish a team and arrange accommodation, tools, etc

The team leader must now establish a group who will work with him on the project over the next three to six months. The team should include individuals from line and staff functions other than the ISD. However the ISD must of course be represented. Many firms use at least one outside consultant. Outside consultants are often useful in order to help generate new ideas or to take responsibility for failure. A project secretary will have to be appointed. Office accommodation will be needed as well as personal computers. There are numerous software tools available on the market which will assist the team and these must now be selected. Software products to consider include spreadsheets, databases, word processors, as well as Computer Aided Systems Engineering (CASE) tools.

12.5.3   Step 3 – Allocate responsibilities and create a timetable

Different members of the team should be made responsible for different steps in the SISP and as some of these may be performed concurrently it is important for each member to know exactly what his/her responsibility is. A detailed timetable should now be drawn up. Project planning and control software is very useful at this stage as it will allow Gantt charts and project networks to be quickly and easily developed.

12.5.4   Step 4 – Determine the Corporate Goals, Objectives, Mission, etc

It is hoped that the firm will have already established its corporate goals, objectives and mission. Many firms will already have these encapsulated in public documents or statements and if this is the case the SISP team can simply use these directly. However, if corporate objectives have not been explicitly developed, it may be necessary for the SISP team to work with the top management team in developing objectives in the manner described in Figure 12.1.

12.5.5   Step 5 – Establish the firm's Corporate Strategy, explicitly or implicitly

Similarly to the firm's goals and objectives the corporate strategy will hopefully have already been developed. If this is the case the SISP team may once again use this information directly. However, if there is no explicit strategy it is possible for an implicit strategy to be derived by observation or alternatively for the SISP team to use the method described in Figure 12.2 in conjunction with the top management group to establish the firm's corporate strategy. If the latter course of action is adopted it must be borne in mind that this is a major exercise and may well delay the SISP for several months.

12.5.6   Step 6 – Define the Critical Success Factors

CSFs may now be defined both for the firm as a whole as well as for each individual function. This process requires extensive discussion with the senior management team, business unit managers as well as with each functional head. An interviewing approach is normally used to collect the information during this step. Group discussions are also used. Some details of this are provided in Chapter 4.

12.5.7   Step 7 – Establish the Key Performance Indicators

For every CSF there will be at least one KPI. The KPI will indicate whether the firm has been able to achieve its CSF. It is essential that KPIs are identified as without them the CSF concept loses much of its impact. Chapter 4 provides a discussion of these points.

12.5.8   Step 8 – Define the Critical Data Set

In order to be able to manage the CSFs it is essential to have regular reports which highlight the KPIs. These reports must be based on the data which will allow the KPIs to be calculated. Before these reports may be designed it is essential to define the data which management requires and this should be undertaken at this stage. This can be a substantial exercise, some of the detail of which is discussed in Chapter 4.

12.5.9   Step 9 – Incorporate the firm's Information Technology Architecture

Although a SISP may be produced without reference to the firm's ITA, such a practice contains the risk of the short to medium term requirements becoming unsynchronised with the firm's long term requirements. In order to prevent this from occurring, an ITA should either have already been produced, or if not, should now be undertaken. Chapter 5 describes what is required for an ITA and if this has not already been done it could add several months to the SISP project. The major purpose of including the ITA at this stage is to ensure that the SISP will eventually focus on appropriate data, software and hardware standards.

12.5.10 Step 10 – Conduct a Systems Audit

The next step in developing the SISP is to analyse the current system situation in order to understand where the present emphasis has been placed. This is achieved by performing a comprehensive systems audit from which a profile is developed which shows how the firm stands with regards hardware, software, communications, data and people. This is essentially a bottom up exercise which requires a list to be created of all the hardware components in use in the firm. Each component should be categorised, it should be aged and its usefulness established. Once the hardware list is complete the same exercise is performed for the communications equipment, the software and the data. The results of a systems audit are often a surprise as many firms do not actually know the extent of their hardware, software, communications etc, inventory. To facilitate the audit process systems are sometimes categorised in terms of portfolio types. There are two main methodologies available for system portfolio categorisation. These are the Nolan Norton iron cross approach and the Warren McFarlan strategic matrix approach. The Nolan Norton approach categorises systems as either institutional, professional, physical, external or infrastructure. The McFarlan approach categorises systems as either strategic, turnaround, factory or support. These categories are discussed in Chapter 6.

During the systems audit special attention should be given to establishing the DC&N and the OA inventories as these are areas of critical importance from the point of view of competitive advantage.

To complete the systems audit a list of staff who are either directly or indirectly involved with information systems should be drawn up. It is quite easy to establish those who are directly employed by the ISD or who have information systems functions within individual user departments. However, this listing should also include non information systems department individuals who make a major contribution to the functioning of information systems within the firm.

12.5.11   Step 11 – Rank current Systems Condition and Prioritise current Systems Proposals

At the end of the system audit the SISP team will have in its possession a clear statement of all the hardware, software and data which the firm currently uses. It is now necessary to evaluate the appropriateness of each of these. Therefore the team needs to evaluate the effectiveness of each of the firm's mainframes, minis and personal computer utilisation. It will have to consider each operating system and each application system and rank its efficiency and its effectiveness. In addition it will have to consider whether the organisation's data is being held in appropriate forms and which databases may need enhancement or modification.

A useful tool in assisting the ranking process is the concept of generic information strategies combined with the strategic matrix. Strategic systems may be seen as being top ranking and requiring central planning attention while support systems may be considered to be low ranking and be treated as a necessary evil.

This ranking process is a substantial exercise which requires obtaining consensus from both ISD professionals as well as systems users. At the end of the exercise the original list supplied by the systems audit will be presented in order of systems which are most beneficial to the organisation. Current systems which are producing a distinct problem for the firm will also be highlighted.

In addition to the actual systems on hand there will be numerous proposals for systems enhancement or replacement. These proposals will now need to be prioritised and the systems ranking can be used as one of the main methods for this purpose.

12.5.12   Step 12 – Brainstorm for new systems and create an IT Opportunities List

The early part of this approach to a SISP has required the application of top down planning. It was a top down planning method which was used in objectives determination, corporate strategy formulation and CSF determination. Bottom up planning was used in the systems audit, ranking and prioritisation steps. In the brainstorming section a different approach is required. This is sometimes referred to as information weapon planning, blue sky planning, or lateral thinking. The objective of this phase is to try to identify as many information systems opportunities as possible. The emphasis here should be on identifying ways and means by which the firm can use its information systems to obtain a competitive advantage. As many ideas as possible should be generated, the emphasis here being on obtaining a long list from which realistic options may be subsequently selected.

The brainstorming session should be attended by groups of four to six individuals, each from different departments. Any idea, no matter how extravagant should be entertained by these groups. The discussion should especially not be limited by the firm's current inventory of hardware and software. Madcap ideas will eventually be eliminated during the filtering workshops, or perhaps even before.

12.5.13   Step 13 – Perform Cost Benefit and Risk Analysis

Wherever possible costs and benefits should be associated with each system identified during the brainstorming sessions. Where it is not possible to identify exact financial numbers or hard benefits, some soft benefits should be listed. With regard to the risk element, this should be assessed under several different headings including:

- Risks associated with new technology
- Risks associated with project size
- Risk of failure, ie the damage which can be done to the firm if the project fails.

12.5.14   Step 14 – Conduct Filtering Workshops

At this stage in the SISP process there is likely to be a substantial list of possible projects. These will include new applications as well as enhancement and maintenance requirements. There will also be a demand for new hardware as well as development tools and the establishment of new databases. However, many of the suggested systems will not necessarily be appropriate and in any event each organisation will have only a limited amount of funds to apportion among its investment opportunities. The first step in the filtering process is to ensure systems proposals match the firm's corporate strategy. Matching means, for example, that firms following a cost leadership strategy should not be extravagent in developing sophisticated IS for the purposes of differentiation. If systems do not match the strategy then they will either consume funds required for other tasks, or will simply not show an appropriate return. The second step in the filtering process is to choose systems with superior returns on investment and/or cash flows. This is generally a relatively easy exercise where hard benefits have been estimated. Where only soft benefits have been identified it will be necessary for the SISP team to make a subjective evaluation. As regards the risk, this must also be used as a final indicator as to which systems to include in the SISP.

12.5.15   Step 15 – Produce an Action Plan

As a SISP is a document which describes how the activities of the ISD will support the general business strategy and thereby help the firm to attain its objectives, it should contain a list of things to be achieved and dates for their completion. Therefore the SISP will state what new hardware and software systems must be acquired, when they should be acquired and from whom they should be acquired. Under separate headings in the action plan there should be details of DC&N as described in Chapter 9, and OA as described in Chapter 10. The SISP will include the cost of this new equipment as well as where possible the actual benefits. These numbers should be included directly into the firm's budgets with the approval of the relevant departmental heads.

A SISP will usually indicate changes in the level of staff requirements and these should be expressed in some detail, including job descriptions, remuneration conditions and dates at which staff are required. The SISP should clearly indicate who will be responsible for specific projects. Responsibility will frequently be held by users as well as by members of the ISD.

12.5.16   Step 16 – Communicate the Action Plan to all appropriate staff

On completion the SISP should be distributed to the members of the top management team who authorised the project and all those on whom it has direct impact. This will offer an opportunity for all concerned to make final comments on the plan before it is presented to the chief executive and he/she is asked to endorse the SISP in public. This commenting exercise is important and is frequently accompanied by a presentation and discussion of the proposed plans.

12.5.17   Step 17 – Identify and appoint Project Champions

Many of the projects identified in the SISP will require project champions and it is now necessary for the SISP team to identify these individuals. Project champions will normally be users who can identify closely with the system. They are often individuals who have much to gain, both professionally and personally, from the system succeeding. The project champion is a vital ingredient in ensuring systems success.

12.5.18   Step 18 – Arrange for Top Management to publicly commit to the SISP

One way of ensuring that a SISP is not just an academic exercise from which no action occurs is to arrange for the chief executive to publicly endorse the proposals. This can be done by having a statement issued from his/her office which may be published in the in-house journal, or perhaps even where circumstances are relevant, have published in the local or computer press.

12.5.19 Step 19 – Create Feedback Mechanisms

At this stage the main work of the SISP team has been completed. However, it is important to ensure that the work defined in the SISP is actually undertaken. For this reason it is necessary to arrange for an individual, perhaps the SISP team leader or maybe the information systems director to monitor the progress of the SISP. To do this, some feedback mechanism must be established through which it will be possible to evaluate how much of the SISP has actually been achieved.

12.5.20 Step 20 – Updating the SISP

As work proceeds on the SISP there will inevitably be a difference between what actually takes place and what has been defined in the plan. It is critical for this to be recorded and for the plan to be periodically updated to incorporate these deviations.

12.6 THE FORMAT OF THE SISP

The format of a SISP varies enormously depending on the scope of the study, the culture of the firm etc. In some cases the plan is presented primarily as a verbal report supported by a series of overhead slides. Generally this approach is not adequate as the issues addressed in a SISP report are sufficiently complex to require considerable thought and reflection. In other instances a 500 page document is written. With many computer reports it is sometimes mistakenly believed that volume represents quality, and this is frequently not the case. If a very large document is produced then it should at least be supported by a succinct summary.

Whatever the approach, the SISP report should address most of the major steps discussed in this chapter. In addition the report should indicate the methodology used by the SISP team, and list the staff who gave verbal or written input to the project. Figure 12.7 shows a possible contents page for a SISP report. In order to ensure that there are no surprises at the end of the SISP project, it is important that there should be regular feedback between the SISP team and top management throughout the duration of the project. This is further discussed in Chapter 13.

12.7 SUMMARY

To successfully undertake and complete a SISP it is important to follow a methodology. Several proprietary methodologies which are sold by consultancy firms were mentioned in Chapter 1, and further details can be found in Appendices 4-11. However it is equally possible for the firm to develop its own methodology. In this chapter a methodology has been described which

SISP REPORT
CONTENTS

Management summary
Terms of reference
Methodology
Corporate goals, objectives and mission
Corporate strategy
Critical success factors
Key performance indicators
Critical data sets
Information technology architecture
Information systems inventory
Appraisals of current information systems
Results of brainstorming sessions
Cost benefit analysis
Short listed systems
Action plan
   Hardware purchases
   Software purchases
   Communications developments
   Office Automation
   Data developments
   Staffing requirements
   Training requirements
Project champions
Figures for budget
How to measure success

Figure 12.7   Typical SISP report contents page

has been used by the author to undertake this type of work. Readers may expand, change or develop these 20 steps to produce their own methodology in order to undertake a SISP study in their own firm.

13 The Implementation of a SISP and Associated Problems

13.1 INTRODUCTION

As well as addressing the main steps required for a SISP which are discussed in Chapter 12, it is important to understand the process required to ensure that the SISP is successful. It is also most important to bear in mind that many firms encounter problems in attempting to conduct a SISP.

A SISP will normally be initiated by either the senior IS executive or by a member of the senior management team. If the project is initiated by the ISD then it is essential that the full support of top management is also acquired. This is critical primarily because a SISP is a very expensive exercise frequently costing as much as £100,000. Furthermore it requires significant amounts of time and people. Unfortunately, top management frequently do not understand what can be achieved with a SISP and therefore it is sometimes difficult to obtain their backing. The top management commitment is also essential because it is difficult to carry out the findings and recommendations of the SISP report without it. Senior management is normally only committed to undertaking a SISP when a public announcement of the firm's intention to embark on one is made. This announcement should be made as early as possible. This announcement is different to the firm's commitment to implement the recommendations of the SISP which was discussed in Chapter 9.

13.1.1 Terms of Reference

Having obtained top management backing for a SISP, the next step is to define its terms of reference. The main parameter to be defined is the scope of the SISP. There are a number of dimensions to the issue of scope.

These are:
- business;
- geography;
- hardware and software;

– applications;

– time.

Most SISPs are fairly general in scope because they are initiated by organisations who perceive the need to have a thorough review of their information systems and general planning procedures. The terms of reference should be reduced to writing and signed by all appropriate managers.

13.1.2 Set a Timeframe

First of all establish the period of the plan, ie, the next 12 to 18 months and then the next three or five years. It is important to note the dual nature of the timeframe. This occurs because typically most of the findings of a SISP affect the medium to long term use of IS in the firm. At the same time a SISP will almost invariably bring to light matters which need more immediate attention. These issues must be handled within the next few months.

As the work which must be conducted during a SISP is substantial and as a team of people are always involved it is very important to plan the workload carefully. This is best done by creating a timetable, specifying the tasks required, their duration and the resources available to the SISP team leader. This timetable is then frequently computerised using a project management system incorporating project management techniques such as critical path analysis, etc. It is unlikely that a SISP can be completed on a medium sized firm in under three months. On the other hand a SISP should not be allowed to extend much beyond six months because, with an extended time horizon for the study, conditions will change which will therefore possibly impact the relevance of the conclusions.

13.1.3 Establish a Team

The next step is to establish a SISP team. This includes appointing a team leader. It is critical to make sure that the team has all the required skills for the job. If a complete team cannot be generated internally then consultants should be considered. Figure 13.1 shows the structure of a typical SISP team. The minimum number of team members should be three, and the maximum could be as many as six. There should be a team secretary or administrator. It is frequently useful to employ an outside consultant who may introduce a degree of objectivity if the situation is changed. Furthermore, the consultant may be able to suggest unpopular decisions to which internal staff might object.

As well as this work team, a management steering committee with representatives of top management should be appointed. This will be the group to which the SISP team leader will report and from whom he/she will seek

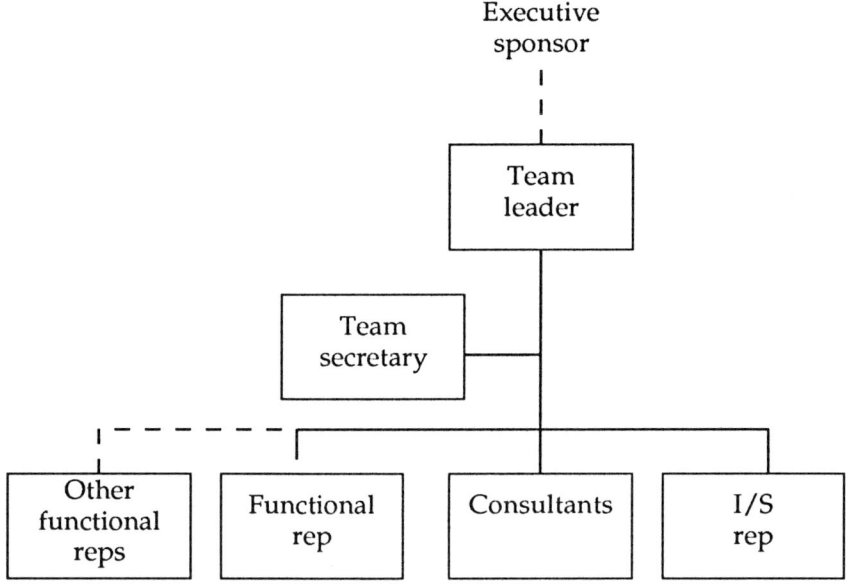

Figure 13.1   The structure of a typical SISP team

regular advice. The management steering committee is most important as it is the conduit through which the SISP team leader keeps top management informed of the work being done and the conclusions as they are being formulated. Also the steering committee is used to update the SISP team leader of management thinking as the project proceeds. At the end of a SISP there should be no surprises and the final presentation to management should only be a formality.

13.1.4   Create Infrastructure

A SISP involves substantial data collection and analysis and therefore support staff will be required. This may be only a SISP secretary or it may be several analysts depending on the scope of the job and of course the size of the firm concerned. In addition a variety of computer programs are available which can help in this respect. These include databases, project management software, spreadsheets as well as CASE or integrated CASE (ICASE) tools. CASE tools are especially helpful in conducting the information technology architecture plan. There are now dozens of such products on the market, ranging from relatively simple tools to very sophisticated ones. Some CASE products have planning modules which can actually assist with the planning process itself. If CASE tools are to be used then hardware and software must be acquired and the relevant members of the team must be trained. The investment in hardware and software can be considerable, and the training requirement substantial, and therefore should not be underestimated.

13.1.5   Budgets

A budget should be drawn up for the project which will become a major control document. This must be monitored on a monthly basis and variances must be examined and fully explained. The cost of a SISP can be substantial and therefore financial control is very important. The costs will typically include time, materials, hardware, software, travel, accommodation etc.

13.1.6   Regular Meetings

A meeting of the team must be held to brief all members about the methodology to be used. There are more than a dozen methodologies available through consultants. Then there are self developed approaches. What is acceptable to management is the key issue when deciding which methodology to choose. As the study progresses there should be weekly meetings between the team members. This will help prevent analysts from straying off course. The team leader should meet formally with the steering committee at least once a month and perhaps more frequently on an informal basis.

13.1.7   Feedback and Report to Top Management

As mentioned above the final plan should not contain any surprises to anyone, especially top management. Therefore regular formal and informal meetings should be held to keep top management informed as to how the SISP is proceeding. Finally the SISP report must be presented to the board of directors. This report should be a substantial document containing details of the current IS situation, an analysis of what is required and recommendations for the future. A few dozen overhead transparency slides alone is generally inadequate to give management a full picture with which it could make a sound decision about the medium to long term future of the firm's ISD.

13.1.8   Plan Presentation

The final SISP should be presented to the senior management team. This frequently takes the form of a visual presentation using overhead slides. This should be supported by a comprehensive written document containing the assumptions and details of the proposed course of action, as well as a synopsis of the likely outcome of the plan.

13.2   DIFFICULTIES ENCOUNTERED DURING A SISP

The following are the results of some research recently conducted in the USA which indicate the type of difficulties SISP teams have in identifying senior management's objectives and goals.

13.2.1   Major Problems

- Firm lacks a formal strategic plan;
- Business objectives change;
- IS management is not a part of the strategy formulation body;
- Top management lacks IS understanding;
- Top management fails to communicate its objectives in IS terms;
- Top management doesn't tell ISD about its objectives;
- ISD and general management have different interpretations of organisation objectives;
- ISD personnel are viewed as 'Techies' and/or 'Turkies';
- Certain objectives must be maintained confidentially by top management;
- Top management is intimidated by automation;
- ISD personnel are not receptive to what top management tells them;
- Business units don't advise corporate IS of their objectives;
- The request for objectives is sometimes seen as threatening.

13.2.2   How to Improve the Above Situations

- Make IS part of the corporate planning process;
- Have ISD report to the president;
- Have top management develop the plan;
- Formally educate top management;
- Informally educate top management;
- Hire a consultant;
- Set up corporate/IS management committees;
- Deliver information projects on time and within budget;
- Refrain from using technical functions.

13.3   ADDITIONAL PROBLEMS ENCOUNTERED IN CONDUCTING A SISP

Numerous problems have been identified with SISP. These problems may be categorised under the headings of Resources, Process and Output.

13.3.1   Resource Problems

There can be difficulty in obtaining top management interest and then backing for the SISP, and then its commitment for the implementation of the plan. From this follows resource problems of time, money, personnel, etc.

Top management sometimes just does not see the need for an integrated approach to IS planning and computer planning and therefore perceives a SISP as an extravagance. Even when top management approves of the SISP project, there may not be the skills and/or the funds available.

13.3.2   Process

Process problems are primarily due to difficulties with the methodology and the analysis associated with it. Many of the published methodologies are too complex. Many require the use of concepts or tools with which most firms are not familiar. Another problem are the difficulties many firms report concerning the forecasting of the change in technology. This is especially the case where firms need to forecast the rate of change in technology.

13.3.3   Output

The main problem associated with the output of a SISP is the comprehensiveness of the report and its appropriateness. It is difficult to balance short-term tactical   issues which must be addressed in the 12 to 18 month timeframe, with the firm's strategic focus which must be developed over the three to five year time period.

Research suggests that overall SISP produce good plans but that firms sometimes do not have the management commitment or the control mechanisms to follow them up.

What makes SISP easier or more difficult? Research suggests the following indicators.

-     Enterprises which have no formal planning or inadequate planning procedures have considerable difficulty with SISP.
-     Enterprises which involve IS executives in the general process of strategic planning have less difficulty with SISP.
-     Enterprises where the top IS executive reports to a high level business

executive cope better with planning.

- If top management initiates the study then it is likely there will be more difficulty with SISP.

- The broader the scope of the SISP the more problems will be encountered.

- Less problems are encountered with specific planning horizons.

13.4 BENEFITS OF A SISP

As this chapter has strongly focussed on the problems which may be encountered in conducting a SISP, it is perhaps appropriate to conclude with a brief list of the benefits which may be derived from persevering with a SISP project. These represent both tangible and intangible improvements in the management of the firm and include:

- A greater commitment on the part of top management to the IS function in the firm. Frequently this results in more funds being made available to the ISD.

- Better allocation of information system resources to meet business priorities. This frequently results in better ROI for the ISD.

- Much improved communications with systems users. Frequently this results in faster systems delivery, fewer complaints etc.

- A clearer sense of the business role of the ISD leading to the identification of SIS.

The four points above should result in an improved position for the firm in the marketplace.

A well conducted SISP will produce multiple benefits for the firm even if its recommendations are not fully implemented.

13.5 SUMMARY

It is not a simple matter to conduct a successful SISP. In the first place it needs a strong management commitment as well as considerable resources of time and money. Although top management may authorise a SISP it is not necessarily the case that they will be able to give it all the support that it requires.

In addition SISP methodologies are fairly complex and are not well understood by many ISDs. A SISP cannot be handed over entirely to a team of consultants or even be dominated by outsiders. The IS literature is now full of research concerning SISP and becoming familiar with this is a good place to start.

Appendix 1
Glossary

4FRONT

The strategic information system planning methodology marketed by Deloitte & Touche.

AI
Artificial Intelligence

An approach to developing systems so that they will function in a way not dissimilar to the human brain. The most frequently encountered application for artificial intelligence is expert systems which allow very efficient rule processing to be performed.

Architecture

In the context of IT, architecture refers to the infrastructure required to support the firm's business objectives. The IT architecture plan is medium to long term, ie five to ten years, and it specifically refers to policies and strategies.

Association Matrix

A planning technique used to describe the ways in which systems interrelate.

Bottom-Up Planning

Bottom-Up IS planning is an approach which addresses the current IS requirements and focuses on priority settings and resource allocation to achieve these requirements.

Bridge

A communications device consisting of hardware and software for the purpose of connecting LANs.

BSP
Business Systems Planning

An information system planning methodology marketed by IBM in some parts of the world.

Business Vision

The business vision is what the management want to achieve with the enterprise in the future. A business vision usually refers to the medium to long term. It is often expressed in terms of a series of objectives.

215

CAD
Computer Aided Design

A computer system or software package providing facilities for simplifying the design of items. Systems may be specialised towards engineering, architectural or electrical/electronic applications.

CAM
Computer Aided
Manufacture

Wide ranging term to describe computer systems that improve the firm's ability to improve its manufacturing efficiency.

CASE
Computer Aided Systems
Engineering

Term used to refer to software products that improve the efficiency of systems planners, systems analysts and systems designers. Some CASE tools will also include code generators which can produce final programs in COBOL.

COBOL
Common Business
Oriented Language

One of the most commonly used computer languages, especially on mainframe systems.

Communications
Blueprint

A plan of how the firm intends to develop its communications infrastructure. This blueprint focuses on policies and standards which will assist the firm in achieving its business vision.

Corporate Strategy

The method through which the firm finds, gets and keeps its clients. In a broad sense it refers to how the firm relates to and interacts with its environment, including its stakeholders.

Cost Leadership

A generic strategy by which the firm presents itself to the marketplace as a low-priced, no-frills supplier.

CSF
Critical Success Factors

Those aspects of the business which must be right for the enterprise to succeed in achieving its objectives. It is also sometimes said that even though all other aspects of the business are going well, if the critical success factors are not, then the business will not succeed.

Data Model

A comprehensive representation of all the data required by the firm to achieve its business objectives. Details of data types, sizes etc are specified in the data model.

Data Communications	The process of transmitting information from one computing device and receiving it at another.
Differentiation	A generic strategy by which the firm presents itself to the market as a high quality supplier, and therefore asks for a premium price for its goods or services.
DP Data Processing	Early term given to the use of computers in business for the purposes of record keeping and providing regular reports to assist in the functioning of the firm. The term was originally referred to as Electronic Data Processing (EDP), but the E was dropped by most members of the industry.
DSS Decision Support Systems	Information system that supports semi or unstructured decisions that are made in the area of strategic planning, management control or operations control.
EDI Electronic Data Interchange	Technology which facilitates computer application to computer application communications. EDI is designed to allow structured messages to be transmitted across a network. It relies on adherence to data communications standards. These standards have to include details of how EDI partners are prepared to receive standard business documents such as purchase orders, sales invoices etc. This means that careful attention must be given to the definition of such documents.
EDIFACT Electronic Data Interchange For Administration, Commerce and Transport	Standard which emerged out of the United Nations commercial trading committees.
EFT Electronic Funds Transfer	Technology which allows funds to be moved instantly from one account to another. For its application it requires a debit card which

allows the user to instantly pay for goods and services. Typical applications are in supermarkets and petrol stations.

Entity Model

A representation of the various business entities which must be catered for by information systems. Examples include clients, staff, inventories etc.

EIS
Executive Information
Systems

Systems used by top executives to assist in the planning and control process of the firm. It involves the use of an information warehouse or repository which is accessed through a series of easy to use tools. EIS also normally implies the use of communications to address external databases.

EPOS
Electronic Point Of Sale

Technology of recording retail sales directly onto a computer. This can be achieved through a variety of devices ranging from computerised tills where operators enter the data, to various forms of scanning machines. EPOS produces instant updates to inventory records as well as valuable sales information. It can also have a very much lower error rate than traditional systems.

EtherNet

A LAN system developed by DEC, Intel and Xerox. It complies with IEEE 802.3 and OSI 8802.3. It is also referred to as CSMA/CD.

ETO
Electronic Trading
Opportunity

Use of computers to buy or sell in the marketplace. This is a wide-ranging term which includes systems such as airline reservations through which organisations can sell their services, as well as applications used for purchasing from a vendor or vendors.

EUC
End User Computing

Term referring to the supply of computer power to management in order to increase its efficiency and effectiveness.

Factory System

A computer system which assists the firm in achieving its required level of efficiency and effectiveness. These systems are also sometimes referred to as critical information systems (CIS).

Function Model
A representation of all the business functions which the information systems must accommodate.

Generic Strategy
One of the basic ways in which a firm can find, get and keep its clients. There are two generic strategies, which are *cost leadership* and *differentiation*. A generic strategy may be broad based or focus on a niche in the market.

Hardware Blueprint
A plan of how the firm intends to develop its hardware infrastructure. This blueprint focuses on policies and standards which will assist the firm in achieving its business vision.

ICASE
Integrated Computer Aided Software Engineering
(See CASE)

IEEE
Institute of Electrical and Electronic Engineers.

IEF
Information Engineering Facility
A CASE product marketed by James Martin & Associates.

IEM
Information Engineering Methodology
A systems analysis, design and implementation methodology marketed by James Martin & Associates.

IEW
Information Engineering Workbench
A CASE product marketed by Ernst & Young.

Industry Driver
Condition which directly influences or affects the performance of all the firms in the industry. Examples include major changes in competition, deregulation and new technology developments.

Industry Value Chain
A concept developed by Michael Porter which shows how the value chains of individual firms within an industry are related. It is an excellent basis from which to find SIS opportunities.

Information Weapon	A term used by a number of authors to describe the firm's efforts to gain a competitive advantage through the use of IT.
Information Technology Blueprint	A plan of how the firm intends to develop its infrastructure. It may be orientated towards hardware, software or communications issues. The blueprint focuses on policies and standards which will assist the firm in achieving its business vision.
IOS Interorganisational System	A computer network system which connects two or more separate enterprises for the purposes of improving effectiveness.
IS Information Systems	General term to describe the use of hardware and software to deliver information to businesses.
ISD Information Systems Department	Department in the firm responsible for managing the information systems function.
ISDN	Integrated Services Digital Network.
ISO International Standards Organisation	Organisation which works in the area of establishing telecommunications standards. ISO is responsible for Open Systems Interconnection (OSI).
ISS Information Systems Strategy	Term to describe long-term planning of information systems requirements.
ISSP Information Systems Strategy Planning	Term to describe the production of a plan which incorporates some of the issues of the firm's IT strategy.
Information Technology	Wide-ranging term to describe the use of computers and telecommunications.
JIT Just In Time	Approach to manufacturing which requires raw material to be delivered to a firm exactly when required. The objective of a Just In Time system is to minimise raw material inventory and work in progress.

LAN **Local Area Network**	The joining together of a number of personal computers or other devices in a network which operates within a limited geographical area.
Method1	The strategic information system planning methodology marketed by Arthur Andersen.
Minitel	The French PTT's home terminal which has replaced the country's telephone directories.
MIS **Management Information Systems**	There is no general agreement in the industry as to a precise meaning of the term MIS. Initially it was used to describe systems which would play an active role in assisting managers make decisions. However with the arrival of Decision Support Systems and Executive Information Systems, the term MIS has been used to describe information systems which perform routine data processing and which supply regular reports.
Methodology	A systematic procedure for problem solving.
MSS **Management Support Systems**	Information system which provides reports which assist management in its decision making function.
Network	A series of important points connected together. In IT terms a network may be defined as a number of computing devices connected together electronically.
Network Manager	Member of staff with overall responsibility for the operation of the network. This term also refers to software products which assist in the management and control of networks. They usually include diagnostic and maintenance functions.
Niche	A clearly defined market segment at which the firm aims its corporate strategy.
OA **Office Automation**	Provision of computer power to white collar workers in order to improve their efficiency and effectiveness. The key to an office automation system is its connectivity whereby data

is shared between a group of people working in the same office or the same firm.

OASIS
Organisation And
Systems Innovation Ltd

Independent consultancy firm specialising in research into the use of IT.

OD
Organisational
Development

How firms manage their internal structure and relationships between staff.

OSI
Open Systems
Interconnection

Structure based on a seven layer model developed by ISO which will allow different computer manufacturer's machines to communicate with one another.

PMW
Project Management
Workbench

Software product used to plan and control projects. It produces various forms of Gantt chart etc.

PRISM
Partnership in Information
Systems Management

Service offered by the Index Group and Hammer and Company to research into IT issues.

Probability Value Matrix

A method used to accommodate uncertain future values of systems. This approach is sometimes used in cost justifying systems.

Repeater

A hardware and software device which is used to interconnect different types of LANs.

ROI
Return on Investment

Accounting or financial management term to describe how well the firm has used its resources. It is usually calculated by dividing net profit after tax by total net assets.

Router

A hardware and software device which is used to interconnect different types of LANs.

SDM
Systems Development
Method

Process modelling technique used in the development of information systems.

SIS
Strategic Information
Systems

Information systems which directly assist the firm in achieving its corporate strategy. These applications are sometimes referred to as competitive edge systems.

SISP **Strategic Information** **Systems Planning**	An approach to planning information systems which incorporates aspects of the firm's corporate strategy and also aspects of the ISD's short-term needs. This technique combines both top-down and bottom-up planning.
SISP Methodology	A SISP Methodology is a systematic procedure for problem solving and intervention into the IS diffusion mechanism influencing: – the dominant issues on the IS planning agenda; – the organisational setting in which the IS decisions are made.
Software Blueprint	A plan of how the firm intends to develop its software infrastructure. This blueprint focuses on policies and standards which will assist the firm in achieving its business vision.
Software Platform	An already existing IS which may be extended so that it acquires a strategic dimension. An example would be a sales order entry system to which clients are given access through an external network so they can monitor the progress of their orders.
SOG **Strategic Option Generator**	A system application developed by Charles Wiseman which may be used to identify SIS.
SNA **Systems Network** **Architecture**	IBM standards of data communication between their major systems.
SPSS **Statistical Package for the** **Social Sciences**	Software package used widely by universities and research institutes to analyse data.
SSM **Soft Systems Methodology**	A systems methodology based on the concept of processors developed by Professor Checkland at Lancaster University.
Standards & Policies	Rules and regulations set down concerning the type of hardware and software which the firm will use.
Strategic Vision	How the top management of an enterprise

	believes it can achieve its objectives in the medium to longer term.
Strategy	The formal use of this word refers to the way a firm finds, gets and keeps its clients. Common usage has reduced the meaning of strategy to be synonymous with plan. See also Corporate Strategy and Generic Strategy.
SUMMIT-D	A strategic information planning methodology originally marketed by Coopers & Lybrand Deloitte.
SUMMIT-S	The strategic information planning methodology currently marketed by Coopers & Lybrand Deloitte.
Support Systems	Basic record keeping systems which the firm requires to function. These systems are also sometimes referred to as vital information systems (VIS).
Systems Formulation	The process of identifying and specifying the requirements and the subsequently expected or forecast benefits to be derived from a system.
TCP/IP	Transfer Control Protocol/Internet Protocol.
Technology Vision	How the organisation considers the application of technology within the business. This term is usually used to refer to a relatively mechanistic application of technology within the firm.
Token Ring	A medium access control technique for communication networks using a ring topology. It is a popular form which is marketed by IBM. The standards for rings are specified by IEEE 802.5 and OSI 8802.5.
Top-Down Planning	Top-down IS planning attempts to develop IS which support business objectives and strategies.
Top Management	A term used to refer to the chief executive and

	other senior members of the board of directors.
Topology	The structure of a data communications network.
TPS **Transaction Processing Systems**	Computer systems which process large volumes of data. These systems are normally on-line or real time.
Turnaround System	Experimental information systems developed by the firm. This is the R & D aspect of the information systems department. It is hoped that turnaround systems will eventually become SISs.
VADS **Value Added and Data Services**	Regulatory term in the United Kingdom to describe a facility which offers both databases and the use of a mainframe and associated communications hardware as a business network which may be subscribed to by members of the public in the same way as a VAN.
Value Activities	The term used by Michael Porter to describe the individual aspects or functions of an enterprise.
Value Chain	A value chain is a method described by Michael Porter for the detailed analysis of an enterprise.
VAN **Value Added Network**	Regulatory term in the United Kingdom to describe a facility whereby a firm may sell its network to third parties, thus allowing them the facility of large scale data communications without its initial setup costs.
Vision	Sometimes referred to as Strategic Vision or Business Vision, this term refers to a view as to how the firm can successfully function in the marketplace in the medium-to-long- term. It usually encompasses how the firm will find, get and keep its clients.
WAN **Wide Area Network**	Term used to describe the connection of computers over large geographical distances.

WP   Term used to describe the entering, manipula-
Word Processing   tion, storage and retrieval of text.

Appendix 2
Bibliography and References

Ackoff R L, 'Management misinformation systems', *Management Science 14*, Vol 4, December 1967

Alter S L, 'A study of computer aided decision making in organisations' cited by Benbasat I, *The Information Research Challenge*, Harvard Business School Press, 1987

Ansoff H I, *Corporate Strategy*, Penguin Books, 1965

Ansoff H I, *Implanting Strategic Management*, Prentice Hall International, 1984

Anthony R N, *Planning and Control Systems: A Framework for Analysis*, Harvard University Press, 1965

Bailey K D, *Methods of Social Research*, The Free Press, 1987

Bell J, *Doing Your Research Project: A Guide for First-Time Researchers in Education and Social Science*, Open University Press, 1987

Belson W A, *The Design and Understanding of Survey Questions*, Gower Publishing, 1981

Benbasat I, 'An analysis of research methodologies', *The Information Research Challenge*, Harvard Business School Press, 1987

Berelson, cited in Krippendorff K, *Content Analysis*, Sage Publications, 1980

Born M, cited in Margenau H, *The Nature of Physical Reality*, Mc-Graw Hill, 1950

Boynton A C, Zmud R W, 'Critical success factors: A case-based assessment', *Sloan Management Review*, Summer 1984

Butler Cox Foundation, *Competitive Edge Applications: Myths and Reality*, Report 61, December 1987

Cash J I, et al, *Corporate Information Systems Management: Text and Cases*, 2nd Edition, Irwin Homewood, 1988

Checkland P, *Systems Thinking, Systems Practice*, John Wiley and Sons, 1981

Christensen A R, with Hansen A J, *Teaching and the Case Method*, Harvard Business School, 1987

Churchill Jr G A, *Market Research – Methodological Foundations*, The Dryden Press, 1987

Cohen M R, Nagel E, *An Introduction to Logic and Scientific Methods*, Harcourt, Brace and World, 1934

Cook T D, Campbell D T, *Quasi-experimentation – Design & Analysis Issues for Field Settings*, Rand McNally College Publishing, 1985

Dillon et al, *Marketing Research in a Marketing Environment*, Times Mirror/ Mosby College Publishing, 1987

Drucker P F, 'The coming of the new organisation', *Harvard Business Review*, January–February 1988

Drucker P F, *Innovation and Entrepreneurship Practice and Principles*, Heinemann, 1985

Earl M J, 'Competitive advantage through information technology: Eight maxims for senior managers', *Journal of Multinational Business*, Summer 1988

Earl M J, *Information Management: The Strategic Dimension*, Oxford University Press, 1988

Earl M J, et al, *Information Systems Strategy Formulation*, John Wiley and Sons, 1987

Edge A G, Coleman D R, *The Guide to Case Analysis and Reporting*, System Logistics, 1986

Einstein A, 'The fundamentals of theoretical physics' in *Out of My Later Years*, Philosophical Library, 1950

Evans C, *The Making of the Micro - A History of the Computer*, Victor Gollancz, 1981

Fowler Jr F J, *Survey Research Methods*, Sage Publications, 1984

Galliers R D, 'Strategic information systems planning: myths, reality and guidelines for successful implementation', *European Journal of Information Systems*, 1, (1), 1991

Glaser B G, Strauss A L, *The Discovery of Grounded Theory*, Aldine, 1967

Gorry A, Scott-Morton M, 'A framework for management information systems', *Sloan Management Review*, 1971

Gould S J, *The Panda's Thumb*, W W Norton, 1980

Green P E, Carmone Jr F J, Smith S M, *Multidimensional Scaling*, Allyn and Bacon, 1989

Greenacre M J, *The Theory and Applications of Correspondence Analysis*, Academic Press, 1984

Hanke J, Reitsch A, Dickson J P, *Statistical Decision Models for Management*, Allyn and Bacon, 1984

Harré R, *The Philosophies of Science - An Introductory Survey*, Oxford University Press, 1972

Hoinville G, Jowell R, *Survey Methodologies*, Heinemann Educational Books, 1977

Jaunch L R, Osborn R N, Martin T N, 'Structured content analysis of cases: a complementary method for organisational research', *Academy of Management Review 1980*, vol 5 no 4

Jocher C, 'The case method in social research', *Social Forces Journal*, 1928

Kasanen E, Suomi R, 'The case method in information systems research', *Liiketaloudellinen Aikakauskirja - Foretagsekonomisk, The Finnish Journal of Business Economics*, vol 4, 1987

Keen P G W, cited in Kwon T H, Zmud R W, 'Unifying the fragmented models of information systems implementation', in *Critical Issues in Information Systems Research*, John Wiley and Sons, 1987

Kerlinger F N, *Foundations of Behavioural Research*, Holt Rinehart & Winston, 1969

Lakatos I, *The Methodology of Scientific Research Programmes - Philosophical Papers Volume 1*, Cambridge University Press, 1978

Lawley D N, Maxwell A E, *Factor Analysis as a Statistical Method*, Butterworths, 1963

Lee A S, 'A scientific methodology for MIS case studies', *MIS Quarterly*, March 1989

Leedy P D, *Practical Research - Planning and Design*, Macmillan Publishing, 1989

Lehmann D R, *Market Research and Analysis*, Irwin, 1985

Magal S, 'Critical success factors for information centres', *MIS Quarterly*, September 1985

Malone T W, 'The logic of electronic markets', *Harvard Business Review*, May–June 1989

Margenau H, *The Nature of Physical Reality*, McGraw-Hill, 1950

Martin J, *Telematic Society - A Challenge for Tomorrow*, Prentice Hall, 1981

Martin P Y, Turner B A, 'Grounded theory and organisational research', *The Journal of Applied Behavioural Science*, Vol 22, No 2, NTL Institute, 1986

McFarlan F W, 'Information technology changes the way you compete', *Harvard Business Review*, May–June 1984

Miles M B, Huberman A M, *Qualitative Data Analysis - A Sourcebook of New Methods*, Sage Publications, 1984

Mintzberg H, cited in Quinn J B, Mintzberg H, James R M, *The Strategic Process, Concepts, Context and Cases*, Prentice Hall, 1988

Nachmias C, Nachmias D, *Research Methods in the Social Sciences*, Edward Arnold, 1989

Nolan Norton, cited by Waller R R, (unpublished paper), presented at Information Systems Conference, 1989

Nolan R, 'Managing the crisis in data processing', *Harvard Business Review*, March–April 1979

Nolan R, 'Managing the four stages of EDP growth', *Harvard Business Review*, 1974

Nolan R, 'The plight of the EDP manager', *Harvard Business Review*, May–June 1973

Onions C T, ed, *The Shorter Oxford English Dictionary*, Guild Press, 1983

Oppenheim A N, *Questionnaire Design and Attitude Measurement*, Gower, 1966

Parker M M, Benson R J, with Trainor H E, *Information Economics – Linking Business Performance to Information Technology*, Prentice Hall, 1988

Parsons G L, 'Information technology: A new competitive weapon', *Sloan Management Review*, Fall 1983

Parsons G L, 'Fitting information systems technology to the corporate needs: the linking strategy,' *Harvard Business School Note* 9-183-176

Patching K, *The Information Centre, Managing the Growth of End-User Computing for Corporate Advantage*, Quiller Press, 1989

Perry N O, cited in Cash et al, *Corporate Information Systems Management: Text and Cases*, Second Edition, Irwin, 1988

Peters T J, Waterman R H, *In Search of Excellence – Lessons from America's Best-run Companies*, Harper & Row, 1982

Popper K, cited in Harré R, *The Philosophies of Science - An Introductory Survey*, Oxford University Press, 1972

Porter M E, *Competitive Advantage – Creating and Sustaining Superior Performance*, The Free Press, 1985

Porter M E, *Competitive Strategy – Techniques for Analysing Industries and Competitors*, The Free Press, 1980

Quinn J B, cited in Quinn J B, Mintzberg H, James R M, *The Strategic Process, Concepts, Context and Cases*, Prentice Hall, 1988

Quinn J B, *Strategies for Change: Logical Incrementalism*, Irwin, 1980

Reid G C, *International Journal of Social Economics*, vol 14, no 11, 1987

Remenyi D S J, *Increase Profits with Strategic Information Systems*, NCC Publications, 1988

Remenyi D S J, *Strategic Information Systems – Development, Implementation, Case Studies*, NCC Blackwell, 1989

Remenyi D S J, *Strategic Information Systems, Current Practice and Guidelines* (unpublished dissertation), Henley – The Management College, 1990

Rockart J, Bullin C, 'A primer on critical success factors', *CISR Working Paper*, Sloan School of Management, MIT, 1981

Rockart J, 'Chief executives define their own data needs', *Harvard Business Review*, March–April 1979

Rockart J, Treacy M E, 'The CEO goes on-line', *Harvard Business Review*, January–February 1982

Schultz R L, Slevin D P, *Implementation and Management Innovation in Implementing Operations Research Management Science*, American Elsevier, 1975

Stalk Jr G, 'Time – The next source of competitive advantage', *Harvard Business Review*, July–August 1988

Synnott W, *The Information Weapon*, John Wiley and Sons, 1987

Toffler A, *Previews and Premises*, Pan Books, 1984

Townsend R, *Further Up the Organisation*, Knopf, 1984

White C, Christy D, 'The information centre concept: a normative model and a study of six installations', *MIS Quarterly*, December 1987

Wiseman C, *Strategy and Computers - Information Systems as Competitive Weapons*, Dow-Jones Irwin, 1985

Yin R K, *Case Study Research – Design and Methods*, Sage Publications, 1989

Yourdon E, *OOA – Object Orientated Analysis*, Bergan, 1990

Zani W, 'Blueprint in MIS', *Harvard Business Review*, November–December 1970

Appendix 3
Methodologies for SISP

There are a number of different proprietary methodologies used to develop a SISP. The following is a list of the better-known methodologies available on the market:

NAME OF METHODOLOGY	SOURCE
Method/1	Andersen Consulting
Information Quality Analysis	Vacca
Business Information Analysis & Integration Technique	Carlson
Business Information Characterisation Study	Kerner
SISP	Database Consultants Europe
Information Engineering	James Martin
Strategic Systems Planning	Holland
Critical Success Factors	Rockart
Ends/Means Analysis	Wetherbe & Davis
Staged Approach	Nolan Norton
Business Systems Planning	IBM
Executive Information Planning	IBM
Information Systems Investment Strategy	IBM
Strategic Investment Methodology	IBM
Strategic Applications Search	IBM
Information Strategic Planning	IBM
Portfolio Management	McFarlan
Strategy Set Transformation	King

NAME OF METHODOLOGY	SOURCE
Value Chain Analysis	Porter
Customer Resource Life Cycle	Ives & Learmont
IEW	Ernst & Young
Summit S & Summit D	Coopers & Lybrand Deloitte
4Front	Deloitte & Touche
SSADM	LBMS plc
SISP	Price Waterhouse
Critical Success Factors	Index Group
SISP	TechTrans Ltd
Information Systems Planning	ICL (UK) Ltd

Appendix 4
Andersen Consulting

INTRODUCTION

Arthur Andersen offers an IS planning methodology and a set of CASE tools under the umbrella name of Foundation. Foundation includes Method/1, Design/1, Install/1, etc.

Arthur Andersen is the second largest professional services organisation in the world. It consists of two primary business units, one of which is Andersen Consulting and the other is an audit and tax practice. In the fiscal year ended 31st August 1989, Arthur Andersen worldwide had a revenue of $3.4b of which Andersen Consulting contributed about $1.4b. It is a worldwide organisation with practices in every major country and typically in several locations within these countries.

Andersen Consulting has been developing systems since 1954. In fact, one of its major claims to fame is that it developed the first commercial data processing system in the USA. It was for General Electric and was a payroll application. The firm has 35 years of systems development experience and now employs over 18,000 people in Andersen Consulting worldwide — approximately 900 in the UK at this time. Eighty percent of Andersen Consulting, some 14,400 people, design, implement and support office information systems. The remainder handle traditional management consulting assignments such as profitability studies, acquisitions, mergers, etc.

Therefore Andersen Consulting is very strongly involved with information systems planning and development, working across all industry sectors. With this volume of work, somewhere in the world Andersen Consulting is delivering two major systems per day. One of the factors that enables it to perform consistently well across the world is that it has a proprietary systems development methodology, Method/1. All 18,000 consultants are trained in Method/1. This provides a standard approach to systems development across the firm.

Andersen Consultancy defines Strategic Information Planning as a process by which an organisation defines how it uses information and technology to achieve competitive advantage and implement strategy.

Method/1 is a top-down approach to systems planning. It begins by identifying the firm's business vision and then develops this into business objectives, business strategies and critical success factors. The planning approach considers where the firm is, where it wants to go, and how it can get there. Executives are encouraged to assess the firm's internal efficiency and compare it with that of its competitors. Method/1 looks to see what information the firm has with which it can assess itself and incorporates this into the proposed reports.

The Method/1 toolset has three components:

- Automated Method/1: an automated methodology system that allows the methodology to be customised, published and examined online.

- Manage/1: an automated project management tool that provides a variety of project management features including project setup, work planning, estimating, scheduling, time recording and reporting.

- Change/1: an automated change control tool.

Andersen Consulting takes a multi-disciplinary approach by supplying teams of consultants with different backgrounds. The result of this blend of different experiences is that Andersen Consulting often suggests changes to the scope of the client's business. In its approach to this work Andersen Consulting uses Michael Porter's Value Chain analysis.

Planning is in Andersen Consulting's view an ongoing process which must be worked at continually. According to Andersen Consulting the steps required for a strategic information plan are:

- Establish a planning team and an executive steering committee.
- Identify broad information resource management issues.
- Determine the scope of the plan.
- Establish the strategy/CSF.
- Assess the present status of the firm's IS.
- Assess the business and competition.
- Search for appropriate IT opportunities.
- Produce the firm's IT strategy.
- Produce a data/application plan.
- Develop a technology plan.
- Write an organisation plan.
- Synthesise into an implementation plan.

Andersen Consulting will customise Method/1 for client's specific requirements.

After the planning is complete the client may require either custom built systems or packaged systems, and Andersen Consultants can accommodate either approach. Figure A4.1 shows the different steps which may be taken.

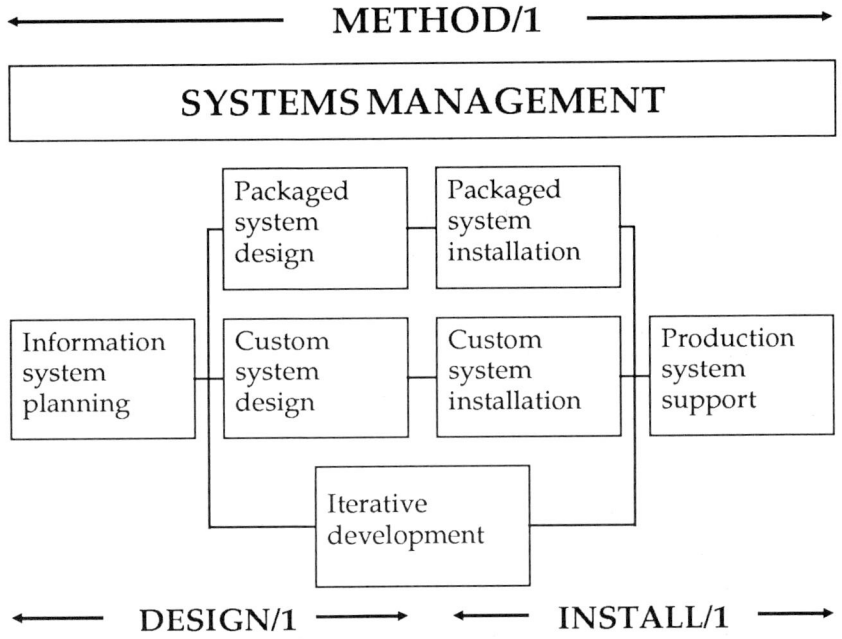

Figure A4.1   Approaches to providing the systems

In addition to the methodology described above Andersen Consulting also supplies ICASE tools which help in the development of code. Part of the concept used in the CASE tools supplied by Anderson Consulting is called Middleware. Middleware represents an approach to developing systems which isolates the unique problems of specific system software from application software. It relieves the developer from having to focus on the detail of specific systems software so that more time is available to concentrate on the business issue. This means that the products produced using these tools are more portable from system to system. Anderson focuses extensively on re-usability and design repository. Anderson Consultancy will forward engineer, reverse engineer and re-engineer systems.

The cost of these tools is about £250,000 and is usually sold with about the same amount of consultancy, ie an equivalent consulting bill.

Method/1 is extremely well documented, being supported by numerous large manuals.

Andersen Consulting provides extensive training to support their clients' use of Method/1. There is a four level training package available which requires a total of eleven days to complete.

Appendix 5
Coopers & Lybrand Deloitte

SUMMIT S and SUMMIT D

Coopers & Lybrand Deloitte (C&LD), which was created in 1990 by the merger of Coopers & Lybrand and certain parts of Deloitte, Haskins and Sells, refer to its approach to IS planning as Summit.

C&LD takes a business management approach in an attempt to integrate IT and business planning, and tries to identify new opportunities and ventures for the client. C&LD looks at investment areas for IT and advises on their appropriateness and on the balance between IT investment and other investment. C&LD recognises that IT planning is a continuous process, and that effective staff management, getting the right number of people with the right skills, is important. It also tries to match its techniques to the skills and knowledge of its clients' personnel.

Therefore the key to the Summit approach is that of business advice which is applied to the IT requirements and functions within the firm. CL&D's services extend into the technical area and in addition to the above general management approach, it also offers detailed IS services including systems design, programming, installation, testing, transition and training.

Summit is a family name for information systems methodologies. Within this family there are two methodologies which are Summit S and Summit D.

Summit S is a strategic planning methodology and Summit D is a systems delivery methodology. These two are the first in a proposed series of methodologies. Summit S and Summit D have been under development since 1987 by an international team drawn from Canada, the UK and the US. They have built on methodologies that have been used by the firm in the past, taken the best methods used by C&LD throughout the world and added new features where appropriate. Summit was built entirely from the group's consultancy experience as well as from internal auditing experience.

One of the important features of the Summit methodology is that it has a bias for action and continually initiates activities which are immediately required. Therefore during the process of a Summit S study, it is common to find urgent projects already being commenced. It is a highly adaptive approach which accommodates both large and small firms as well as enterprises in any industry or public sector. This is achieved by the use of a concept referred to as route maps. Route maps allow the methodology to be customised to the environment while ensuring logical processes are followed, which means that the methodology can in fact be tailor made to suit particular client situations.

Summit incorporates and accommodates a wide range of tools and techniques. It allows clients to use their own favoured tools. It uses data dictionaries, data modelling, network architecture, strategic planning software and economic justification methodologies. Modelling is one of the key techniques and C&LD model the business using various approaches. All these approaches are particularly well documented within Summit.

Summit presumes a developed multi-disciplinary team of consultants and client staff. It is supported by a computerised project management system.

The actual process of Summit S is best described diagrammatically and is shown in Figure A5.1.

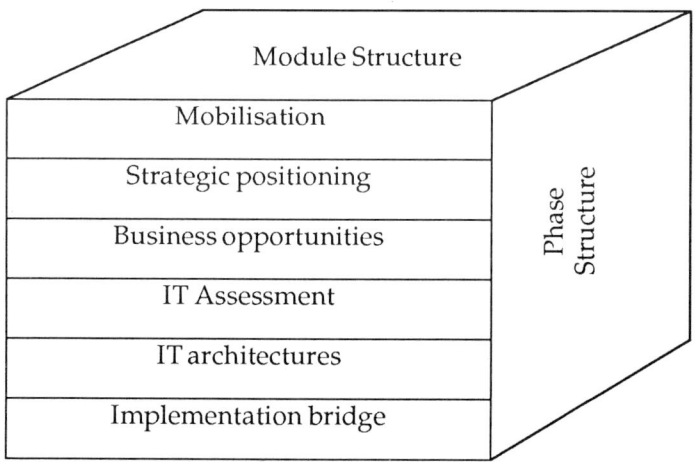

Figure A5.1　　An overview of the Summit S process

C&LD define some of the deliverables of Summit S as follows:

–　Opportunities to employ IT to the best effect in the firm.

–　An understanding of the firm's competitive position in its use of IT.

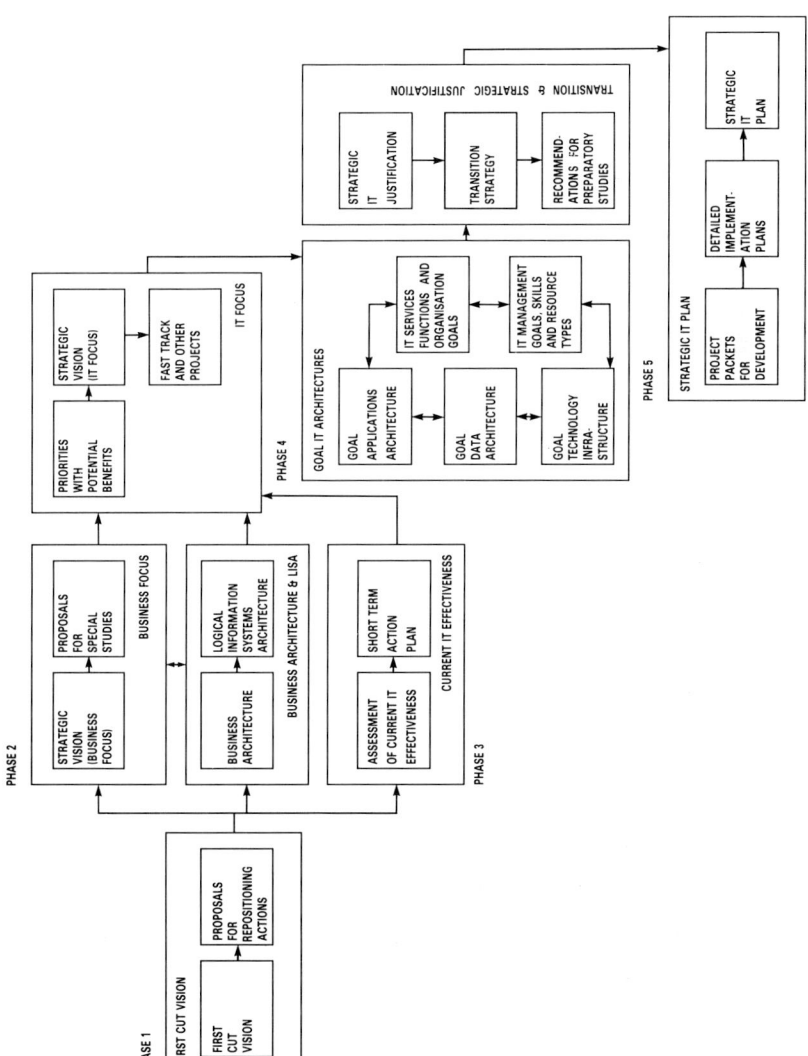

Figure A5.2   The detail of the Summit S process

242 STRATEGIC INFORMATION SYSTEMS PLANNING

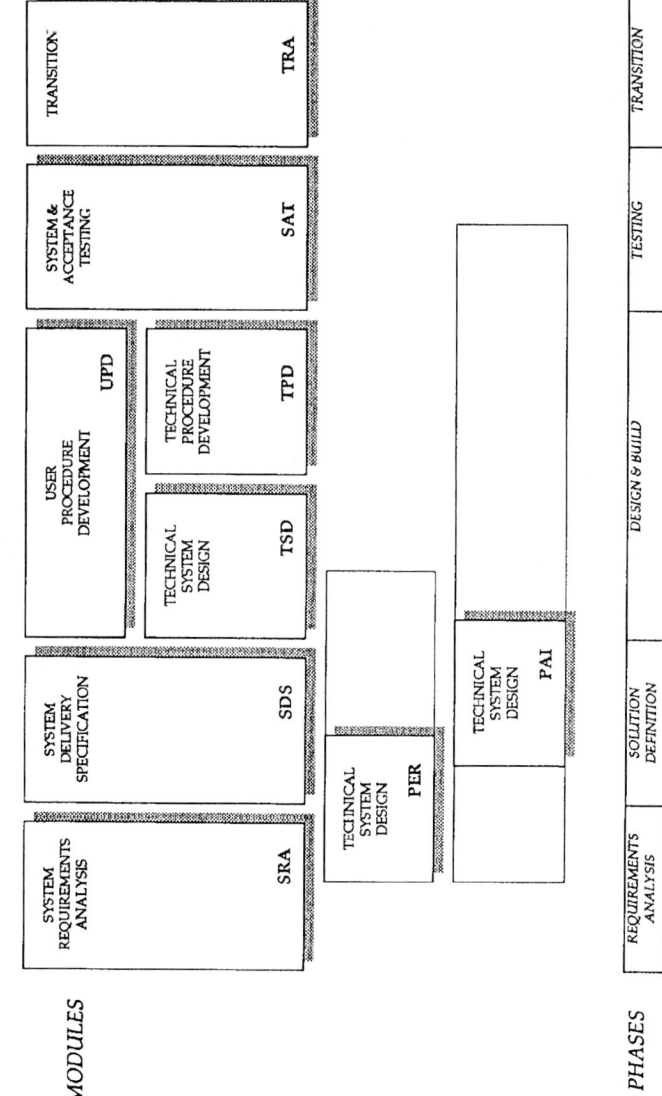

Figure A5.3   The Summit D process

- A data model of the enterprise showing basic processes and what information is required to support these processes.
- A long term technology direction.
- An architecture and blueprint for the firm's systems.
- A series of work packages to respond to urgent needs identified during the project.
- A well briefed top management team.
- A highly motivated ISD.
- A step by step implementation plan.

The detail of this approach is expressed diagrammatically in Figure A5.2.

The same structure applies to both Summit S and Summit D. The two are very closely linked. With regard to CASE tools for instance, taking a job from Summit S through to Summit D, the same set of tools would be used on the strategic side as well as on the delivery side. Thus there are fundamental links between the two methodologies.

Summit-D is expressed diagrammatically in Figure A5.3 This diagram gives an impression of the technical nature of the Summit-D methodology. Summit-D may be used by a client in whole or in part to accomplish its systems production. C&LD will provide either the whole service or just the components required.

Coopers & Lybrand Deloitte uses the following CASE tools: NEWPRO deals with all the Summit S methodologies, Teamwork Analysis and Design handles analysis and design, and Telon produces Cobol and PL/1 code. These products will also run under MS-DOS, OS/2 and UNIX.

Appendix 6
Deloitte & Touche

CONCEPT/90

Deloitte & Touche (D&T) in conjunction with Holland Systems Corporation developed and now market an integrated line of information systems products and services. The umbrella term for these products and services is Concept/90.

D&T employs 28,000 people in 440 offices in 63 countries. It considers itself to be one of the top four firms in the accounting, auditing and consulting professions. The methodology marketed by D&T is called 4FRONT and there are several companion products such as Design4data and Design4applications.

D&T offers not only the methodology but also software which automates the planning stage. There is a series of on-going courses which train clients in the skills necessary to apply 4FRONT.

In developing the IS plan, 4FRONT uses a number of models and reports. These include:

- *Functional Model*, which shows business actions and how they relate to one another. It identifies the information needed to perform each activity.

- *Organisation Model* identifies corporate directions, pertinent issues and business objectives. It shows where information supporting specific actions could provide a competitive advantage in the marketplace. This can be seen in Figure A6.1.

- *Data Architecture* consolidates and standardises the data identified in the function model. 4FRONT reviews data combinations required to support the business, identifies data frequently used together and clusters them. Thus data architecture is a step towards the development of a non- redundant data resource.

- *Applications Architecture* is a descriptive model of the current and future application systems required to support the business activities specified in the function model. The result is a target environment towards

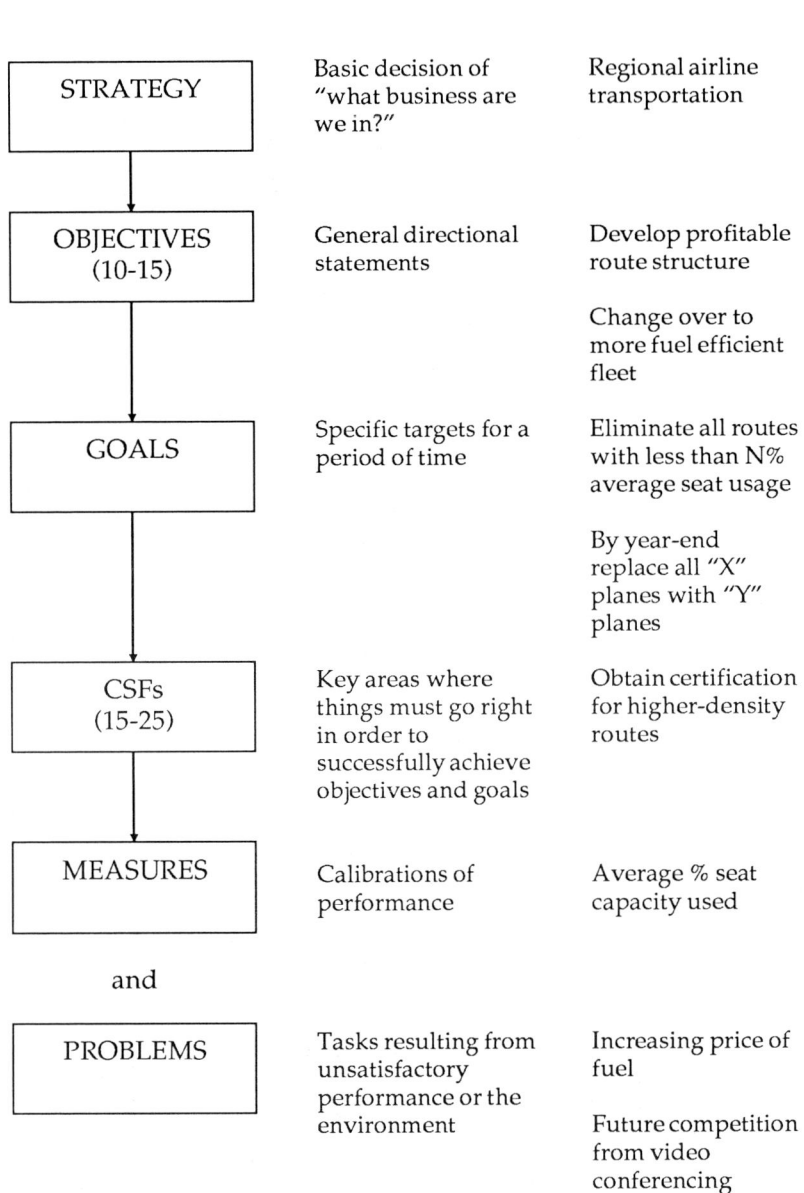

	BRIEF DEFINITION	**BRIEF EXAMPLES**
STRATEGY	Basic decision of "what business are we in?"	Regional airline transportation
OBJECTIVES (10-15)	General directional statements	Develop profitable route structure Change over to more fuel efficient fleet
GOALS	Specific targets for a period of time	Eliminate all routes with less than N% average seat usage By year-end replace all "X" planes with "Y" planes
CSFs (15-25)	Key areas where things must go right in order to successfully achieve objectives and goals	Obtain certification for higher-density routes
MEASURES	Calibrations of performance	Average % seat capacity used
and		
PROBLEMS	Tasks resulting from unsatisfactory performance or the environment	Increasing price of fuel Future competition from video conferencing

Figure A6.1   **An example of an organisation model**

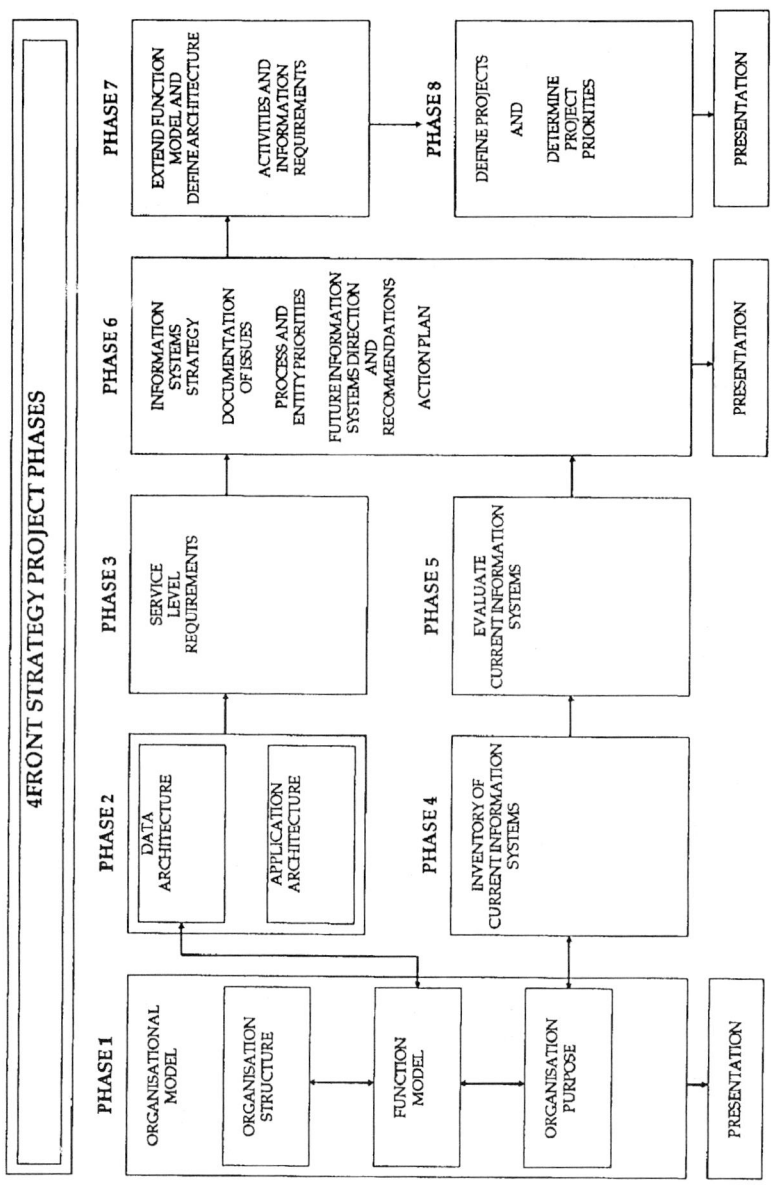

Figure A6.2   The 4FRONT process

which all future systems development can be directed.

–   *Project Plan* specifies the order of applications and database development. Priorities for development based on business objectives and technical factors are specified. This plan ties future systems development to business needs.

This process is described by the diagram in Figure A6.2.

During the analysis processes of 4FRONT data modelling is extensively used. D&T has an automated tool for creating Logical Data Models (LDM) which is called Design4data. This is separate from the physical implementation, and is thus hardware and software independent. Techniques used during the preparation of a LDM include Conical Synthesis and both top-down and bottom-up analysis. Design4data uses a four step structured method to integrate data elements, user views and relationships.

Tools used by D&T include PC Prism, Excellerator, ABT Workbench and Micro Focus.

Appendix 7
Ernst & Young

THE ERNST & YOUNG APPROACH TO STRATEGIC INFORMATION SYSTEMS PLANNING

Ernst & Young is one of the foremost vendors of information systems planning methodologies. It is a large firm with branches throughout the world.

Its main planning product is referred to as Information Engineering Workbench (IEW) of which there are several modules. The philosophy on which the techniques used in these software products is based is explained below.

THE PLANNING ENVIRONMENT

The system development process is subject to a number of influences, including:

- political and commercial pressures;
- technology available in the market;
- internal and external cultures affecting the organisation's human resources.

E&Y's experience indicates that the organisation's business strategy should consist of component strategies corresponding to the key influences, and covering:

- corporate business functions;
- the organisation's use of IT;
- human resources.

The balance between the influences on systems development, and the strategies required to achieve success is shown in Figure A7.1.

During the planning phase, the nature and extent of each of these influences on the organisation is reviewed and analysed to provide a diagnosis of which aspects of the various component strategies should be given priority. A key feature of the future maintenance of the strategy is that these aspects

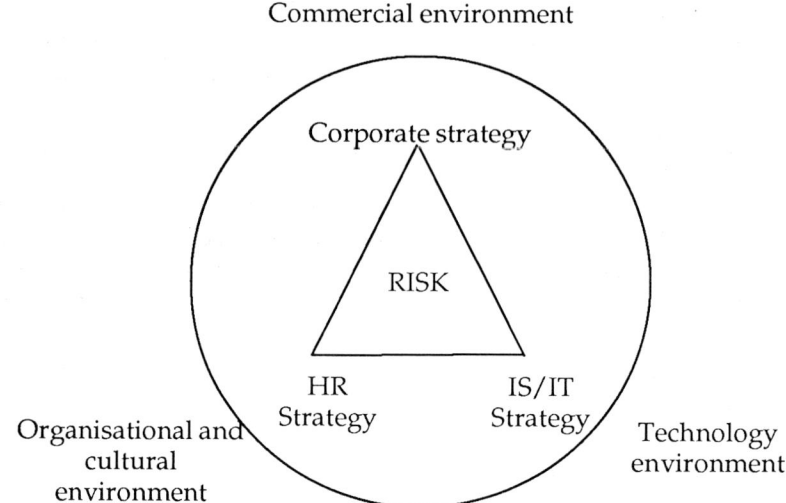

Figure A7.1   The planning environment

must then be monitored for their continuing relevance, and for their impact on the strategic direction.

E&Y's approach recognises that 'hard' information (eg facts and definite information) and 'soft' information (eg opinions, views and feelings) are both relevant in the management process, and techniques are employed to cover the spectrum of types of information. This ensures that right from the start the strategy is firmly rooted in reality and takes account of the dynamic nature of organisations as well as the underlying and relatively unchanging structure of the information that they use. Technical implementation of the strategy can then be linked to the management of change in the organisation.

SISP IN THE CONTEXT OF INFORMATION ENGINEERING

During the 1990's and into the next century, the formative stages of systems development (planning and analysis) will receive greatly increased emphasis. As the later stages increasingly become the province of sophisticated programming tools or application generators, there will be a need to prove that this development is soundly based on a thorough analysis of business needs., This is the rationale behind the concept of Information Engineering (IE).

IE may be defined as a comprehensive, formal, rigorous approach to the planning, analysis, design, construction, and evolution of business information systems in an enterprise or organisation. The comprehensiveness and rigour of the approach are achieved in practice by the use of supporting CASE tools, in conjunction with a broad framework of logically inter-related tasks and deliverables.

E&Y has developed and expanded the basic ideas of IE into a complete methodology (EY/IEM) for the management of the software development lifecycle, from strategy through to the control of the evolution of installed applications. This incorporates the benefits of hundreds of staff years of practical experience, and makes EY/IEM an approach that is both rigorous and flexible enough to address all sizes of project in a wide variety of Information Systems environments.

The basic framework of EY/IEM may be illustrated as the pyramid in Figure A7.2.

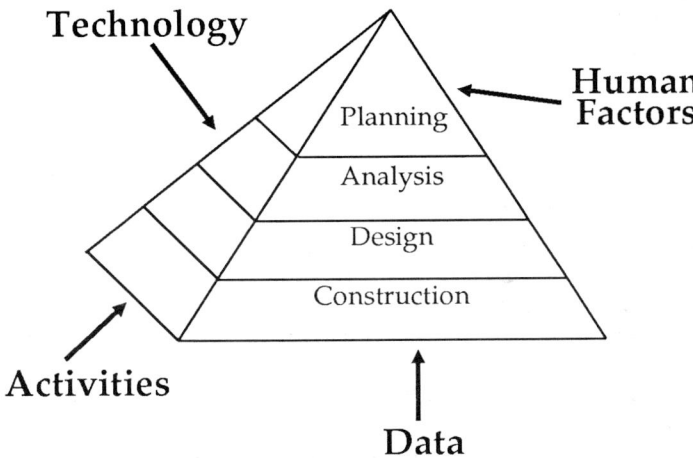

Figure A7.2   The information engineering pyramid

The pyramid has four levels, each corresponding to a major phase in the IE approach – Planning, Analysis, Design, and Construction. Each phase involves the building and/or refinement of computerised 'information models' which provide a basis for evaluating the alternative options for subsequent work. During each phase, options are assigned priorities reflecting their respective values to the business, so that the best possible business return on the investment in systems may be achieved.

The pyramid may also be used to illustrate the inter-relationship of four key components of IS development which must be correctly integrated at all stages of the development:

- Data: the information used by an organisation
- Activities: the functions, processes and procedures making up the organisation
- Technology: the hardware, software and communications
- Human Factors: the methods, organisation, techniques and job design factors which ensure the usability and effectiveness of an application, and the culture needed to support specific systems philosophies

The broadening of the pyramid from its apex (the Planning phase) to its base (the Construction and Implementation of the applications) represents the increasing level of detail involved in the development life cycle.

PORTFOLIO OF E&Y STRATEGIC PLANNING APPROACHES

A diagnosis is made early in the Planning process as to which aspects of the strategy require attention. Each of these can then be addressed by a specific 'tool' in the E&Y portfolio of Planning approaches.

The diagnosis may indicate a number of problems which would cause a specific route to be taken through the planning phase. Where the corporate strategy is insufficiently well developed, proceeding with the development of an IS strategy would be tantamount of building on sand. E&Y's FOCUS methodology provides a practical workshop approach to the development of a corporate strategy. This provides the top level management direction for the IS strategy in a form that can be handled by EY/IEM and by associated software tools.

Human Resources issues will always be raised during the Enterprise Strategy Analysis and in the programme of change management to support the implementation of the strategy. Attitude survey data is considered at the planning stage together with changes in structure, roles and job design needed to support particular strategic objectives. IS may be used to automate existing manual processes and to give people better information to do their jobs. The concern with both is – what information will be required and how will it be used?

Information Systems Strategy must provide an input to IT strategy covering hardware platforms, communications and security issues. E&Y's approach is to assess the resource requirements and to align the technologys strategy to Corporate and Human Resources strategies as well as to the Information and Applications architectures.

Analysis of current Information Systems may indicate that the existing information systems provide a reasonable basis for immediate operational needs. In such a case the emphasis should be upon making the systems in place work better, using E&Y's Management Review of Information Technology (MRIT).

THE E&Y APPROACH TO INFORMATION ENGINEERING

During the planning phase, a high level model of the organisation's main business functions and information requirements is constructed. This Enterprise Model links information requirements to the strategic business plans and corporate objectives of senior management.

The planning phase allows an organisation to make effective decisions in several key areas including Information Needs, Applications, Technology Strategies and Resources, Organisation of IS Resources, Management Practices and Migration.

– *Start Up and Preparation:* The project charter and terms of reference are agreed and sponsorship arranged, and all aspects of resourcing the project are considered, including team selection and training (for both user and IT staff members). Detailed project plans and schedules are constructed.

– *Enterprise Strategy Analysis:* Strategy information is gathered from Executive Management of the business segments within the scope of the project. The collected information is analysed to ensure a complete and consistent model of the enterprise strategy. The strategy is expressed by the following concepts:

  • Business Functions and Processes

  • Goals

  • Critical Success Factors

  • Critical Assumptions

  • Strengths Weaknesses Opportunites and Threats (SWOT) Analysis

  • Executive Information Needs

– *Current Information Systems Assessment:* This stage covers the development of profiles of the functionality and performance of the current Information Systems in use in the enterprise, as well as an assessment of the technology used to operate the systems and the resources available to the IS management function.

Current applications are profiled and assessed according to:

- Technical criteria, obtained by surveying members of the IS department to collect views on the efficiency and reliability of the system, its ease of maintenance and technical obsolescence.

- User view: end users of the systems are surveyed to ascertain their views as to the system's usability, functionality, reliability and response time.

- *Operational Information Needs Assessment:* The operational information needs are obtained initially in interviews with operational managers. Here, the information needs for the basic conduct of the major processes are identified.

Business events are analysed and related to the major processes which they trigger. Each process is considered to define:

- Processing Information Needs as input to the process.

- External Information Needs as output from the process, eg from other departments or external contacts.

- Management Information Needs required to monitor and control the performance of the process.

- *Enterprise Model Refinement:* The Enterprise Model is refined using as input the information gathered during the previous stages.

The Function Model is developed to reflect the structure of the business activities, rather than the organisation structure which is more likely to change.

The Enterprise Data Model describes the things about which the enterprise needs to hold information (Entities) and the relationships between these entities.

- *Enterprise Information Architecture Development:* Four components of the Information Architecture are developed which provide a strategic framework for IT in the enterprise. This provides the 'vision' of where the enterprise is headed in terms of information systems. The four components are, Information Systems Architecture, Data Architecture, Technology Architecture and Management and Organisation Architecture.

In addition to Information Architecture, a Migration Strategy is developed which defines, in terms of Strategic Implementation Phases, how to progress from the current environment to the future architecture.

- *Strategic Information Systems Plan Development:* An Information Systems Plan is developed which will implement the Information Architecture, including:
  - Project definitions
  - Strategic IS Plan
  - Tactical IS Project Plan
  - The policies and procedures required
- *Phase Review and Assessment:* The planning phase project is reviewed by Quality Assurance and the project team to determine what went well and what aspects could be improved.

THE USE OF AUTOMATED TOOLS IN EY/IEM

EY/IEM provides a framework for the use of state-of-the-art Information Engineering tools to help ensure that information systems serve as a central and key resource for the enterprise. While EY/IEM addresses a variety of technological environments, certain industry tools bring speed and efficiency to many tasks in the methodology.

The Information Engineering Workbench (IEW) is a range of software products that can be purchased and used individually, or alternatively combined to form an integrated toolset for the entire software lifecycle. The IEW is unique in using Expert Systems technology that not only automates structured techniques, but also co-ordinates work being carried out and provides automatic quality assurance. The result is greatly improved quality of work, as well as reduced development timescales and costs.

The component parts of IEW include:

- Knowledge Co-ordinator and Encyclopaedia: these are the IEW expert system and knowledge base, which tightly integrate other IEW components.
- Planning Workstation: supports the development, monitoring and maintenance of an Information Strategy Planning study.
- Analysis Workstation: automates structured analysis techniques, using the Knowledge Co-ordinator and Encyclopaedia to create rigorous logical models and eliminate manual checking.
- Design Workstation: automates structured design techniques, using the IEW expert systems to carry forward analysis deliverables and generate correct designs.

–   Applications Generator: uses information accumulated during the previous phases to generate complete working applications.

Appendix 8
IBM Corporation

IBM AND PROPRIETARY IS PLANNING PRODUCTS

IBM is a large scale supplier of a number of IS planning methodologies and services including products such as Business Systems Planning (BSP), Information Systems Investment Strategy (ISIS), Strategic Investment Methodology (SIM) and Strategic Applications Search (SAS).

BUSINESS SYSTEMS PLANNING (BSP)

IBM's work in the area of consultancy dates back to BSP in the 70s when a number of consultants began working with customers using this methodology.

The fundamental principle of BSP relies on two sets of analysis:

– the business processes analysis;
– the data elements analysis.

According to IBM many firms will typically have anything from 50 to several hundred individual business processes and perhaps several hundred data elements within the business. BSP is a methodology for a comprehensive overview of all the business processes and all the data elements which are then combined in a matrix to find which elements are used in which processes.

An example of the above is a business process such as producing invoices; the business elements related to this activity are customer name and address, price, etc. The methodology requires the processes and elements to be grouped in a relatively unstructured manner in a matrix which is then analysed to try to identify which elements are used in which processes. There are always overlaps, but by analysing the density of the matrix, an application grouping appears which identifies the effective basis for the introduction of computer systems with as few interfaces as possible between applications so that they are relatively self-contained.

This technique of association analysis is also used by most of the other management consultancies. It proved a successful way of obtaining an overview of an organisation's business in order to develop a structured framework for ISD support in its development of first generation business applications (ie transaction processing). However BSP does not readily identify requirements for second and third generation applications such as office systems support or personal computing. Although it is still marketed by IBM it is in much less use today because in many organisations much of the basic groundwork is already in place.

MULTIPLE METHODOLOGIES

IBM's approach to SISP is not based on a single methodology but on a three legged model which says that there are three parallel approaches which need to be pursued, perhaps at different times, but each contributing its part.

These three legs are top-down, bottom-up and inside-out-planning.

The top-down approach begins with the board of directors and analyses the firm's overall business objectives. From this it is possible to establish what the real IS requirements are. The bottom-up approach says that it is necessary or rather essential, to look at the current position and to plan from that point. Portfolio analysis is an important technique which looks at existing systems, compares them with the running of the business and thus determines where there are gaps. The third approach is referred to as inside-out, which believes that it is also necessary to look at the technology, and establish what opportunities the firm might take advantage of in terms of new systems, new equipment and so forth.

All of these approaches are relevant and to focus only on one methodology is in the view of IBM highly questionable.

Starting with the top-down approach, the methodology used by IBM is based on the use of CSFs linked to business processes.

This concept involves bringing the board together to confirm the corporate strategy of the organisation and then to define the CSFs. Although this is a valuable exercise, CSFs themselves do not tend to be things that can actually be managed. They tend to cut across management lines. For example, a firm may consider that it must be seen to provide a superior service to its customers as compared with its competitors and this could be a CSF. Turning that into something that can actually be managed is difficult. The line IBM has taken is to relate the CSFs to business processes so that having identified them, the broad business processes which must be addressed to achieve the CSF are written down.

CSFs are one of the key elements of the top-down approach. There is a technique called Executive Information Planning which uses a shorter timescale and is more objectives and goals-oriented. It is a process which involves the board of directors defining the goals of the organisation, the specific objectives supporting those goals and the restraints preventing the firm achieving them. It also assesses the role of improved IS in helping to overcome those constraints. Because it is objective rather than mission-oriented it tends to produce a rather shorter term strategic plan – typically 1 to 2 years. It looks at what the systems are designed to address rather than the details of how objectives will actually be achieved.

INFORMATION SYSTEMS INVESTMENT STRATEGY (ISIS)

ISIS was originally developed in the US and can be used in two ways. It is sometimes performed by accountants or financial managers, working with the customer through an interview approach which gathers the data and then working with an internal team to analyse it. This team looks at the whole portfolio of application systems and compares it with the database of applications in that particular industry, assessing where the firm's weaknesses are. Possible areas for exploitation are as a result highlighted.

The next stage is to evaluate the possible financial impact of remedying these weaknesses. This involve moving away from portfolio analysis to some form of financial modelling. This has been done in an approximate or indicative way internally with the people who have worked on it going back to the customer, discussing the outcome with them as a basis for saying 'if it looks interesting let's do it properly and thoroughly'. It is a pilot study first approach to see what the indicators are in order to ensure that there are sufficient reasons to go further.

STRATEGIC INVESTMENT METHODOLOGY (SIM)

One other approach offered is based on a methodology IBM has used extensively internally. This is SIM which was originally developed by a consortium of companies including Du Pont and Nolan Norton. IBM can offer it as an original participant. SIM tries to relate the existing spending on IT with the strategic needs of the business. It analyses spending in the various functions of the business and it looks in a broad-based way at the type of computing that is being supported.

STRATEGIC APPLICATION SEARCH (SAS)

There is a major application of the inside-out approach called SAS, which is a workshop for a selected group of executives, but not necessarily the board of directors. This group is briefed by IBM and then the team is invited to work with IBM for, typically, about three days. The method looks at the group's environment and uses the Porter Link Analysis quite extensively to analyse links in the value chain and to examine external linkages. The aim is to derive new ideas and new approaches. The method uses some structured brain-storming techniques such as meta-planning which involves planning plans. An example is a motor manufacturer who used this method to look at the crucial linkage between the sales and the customer. The next step is to see exactly what the links are – advertising, finance company, dealers, spares. The mould is broken and the firm starts to look at what the possible connections are and how to address them. What opportunity does technology offer to address the links that are weak or those that could be improved?

Round the IBM countries there are various mixes of these methodologies. The same name in different countries can be a different program and the same program can have different names everywhere.

The business objectives, business processes and data elements come together in an overall architectural statement. The problem with this is that it doesn't actually make anything happen. To make things happen it is necessary to look at specific opportunities, scope out individual applications, look at the priorities coming from the business, costs and benefits, define the projects and put them into some kind of operating plan and then actually go ahead. If that is in place then it will condition and guide the way in which these things are made to happen. However, there are a lot of organisations who mistake that for *that*. This is an important distinction to make between the two.

The perspective is frequently met whereby organisations have a strategy but nothing much seems to have happened. On the other hand there are companies who say they are doing a lot of work, but nothing seems to fit together. Therefore, in IBM's view methodologies and SISPs are not enough, but require a management will to succeed.

THE INFORMATION STRATEGY PLAN (ISP)

In an ISP the aim is to interpret and firm up the business strategy. If there is no business strategy then IBM help the firm define one.

It is necessary to establish what information needs the business has in order to achieve the business strategy, so the ISP is oriented around business needs analysis. In terms of working with the organisation, the methodology is introduced through a series of techniques introduction sessions to find what information is required about a business objective or organisation function. Joint Application Development (JAD) sessions, or facilitated workshops are used to establish this. This approach gets organisations to get consensus of what the business objectives are from the business strategy, what are the business needs or how does a particular business function operate. What existing business mechanisms are there and what are the problems with the existing process. These workshops generate a multi-faceted model which can be put into the planning workstation. The idea is to interpret the business strategy through to a level of detail that can drive the analysis project.

This process is necessary when a firm does not have a strategic business plan, or if it has not been recorded in a tangible form. Therefore even when a firm thinks they have a strategy plan IBM goes through the interpretation phase to get the IE object types such as entity, goal, CSF, organisational unit, function etc., because the methodology needs the meta model of the organisation to drive the tool set and the rest of the IE concepts.

The information needs analysis is a human technique of being able to interpret, for example, the way in which the financial director has been spoken to about the way he needs to direct his division within the organisation, into a series of information needs. It involves acquiring a statement of categorised information. The format it should be in depends on whether it is market analysis based on competitive products or something else. This information is gathered through the ISP process.

Throughout the process, information about how the business works and what it is trying to achieve is being captured and the back end of the ISP process is to set out a tactical plan to show what has to be done to achieve the business objectives.

The main deliverable is actually a model of the business giving a statement of each of the above four elements. This provides a series of prioritised projects which are all about improving the way the business works.

This ISP is a live document requiring constant change and adjustment. The concept of the ISP phase must be completed within three months but it must be constantly updated. The analysis projects are typically about six months in duration, but this does depend to some extent on the scope of them. These two phases must be completed in a short period of time as the business requirements are likely to have changed if a longer period is taken. The design and construction is a technical issue based on the size of the database etc but typically design will be about six months and the construction period is very variable.

Appendix 9
The Index Group

THE INDEX GROUP

Index Systems Inc was established in Boston approximately 20 years ago by a number of members of staff of the Massachusetts Institute of Technology (MIT). It was founded in order to offer a service to firms which need to bridge the gap between senior management and IT. Index quickly developed into a firm which offered both management consultancy and also developed systems.

In 1983 Index Systems was restructured with the Excellarator CASE product and Applied Expert Systems being sold. The name of the firm was then changed to Index Group Inc and the firm then focused on management consultancy with no implementation capability.

In October 1988 the Index Group was acquired by the Computer Science Corporation which is based in Los Angeles and has offices around Europe. Computer Science Corporation is extensively involved in systems implementation and integration. It has a turnover of approximately $1.2b.

The business of the Index Group may be divided into three groups which are:

- Management consultancy;
- Multi-client services;
- Executive education.

MANAGEMENT CONSULTANCY

Most Index staff work in this area. The clients are large and complex organisations and Index helps them to manage change especially in the area of assisting them in recognising how IT can be used to restructure or redesign the way of doing business. A large number of Index assignments are commissioned by board members or the top IS officer in the firm.

Index worked with Roquart in developing the Critical Success Factor (CSF) approach to both business and IS analysis. Index believe that their approach to CSF is unique providing better results than anyone else by obtaining a degree of participation, involvement and commitment from top management which is hard to achieve. Michael Porter type concepts are also used. Index has experience of most industries and this enables it to understand the business drivers faced by most firms.

Index designs Business Blue Prints for clients which map out how the organisation needs to change to take advantage of new opportunities. From this Blue Print a Road Map or strategic plan is developed which will take the firm into the future.

The consultancy style is based on forming a joint team consisting of Index and client staff. Index provides the ideas and approaches which they have developed over the years. Participative processes such as workshops and interviews are used. Work is usually performed on the client's premises. This approach helps ensure that the client is committed to the solution as it will have helped develop it.

MULTI-CLIENT SERVICES

Index has over 200 firms which participate in Multi-client services in the USA. There are two types of services. The first is pure management research which looks at such issues as how some firms have been able to apply competitive systems successfully.

The second type of service offers to a limited number of firms the opportunity to share IS experiences. There are four distinct services which offer this. These are referred to as Forum, Alliance, Centrum and Institute. These offer their members conferences, local meetings and reports. There is a separate organisation in Europe called Interchange which provides a similar service. Forum is limited to 100 firms, Alliance to 40 and Centrum also to 40.

EXECUTIVE EDUCATION

This is designed for board members or senior managers. It is to help company management become more comfortable in their role of directing IS. It explains how IT may be used as a competitive weapon or how it can be used to help them restructure their business, what it takes to make change happen in their companies. Leading academics and speakers from within Index lead these courses. Members of the various groups also discuss their experience with other members.

Index will continue to operate as a separate entity within the Computer Sciences Group. It will not attempt to sell Computer Sciences services but will introduce Computer Sciences where it appears that a client could benefit from its services.

Index employs 150 consultants worldwide and has been active in the UK for three years where it employs 12 consultants. It has offices in Boston, Los Angeles and London.

Assignments range in size from £50,000 to £500,000 with an average of about £150,000. They are charged on a time and materials basis which is based on a daily rate depending on the consultant concerned.

Appendix 10
James Martin and Associates

IEM AND IEF

Information Engineering Methodology (IEM) has been developed by James Martin Associates. This approach relies on the building of enterprise models, data models and process models. The creation of these models produces a database from which the balance of the analysis is performed. IEM is a planning methodology which is closely associated with Information Engineering Facility (IEF) which is an Integrated Computer Aided Systems Engineering (ICASE) product.

IEM is a top-down approach to IS planning. This means that it focuses on the needs of the business as a whole and not just the ISD. It is a methodology based on the IS problem with a determined move towards automation. The methodology starts with the consultant understanding the firm. Then diagrammatical modelling is used to produce different views of the business. It is a graphics-orientated discipline. During the analytical stage of the project the business models are redefined so that they may be directly translated into systems code.

IEM goes through several stages including:

- Information Strategy Planning;
- Business Area Analysis;
- Business System Design;
- Technical Design/Construction.

It is expressed diagrammatically in Figure A10.1.

IEM is generally considered to be one of the more technical approaches to SISP. One of the keys to the success of IEM is the precise rigorous disciplines which it imposes on the IS function. CSFs are also used in conjunction with the IEM approach in order to identify which issues are most important in ensuring the success of the organisation. A measure of success is associated with each CSF.

Information Engineering Facility (IEF) was developed by Texas Instru-

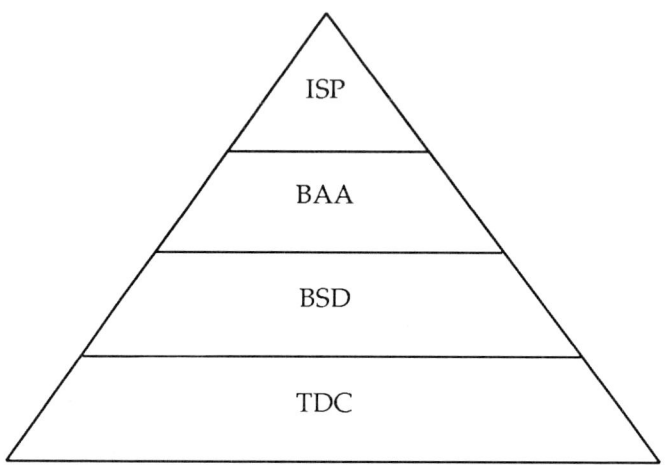

Figure A10.1   Different stages of IEM

ments in association with JMA. IEF has two main objectives which are to improve the quality of systems and to improve the productivity of systems developers. Effective use of IEF should lead to systems being right first time, easy to change, quick to develop and should give the firm tight control.

This process involves the creating of a Central Encyclopaedia which contains all the business definitions and relationships relevant to the enterprise. The Encyclopaedia also contains detailed systems information and systems building rules on issues as diverse as strategic objectives and the required contents of invoices.

The steps comprising the Stage Framework are shown in Figure A10.2.

JMA places considerable emphasis on Technical Architecture Diagrams. Figure A10.3 gives an impression of its approach to this subject.

An important aspect of IEF is the ICASE dimension. ICASE integrates the complete systems life cycle from strategic information system planning through analysis and construction to code generation and implementation and maintenance.

ICASE is a generic term for a wide range of products which are designed to provide automated support for those involved in the software development process. There are a considerable number of these products on the

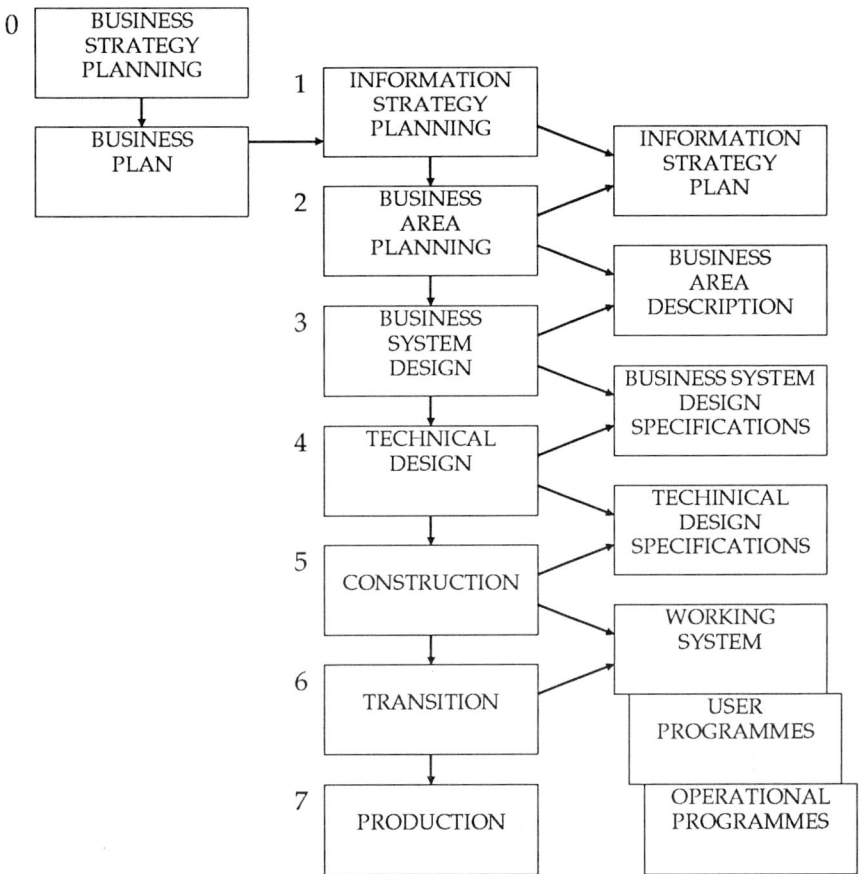

Figure A10.2   The Stage Framework

market and the facilities they offer vary considerably. Some of the wide variety of facilities offered in ICASE products include analyst workbench products, word processing and editing tools, compilation and testing facilities, flow chart production, etc. The JMA ICASE product is regarded highly in the marketplace.

There are several software packages available in conjunction with IEF. These tools link data input with various systems development efforts. An applications generator is integrated with IEF which produces systems in VS

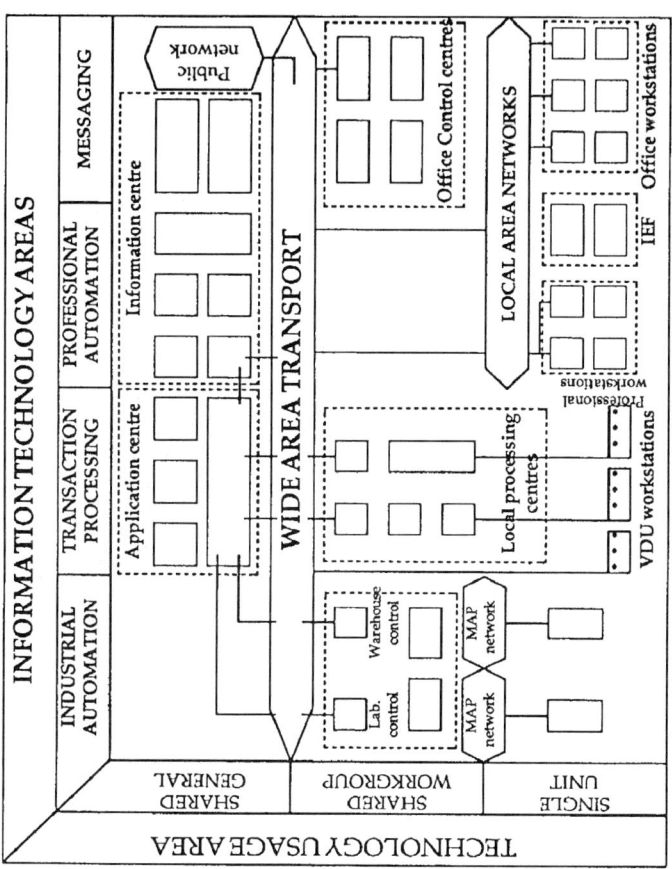

Figure A10.3   A Technical Architecture Diagram

COBOL II running under IMS/DC or CICS. Many of the products use an interface based on an RAEW matrix, as shown in Figure A10.4. IEF is currently implemented to work under IBM's MVS mainframe operating system using DB2 or other SQL-based DBMS products.

The average cost of IEM and the ICASE is £500 000.

IEM and IEF have an entire jargon of their own which requires considerable learning. JMA offer a full range of training to clients and consultants wishing to master these systems.

LEGEND	
R Responsi-bility	**A** Authority
E Expertise	**W** Work

ORGANISATION UNIT

INFORMATION FUNCTION	Board of directors		Information steering committee		ISDP department headquarters		DP department service		Information user department		Systems design department		Office services department	
Information planning & control	R	A	R		R									
			E	W	E	W	E	W	E	W	E	W		
Information systems development											R	A		
					E	W	E	W			E	W		
Development coordination			R	A	R	A								
			E	W										
Information systems user management											R	A		
									E	W	E	W	E	W
Communications planning	R	A							R					
			E	W	E	W			E	W	E	W		

Figure A10.4   An RAEW matrix

Appendix 11
Nolan Norton & Co

NOLAN NORTON

Nolan, Norton & Co was founded in 1974 when David Norton and Dick Nolan began collaborating on DP management studies at the Harvard Business School. The initial work led to the classic papers on the 'S' shaped curve and the stages theory which are still key concepts of NNC work: these state that development of a company's DP capability starts slowly at the 'initiation' stage; grows fast in the 'contagion' stage; and then slows up again at the 'control' stage.

Experience with growth of the microcomputer in business led to three further stages: 'integration' where new technologies and existing applications are brought together to share data and communicate; 'architecture' where long term goals are specified towards which all future IT applications will be built; and 'demassing' which follows the thinking of Alvin Toffler where new technologies serve personal or individual markets.

The objective is to harness IT to practical and profitable applications in the business, to draw together the growing capabilities of IT and the needs of management to run a competitive and profitable business enterprise.

Like most consultancies, NNC offers baseline studies to create a knowledge base about IT in the company. This baseline will position a company on the 'S' curve and ensure that the recommendations for the next steps in IT are relevant to the company's particular environment.

NNC has approximately 300 staff in the United States, 30 in the London, and has branches also in Milan, Utrecht and Madrid. It offers a range of services to support the growth of strategic thinking in an organisation. There is no one best sequence for using these services; they can be selected and tailored according to the needs of the company at that time.

NNC merged with Peat Marwick in April 1987 and can now offer a full range of services to companies using IT. NNC offers study groups to develop the client staff's understanding of baseline, business vision, 'do-well' identification, application opportunities, architecture, implementation strategy, benefit analysis, IT productivity, data centre efficiency, human resource management. Peat Marwick complements these study groups with implementation support or contract work, operating plans, and with business, industry or financial consultancy.

NNC architecture studies will always start with a programme to document or generate a business vision for the company. From this a Business Strategy is generated. Only after this is it possible to align business functions with the most logical location for their performance; the how and where for each thing that the business does. IT architecture follows from this, matching a conceptual, ideal architecture for say ten years ahead to the present baseline. There will be architecture documents for the data, applications, hardware and telecommunications.

Baseline and architecture studies rely heavily on a proprietary application program run on a PC. All NNC staff are trained in the use of the baseline and architecture methodologies, associated forms, analysis techniques and the PC program.

Each study will always involve at least 50% client participation, with client staff being trained to use the tools according to their needs. The program is available for use by the client in subsequent studies. Studies will always start with a main board briefing, and end with a presentation by NNC and client staff of the findings and recommendations. NNC seldom produces a written report; instead the results are presented to management supported by graphics, copies of which are provided to members.

To take the full menu of services might involve several client and NNC staff for several months. Most clients take one or two services in any one year with projects that last four to six months and cost £30,000 to £100,000, but some ongoing associations with clients have lasted for several years.

Education is a key area in supporting the consultancy activity. In addition, a separate group of staff are assigned to research at centres in Boston, and in Belgium. Both activities are focused on IT opportunities and strategy and competitive advantage.

NNC tends to address larger companies. Because of the size and diversity of the largest multi-national companies, studies tend to focus on single divisions or individual companies of these at any one time.

The same techniques, selected and tailored as appropriate, are also offered to middle range companies by another specialist group in Peat Marwick.

Appendix 12
Acronyms

AA	American Airlines
AHS	American Hospital Supplies
AI	Artificial Intelligence
APPC	Application Process to Process Communication
BSP	Business Systems Planning
CAD	Computer Aided Design
CAM	Computer Aided Manufacturing
CASE	Computer Aided Software Engineering
CIM	Computer Integrated Manufacture
CIO	Chief Information Officer
CPU	Central Processing Unit
CSF	Critical Success Factor
CSMA-CD	Carrier Sense Multipe Access - Collision Detection
CSS	Customer Support System
DBMS	Database Management System
DCE	Database Consultants Europe
DC&N	Data Communications & Networks
DEC	Digital Equipment Corporation
DOS	Disk Operating System

DP	Data Processing
DRM	Data Resource Management
DSS	Decision Support System
DTP	Desk Top Publishing
EBC	English Banking Corporation
EDI	Electronic Data Interchange
EIS	Executive Information System
EPOS	Electronic Point Of Sale
ETO	Electronic Trading Opportunity
EUC	End User Computing
IBM	International Business Machines
IC	Information Centre
ICASE	Integrated Computer Aided Software Engineering
ICL	International Computers Ltd
IEEE	Insitute of Electrical and Electronic Engineers
IEF	Information Engineering Facility
IEM	Information Engineering Methodology
IEW	Information Engineering Workbench
IO	Input/Output
IOS	Inter Organisational System
IP	Internetwork Protocol
IRM	Information Resource Management
IS	Information Systems
ISD	Information Systems Department
ISDN	Information System Digital Network
ISO	International Standards Organisation

ISP	Information Systems Plan
ISSP	Information Systems Strategic Plan
IT	Information Technology
ITA	Information Technology Architecture
IW	Information Weapon
JAL	Japan Airlines
JIT	Just In Time
KPI	Key Performance Indicator
LAN	Local Area Network
LU	Logical Unit
MIS	Management Information System
MIT	Massachusetts Institute of Technology
MSS	Management Support System
MS-DOS	MicroSoft Disk Operating System
NFS	Network File Server
OA	Office Automation
OASIS	Organisation And Systems Innovations Ltd
OSI	Open Systems Interconnection
OSS	Operating Support Systems
PC	Personal Computer
PMM:MC	Peat Marwick McClintock: Management Consultants
PRISM	Partnership in Information Systems Management
ROI	Return On Investment
SAA	Systems Application Architecture
SNA	Systems Network Architecture

SDM	Strategic Data Model
SIS	Strategic Information System
SISP	Strategic Information Systems Planning
SOG	Strategic Options Generator
SMB	Server Memory Block
SPF	Single Point of Failure
SWOT	Strengths Weaknesses Opportunities and Threats
TCP/IP	Transmission Control Protocol / Internetwork Protocol
VADS	Value Added and Data Services
VAN	Value Added Network
WAN	Wide Area Network

Index